Taking
Care
of the
Law

Taking Care of the Law

GRIFFIN B. BELL
with
Ronald J. Ostrow

WILLIAM MORROW AND COMPANY, INC.
New York   1982

Library of Congress Cataloging in Publication Data

Bell, Griffin B., 1918-
  Taking care of the law.

  Includes index.
  1. Bell, Griffin B., 1918-   . 2. Attorneys-
general—United States—Biography. 3. United
States—Politics and government—1977-
I. Ostrow, Ronald J. II. Title
KF373.B42A37   353.5′092′4 [B]   82-2245
ISBN 0-688-01136-5   AACR2

Printed in the United States of America

First Edition

1 2 3 4 5 6 7 8 9 10

BOOK DESIGN BY BERNARD SCHLEIFER

To President Carter, who gave me the opportunity to
serve our country as attorney general, and to the men
and women who served with me—GRIFFIN BELL

For Alyce, Alison, Kalin and Kathy—RJO

FOREWORD

You will notice that this book is written by me "with Ronald J. Ostrow." Some explanation is appropriate. I first met Ron Ostrow shortly after my nomination as attorney general was announced, but I already knew of him by reputation since one of Ron's greatest advocates is Jack Nelson, *The Los Angeles Times*'s Washington bureau chief. Nelson is a longtime friend of mine from his own days in Atlanta and the South for *The Atlanta Constitution.* Ron covered the Justice Department for *The Los Angeles Times* throughout my tenure as attorney general. He was tough, critical, incisive, extremely knowledgeable about the history and inner workings of the department, but always balanced and fair. He would frequently travel with me while I was on official trips, and we got to know each other well. Ron is an unusually likeable person, and it was not surprising to me that my respect for him as a reporter began to be equaled by my respect for him as a patriot and as a friend. I hope such a statement does not now embarrass him. Moreover, I know few reporters who enjoy the universal respect of their peers in the reporting profession that Ron has earned through the years. He has worked for *Business Week, The Wall Street Journal* and, for the last twenty years, for *The Los*

Angeles Times; he was a Nieman Fellow at Harvard University; and he coauthored with Jack Nelson a book, *The FBI and the Berrigans.* Near the end of my term as attorney general, I approached Ron and asked him if he would be interested in helping me write about some of the lessons of my experience with government as a federal circuit judge and attorney general. I was gratified by his acceptance. He has labored long and hard on this project. We have spent many hours discussing the material that follows, often with Ron's tape recorder running. His contributions to this project are prodigious, and without him, there would be no book. It should be emphasized, however, that the ideas, conclusions, observations, opinions and recommendations I make in this book are my own and not necessarily the views of Ron Ostrow. For his invaluable efforts, I thank both him and his beautiful and patient wife, Alyce, and their family. I cherish their friendship.

—GRIFFIN B. BELL

Atlanta, Georgia
March 15, 1982

ACKNOWLEDGMENTS

The authors benefited from the assistance of a score of people who made suggestions, raised questions, provided answers and helped locate material. The special assistants to Judge Bell at the Department of Justice and several of his former law clerks were especially helpful. They included Frederick Baron, Nelson Dong, Walter Fiederowicz, John Harmon, Jim Jardine, Phil Jordan and Mike Kelly. Tread Davis and Mike Egan gave of their memories. William H. Webster, director of the FBI, and Roger S. Young, assistant director for public affairs, helped fill in a substantial gap. John L. Martin contributed his experience and knowledge. Attorney General William French Smith and his staff at the Department of Justice helped us in reviewing any national security implications of materials in the two chapters on foreign intelligence. Fay Cain, Karen Garber, Libby Gallagher, Ida Cerra and Nancy Lewis provided early assistance. The librarians of *The Los Angeles Times*'s Washington bureau—Gloria Doyle, Diana Moore and Barclay Howarth—extended their fact-finding skills with their usual cheer. Dennis Britton, the newspaper's national editor, and Jack Nelson, chief of its Washington bureau, were encouraging throughout the project. Linda Sandy

11

raised substantive questions as she typed and retyped, and all of her work helped. Harvey Ginsberg's insistent editing improved the manuscript immensely. Mike Hamilburg, our agent, was sunny when all else was gray. Bob Barkdoll provided helpful editing at an early stage. The book could not have been done without the untiring assistance of two friends —Terry Adamson and Richard T. Cooper. Adamson helped throughout the book with questions, suggestions and recall, and Chapter IX in particular depended heavily on his files. Cooper, deputy chief of *The Los Angeles Times*'s Washington bureau, provided his insightful editing skill and significantly changed the book. To all of you, thanks. We take the blame for any errors.

—GBB *and* RJO

CONTENTS

PROLOGUE

In 1831, a young French lawyer, Alexis de Tocqueville, destined to be a great journalist and statesman, spent several months in the United States. He reflected upon our form of government and published *Democracy in America,* a book that depicts a vision of despotism that might be established in a democracy.[1] This despotism would degrade man without tormenting him. It would come about through a humane and gentle society whose citizens would be alike in power and wealth and opportunity. It would make man's pleasures simple and circumscribe his imagination, all for the common good. The government would not be tyrannical; rather, it would be a guardian. Like a parent, it would watch over the fates of its children in an absolute, minute, regular, provident and mild manner. The government would be the arbiter of happiness and provide for man's security. People would come to depend upon such a government and look to it for benefits. Sumptuary laws would control everyday existence. Even the most energetic and imaginative would not be able to rise above the crowd. Their will would not be shattered, but softened, bent and guided. In the end, man would be timid and soulless. The government would be his shepherd.

INTRODUCTION:
THE CITIZEN AGAINST
THE GOVERNMENT

Oftentimes, the citizen is cast in the role of being against the government the way our system operates today. That may seem unusual coming from a man who sat as a federal appellate judge for nearly fifteen years and who served as the nation's chief law enforcement officer for the first three years of the Carter administration.

But it is not so strange if you believe in exalting the Bill of Rights. To do that, you have to be for the individual, even if it means being against the government. That was the stance of those who created the Bill of Rights and drew up a series of "Thou Shalt Nots" to safeguard themselves and their descendants against the oppression they had known under a monarch who lived across the ocean. The authors also looked at what other governments had done to their people and learned from what they saw. Through the Bill of Rights, they put their fledgling government on notice that the individual citizen stood protected against government excesses.

I was reared to think a liberal was somebody who would fight the government on behalf of the individual. Someday, liberals again are going to decide that they believe in the Bill

15

of Rights, which means they are going to have to oppose government.

The true liberal is a person who stands for the individual, as against the government. Yet what we have now is a generation of "liberals" who are progovernment and against the individual. I trace this change back to the New Deal, when the government began to act on behalf of groups, as opposed to the individual, all in the name of the common good. Many of the New Deal programs departed from the free enterprise spirit that would allow the individual to grow or produce whatever the marketplace would support, with the individual bearing the risk.

I am not saying the programs, the restrictions and the subsidies they came up with were all wrong. I am saying that the process needs to be improved so that groups are not automatically more important than individuals. It is a matter of balance. The basic rule should be that government provides for maximum freedom for the individual. Anything that runs counter to that principle should be suspect and examined closely.

But as matters stand now, the great liberals who conceived the Bill of Rights, were they once more blessed with life, would think that radicals had taken over our country.

When we were searching for a title for this book, I initially turned back to the Declaration of Independence and drew from it the words "to harass our people." The full sentence reads: "He [George III] has erected a multitude of New Offices, and sent hither swarms of Officers to harass our people, and eat out their substance." As serious as excessive government is for our people, we decided that a book carrying the word "harass" in its title would communicate a more negative tone than we intend. So we returned to that glorious document that distinguishes us from all other governments in the world, the United States Constitution. Article II, which lists the power of the President, states in Section 3 that "he shall take care that the laws be faithfully executed." In our constitutional democracy, no mandate exceeds that in importance.

Over the years, government overreaching in America has become a more subtle brand of oppression than the arbitrary rulings of an overseas monarch. But particularly in a land where government was created by the people and for the people, we should be free from such oppression.

The generation of progovernment people that traces its origin to the New Deal has ascended to high places. Its members have risen in the government because they place the government over everything else. We need a new generation of leaders, bona fide liberals, who believe in the Bill of Rights and feel bound by it. Once we have them, we will bring the government under control.

We may be near the point that the Romans reached under Emperor Caligula who, in his arrogance, ordered that all laws were to be posted in small print and high places to better confuse the populace. A good many readers of the *Federal Register,* that daily compilation of government rules and regulations, no doubt believe we have outdone the emperor already. But the United States is no Roman Empire, and this system of governing by confusion will not endure. If large numbers of our people are confused by the law, they will ignore the law. We then will lose that cohesive respect for the rule of law that is so fundamental to our system.

Everywhere in our land, we see the realities of a bureaucracy out of control. This lack of control has a good deal to do with the scourge of inflation, fueled in part by government spending; it produces today's flood of stultifying federal regulations; and it generates citizen frustration over our seeming inability to govern ourselves.

Listing our ills is not so difficult; proposing remedies is a calling of a higher order, and I shall do so in this book.

Aside from my main themes—that we must return to extolling the individual, that we are regulating ourselves to death—I want to develop the related idea that there is too much law abroad in the land, that we are relying too heavily on our legal system to handle our problems. I also include a chapter on the special problem of regulation presented by intelligence and foreign counterintelligence in our democratic society. Finally, I examine crime and how we deal with it in our federal system.

One of the values of a book like this is that it can be a road map for those who may want to join the government and reassert control over it. Where else are you going to find anybody to tell you how to do it—unless it is somebody who has been in the government and knows enough to explain it?

One of the first things likely to strike a newcomer to Washington service is a contrast: There are the monuments to the great heroes and ideals of America's heritage, but there are also the nitty-gritty details, the often narrow and selfish realities, of daily governing. The city is like an enormous cathedral, celebrating what is best and most hopeful in us—the Capitol shining on the hill, the spacious avenues stretching out to the White House, the etched-in-granite words of Lincoln, Jefferson and the rest. From the schoolchildren who pour in by the busload to the crustiest of federal bureaucrat, the emotional pull of Washington never fails.

Yet for those who work there, the day-to-day business of government has a practical side that threatens to drown out the larger message of the capital. The marble corridors of Congress may be crowded with the statues of bygone heroes, but the business of individual congressmen on any given day is likely to revolve around the size of a federal subsidy for one constituent group or the question of special tax breaks for another. And many of the issues that concern officials in the Justice Department, at the Treasury, or even the man in the Oval Office, are usually just as worldly.

The task for those in government is somehow to retain their commitment to the lofty and fundamental principles enshrined in Washington while they deal with the reality of their daily agendas. Fortunately, history provides examples of leaders who had the capacity to do just that. In this regard, as in so many others, Lincoln towers above all.

My mind goes back to the Civil War, to a time late in that desperate, all-consuming struggle when Lincoln met Alexander H. Stephens, Vice-President of the Confederacy, at Hampton Roads, Virginia. The question was a possible agreement to end the bloody conflict. By then the war had become a seemingly hopeless tangle of motives and emotions: states' rights, slavery, regional rivalries, economic interests, political ambitions, hatred bred of so much failure and death. Yet what counted most to Lincoln remained as clear as ever. Lincoln handed Stephens an envelope on which he had written just one word—union. Accept that, he told Stephens, and you may write the other terms. It was characteristic behavior for Lincoln to be flexible, fair and generous on details, but to insist that fundamental principles be observed.

There are people in *all* parts of the federal government who strive to meet that high standard of public service, but they seemed to be especially numerous in the Department of Justice. Indeed, I found the dominant spirit there to be a sense of personal responsibility for taking care that the laws were faithfully executed. As a result, the ultimate loyalty of these people is not to any one man or party or faction. Rather, their loyalty is to the fundamental concept of the rule of impartial law—the crowning achievement of our government. Despite my fifteen years of experience on the federal bench before moving to the department, I did not fully appreciate until I came to Washington just how deeply the men and women of the Justice Department were committed to the idea that, in order to survive, our government has to be right with the law.

Finally, I would like to speak briefly about the background I brought to my experience in Washington and about what— out of that experience—seems most important.

As a judge, I was required to examine in minute detail such problems confronting America as the antiquated, overcrowded prison system, school desegregation, other kinds of discrimination, tax disputes, oil and gas controversies, as well as the general run of problems that citizens ask federal courts to resolve. As attorney general, I had a vantage point that was even broader. I had a close association with the President and my colleagues in the Cabinet and I served as a lawyer for many of the government's high offices. I was also deeply involved in law enforcement and foreign intelligence.

From my close observation of particular government problems while on the bench and from my overview as attorney general, I now want to write about the government as it relates to individual liberty.

I

WHAT WENT WRONG

Looking back to 1976, one sees that President Carter ran for office and won election on the pledge of regaining control of the government in Washington. But he was unable to deliver on the pledge, and that, I submit, is the main reason why he was driven out of office in the 1980 election.

What is puzzling about President Carter's failure is that he does not take his promises lightly. But in fact he promised too much during the 1976 campaign, and compounded the problem by having his staff publish a compilation called "Promises, Promises." Only after the compilation did we realize the excessive number he had made.

One of the greatest errors he committed as President was attempting to carry out all his promises. President Carter argued that the people believed his campaign pledges, and being an honest man he felt he had no choice but to try to carry them out.

Actually, Americans don't want everything politicians say they will deliver. The consumer protection bureau Carter promised offers a good example. Congress, reflecting the mood of the American people, could not even begin to enact the necessary legislation to create the bureau. While trying to fulfill scores of promises, President Carter missed carrying out basic reforms.

President Carter sincerely believed in the need to regain control of the government. But he failed, partly because he staffed the government with McGovern people, with Kennedy people—people with no feelings of loyalty toward him and, more important, with a different view of government. President Carter did this unwittingly by accepting the so-called Washington government-in-waiting.

The members of the government-in-waiting sometimes work on Capitol Hill or the various think tanks of the Left and Right or in Washington's dominant private industry, law firms, when they are not employed by a President. When the opposing political party moves into the White House, they move to these other jobs and bide their time until their next opportunity. The government-in-waiting is made up of people who are permanently entrenched in Washington. I'm talking about the lower-level people. They would have gone in with McGovern just as easily as they went in with Carter. They were not prepared to carry out the kind of reform that I am talking about.

This phenomenon of a government-in-waiting that hovers around Washington is not restricted to Democrats. Less than a week after the 1980 election, Richard Viguerie, an expert at raising political funds through direct mail appeals and a leader of the "New Right," was complaining that President-elect Reagan and his top aides were relying too much on moderates and Ford-Nixon appointees in setting up the transition mechanism.

One way to overcome the problem would be to staff the government, as best you could, from people who have no vested interests in Washington. But that is virtually impossible, because it is hard to lure folks to Washington. Not everybody wants to be in the government. I do have suggestions for a practical way of staffing the government from non-bureaucrats outside of Washington, and will present these suggestions in the last chapter, which deals with reforms.

After staffing the government with the Washington-in-waiting people, President Carter made another crucial error. He moved Vice-President Walter F. Mondale into the White House. Vice-Presidents traditionally have two sets of offices. One is in the Executive Office Building, an architecturally splendid structure next door to the White House; the other is in the Senate, where the Vice-President carries out his largely ceremonial duties as president of the Senate.

Moving the Vice-President into the White House had a profound and adverse impact on the Carter presidency. I know that President Carter repeatedly praised Mondale as the most effective Vice-President in the nation's history and said, in the week following the 1980 election, that he and Mondale were as close as brothers. But Mondale's and Carter's views were not the same. Mondale came from the liberal bloc of the Democratic party, the folks that Jimmy Carter defeated in the primaries of 1976 and again in 1980, when Senator Kennedy carried their standard. Jimmy Carter never presented himself as a liberal in the Mondale-Humphrey mold, though he did from time to time depict himself as a populist. The idea of a millionaire populist has always amused me, since the two persuasions seem contradictory. Yet whatever pigeonhole President Carter belongs in, it is well to the right of Vice-President Mondale's.

But the Vice-President tried to shape administration policy to his way of thinking in important areas, and in some instances he succeeded. He managed to do this because of his physical location in the west wing of the White House and because of placing some close aides in crucial posts in the presidential policy-making apparatus. Two such aides were Bert Carp, Number 2 man on the domestic policy staff, and David Aaron, deputy assistant to the President for national security, one step down from Zbigniew Brzezinski, the President's national security adviser. Both men moved with Mondale from Capitol Hill to the White House. Carp had been Mondale's top domestic affairs adviser in the Senate, while Aaron had been Mondale's leading foreign and military affairs aide.

This placement of Mondale men in key spots led, in part,

to President Carter's views being subsumed by those of his staff. The attempt by Carter and Mondale to gloss over fundamental differences in their political philosophies also helped produce the unclear, all-things-to-all-people voice that the public heard so often from the administration.

President Carter, who privately articulates strong beliefs, was not perceived as a leader with deeply held convictions. Certainly his administration was not viewed as holding a discernible, consistent philosophy, in contrast to the public's perception of the Reagan administration. The difference lies in part in President Reagan's staff sharing a single view, that of its Chief Executive.

If the system of elevating the Vice-President's office is going to be followed by future Presidents, people ought to look more carefully at who the Vice-President is, and he or she will have to take less of a backseat in the election campaign.

I played a role in some of the incidents where Vice-President Mondale tried to use his office's newly won clout to shape or reshape White House policy. To appreciate them, you must remember that in the 1976 campaign President Carter promised, and then instructed me to establish as far as constitutionally possible, an independent Department of Justice. The administration's views on matters of law, then, were to be decided at the Justice Department, not at 1600 Pennsylvania Avenue. Of course, the President, being constitutionally charged with faithfully carrying out the nation's laws, had the ultimate authority and could always fire me.

Vice-President Mondale attempted to exert his influence and that of the White House staff on the independent Justice Department in a ticklish Church-State matter, in two civil rights cases and in writing a charter of dos and don'ts for the Federal Bureau of Investigation.

The Church-State issue arose from the question of whether the federal government constitutionally could extend aid under the Comprehensive Employment and Training Act to sectarian—in this case, mainly Catholic—schools. CETA was enacted in 1973 to provide funds for "job training and employment opportunities for economically disadvantaged, unemployed and underemployed persons."[1] Steps were to be taken "to assure that training and other services lead to maximum employment opportunities and enhance self-sufficiency by establishing a flexible and decentralized system of federal, state and local programs."[2]

The Department of Labor, which approves grants to employers under the act, asked the Justice Department's Office of Legal Counsel in December 1978 for an opinion on the constitutionality of using CETA funds to pay the salaries of disadvantaged persons in sectarian schools. Labor wanted the opinion for two reasons. It planned to issue regulations governing such use of CETA funds, and the Wisconsin Civil Liberties Union had sued the department on grounds that using federal funds to employ persons in church schools violated the "Establishment Clause" of the First Amendment, which states that "Congress shall make no law respecting an establishment of religion, or prohibiting the free exercise thereof . . ."

On January 25, 1979, John M. Harmon, assistant attorney general in charge of the Office of Legal Counsel, responded in a twelve-page memorandum that using the funds for such CETA positions in church schools as health aides and kitchen personnel would pass constitutional muster under Supreme Court decisions. But funding positions that involve teaching or counseling, maintenance work or most clerical responsibilities is "precluded under recent decisions of the Supreme Court."

Protests were not long in coming, particularly from New York and Chicago, where cutting off CETA funds would have a significant impact on Catholic schools and the large Catholic population. Senators Jacob Javits of New York, Harrison A. Williams, Jr., of New Jersey and Richard S. Schweiker of Pennsylvania wrote me a joint letter, urging that I have the opinion reconsidered and charging that it ran counter to Congress's intent. I also heard critical comments from Congressman Carl D. Perkins, chairman of the House Committee on Education and Labor, and Jonathan B. Bingham of New York, as well as from the U.S. Catholic Conference.

But the broadest attack on the Justice Department position was mounted by Vice-President Mondale, who asked me to intervene in the matter.

In response, on May 15, 1979, Harmon, at my direction, explained, in twenty-three pages of memoranda, why he was sticking with his original position.

On June 14, 1979, President Carter, in a two-paragraph letter to me, flatly overruled our decision. His action, which came at the recommendation of Mondale and Stu Eizenstat, who headed the President's domestic policy staff, brought me so close to the brink of resigning that my special assistant, Terrence B. Adamson, carried the CETA file with him when we traveled to Russia in the summer of 1979 in case events required that we resign over the issue while abroad.

Harmon called Eizenstat for clarification, and was referred to Mondale's longtime aide, Bert Carp, now Eizenstat's deputy. Harmon's memo to me on his conversation with Carp lifted the curtain on the backstage maneuvering that resulted in the only instance of President Carter overruling me.

"He [Carp] said that the reason Eizenstat and the Vice-President took this matter to the President was because they frankly were upset that the AG had not consulted with the White House staff or the Vice-President before issuing his opinion, despite the fact that the Vice-President had called the AG three times about the matter and the AG was aware of Eizenstat's interest in the question.

"In sum, he said that Eizenstat and the Vice-President did not feel that the AG should have an opportunity to present his position to the President because the AG had given up that opportunity when he issued the opinion without consulting Eizenstat and the Vice-President. Carp said that he and the Vice-President learned about the opinion when the Catholic Conference confronted them with it the day it was issued."

I dealt with the complaint of the Vice-President and Eizenstat in a June 15, 1979, letter to the President. "According to Mr. Carp, Mr. Eizenstat and the Vice-President were upset because I did not clear my final opinion with them and give them the chance to take the question to you before it was issued. Implicit in this complaint is the notion that the proper way to proceed was for you to direct, on their recommendation, the conclusion I would reach in my legal opinion. Because I failed to follow that course, you have now taken the extraordinary step of overruling the opinion of the attorney general."

Later in the five-page letter, I reminded the President that he had "directed me to establish an independent Department of Justice, a neutral zone in the government where decisions will be made on the merits free of political interference or influence. I was asked for my opinion on a question of law. I was under the professional obligation as a lawyer and under an official obligation as your attorney general to state my frank and candid legal opinion on this question.

"While no one likes to be overruled, I respect your authority to do so, for you, as President, are the one who is ultimately responsible under the Constitution, and to the people, for the actions of this government.

". . . there is nothing inconsistent with my concept of an independent attorney general for you to overrule my decision, even on a question of law. However, the notion reflected in your staff's complaint that I should have given you the opportunity to direct what my legal opinion should be flies in the face of all that we have been trying to do since coming to Washington to rebuild the Department of Justice.

"I will advise you at an early date whether I can defend the CETA regulations in question. This will depend on my judgment whether ethically there is enough of an argument in favor of the regulations to allow me to assert their validity in court."

I closed the letter, telling the President: "I regret this entire turn of events and that you have to bother with it."

My successor, Attorney General Civiletti, decided to defend the CETA funding in the Wisconsin case on the strength of regulations that the Department of Labor had issued. The regulations set strict limitations on what use the money could be put to in church schools.

Not strict enough, however, for John W. Reynolds, chief

judge of the U.S. District Court for the Eastern District of Wisconsin. In 1979, Judge Reynolds enjoined the Labor Department from "granting, awarding or contracting for payment of any CETA funds for full-time or part-time employees of any elementary or secondary school operated by or for any religious or sectarian organization." What's more, Judge Reynolds made the injunction a nationwide prohibition rather than limiting it to Milwaukee County where the case arose.

In September of 1980, the U.S. Court of Appeals for the Seventh Circuit affirmed Judge Reynolds's ruling, and directed him to make the preliminary injunction he had issued a permanent ban. The Justice Department decided not to appeal the decision to the Supreme Court.

There's a footnote to President Carter's pledge to establish an independent Justice Department. During the 1976 campaign, candidate Carter was to appear on NBC Television's "Meet the Press." I suggested to him that he mention the Justice Department pledge, adding that it could be implemented by giving the attorney general a term of office that was not coterminous with the President's—say, five years. The candidate broached that idea to a nationwide television audience, and after taking office kept asking me when we were going to fulfill that promise. Unfortunately, the Office of Legal Counsel had, at my request, looked into the proposal for creating a noncoterminous attorney general, and reported back that it would be unconstitutional. The President, under the Constitution, is responsible for faithfully executing the laws, and he couldn't discharge that responsibility if the attorney general did not have to answer to the President.

Despite this obstacle, we did deliver on the President's pledge to establish an independent Department of Justice, devising systems to bar interference by members of Congress and their staffs and the White House staff with the work of career department attorneys. Our objective was to make the department a neutral zone in the government, free of political interference or influence.

The first civil rights case in which Mondale made the weight of his office felt was probably the most important legal issue that confronted the Carter administration—affirmative action and how far government can go in redressing the wrongs of two hundred years without itself engaging in reverse discrimination.

The case that came to the Supreme Court involved Allan Bakke, a thirty-eight-year-old civil engineer and former marine captain who twice had been turned down for admission to the medical school of the University of California at Davis. The California Supreme Court had ruled that Bakke, a white, had been unconstitutionally discriminated against by a UC-Davis special admissions program that set aside sixteen of one hundred medical school openings a year for blacks, Chicanos, Asians and American Indians. The university, defending the policy as the only effective way to make up for pervasive discrimination against minorities, appealed to the U.S. Supreme Court. On February 22, 1977, only a month after President Carter took office, the justices agreed to decide the issue, the most significant civil rights controversy to come before them since the school desegregation cases of 1954.

Once the court granted certiorari, or review of the case, I asked Judge Wade H. McCree, Jr., the solicitor general, and Drew S. Days III, assistant attorney general for civil rights, to work out the position the federal government would take before the High Court. The U.S. government was not a party to the case, the dispute being between Bakke and the state of California in the form of the university. But clearly the issue was both crucial and timely in the development of civil rights law, and the federal government would want to lend its assistance in the form of a friend-of-the-court, or amicus, brief.

McCree and Days are both black, but that had nothing to do with my assigning the development of the position to them. As the solicitor general, the government's chief advocate before the court, and as the assistant attorney general for civil rights, McCree and Days were the two officials who would naturally be assigned the mission.

After a good deal of writing and rewriting, McCree gave me the initial draft. I then made perhaps my greatest mistake with regard to the power centers at the White House. Nowhere is the tug of power between the White House and a Cabinet department more apparent than in a dispute between the Justice Department and the President's staff over what is law and what is policy. If the staff had its way, no doubt every major issue that naturally fell to the Justice Department would be considered policy rather than a legal matter. Then the White House would be making all the decisions, because it is the White House where policy is made.

My mistake was in taking a copy of the draft friend-of-the-court brief with me to the White House when I went to tell the President what position we were developing. Bob Lip-shutz, the President's counsel, sat in on the session, and President Carter gave the draft brief to him. I told the President that the government would stand for affirmative action but would oppose rigid quotas to carry out affirmative action programs, a position that meant Bakke would have to be admitted to the medical school.

That started wide circulation of the brief. Stu Eizenstat, chief of the domestic policy staff, and Vice-President Mondale were among those who received a copy. Calls began to flow into the Justice Department with suggestions. It immediately became apparent there was tension between affirmative action proponents and those who were antiquota, particularly Jewish people, who feared quotas would strike a blow at the quality education they seek for their offspring. This, incidentally, contributed to the breach between many Jewish leaders, long a mainstay of the civil rights movement, and blacks, who see affirmative action as a promising avenue of escape from the ghetto.

At the Justice Department, Wade McCree and Drew Days were into their third-draft brief, incorporating some of the suggestions that had been advanced. We had learned enough not to circulate these later drafts. The proposed government stance had changed. Judge McCree was pursuing the idea of arguing that the case came to the Supreme Court with inadequate facts and should be returned to the lower court for further hearing. But at this point, a copy of the initial draft was leaked to *The New York Times,* intensifying the controversy.

Joseph Califano, the secretary of health, education and welfare, the Cabinet department that shares school desegregation enforcement with the Justice Department, met with McCree to express concern over any legal brief that would advocate admitting Bakke. The Black Congressional Caucus, equally exercised over that position, met with me, Judge McCree and Drew Days. Clearly and simply, there were attempts to pressure us.

Not long after, my special assistant, Terry Adamson, and I were at the White House on other business, and I was asked to meet with the Vice-President. Eizenstat, Lipshutz and, for a brief time, Hamilton Jordan huddled around a coffee table in Mondale's White House office with me, Adamson and the Vice-President.

Mondale got to the point quickly. He said the Bakke case represented an extremely important policy decision and that the President wanted to be consistent with the stand he took on affirmative action during the 1976 campaign. Eizenstat, the policy man, quickly summarized that—for affirmative action, against quotas.

I responded that I was aware of the President's position, I agreed with it and that McCree's brief would be in accord with the position.

Riding back to the Department of Justice, I instructed Adamson not to tell McCree of the meeting or the Vice-President's comments. The pressure on him was heavy enough without adding the weight of one of the White House's centers of power.

Judge McCree and Drew Days spent much of the next week meeting with individuals and groups who had strong positions on affirmative action and quotas, but they didn't produce any draft. I told them we had to complete the work and to lock themselves in a room until the job was done.

Finally, when on the next Saturday I was still without the brief, I asked for McCree and learned that he was in Detroit. I was scheduled later that day to fly with Mondale on a helicopter to Buck Hill Falls, Pa. (where we would be speaking to a conference of the Second Federal Judicial Circuit), and I anticipated that he would ask me about Bakke. Adamson, who had been in daily touch with McCree, summarized for me the position McCree was developing. Together, Adamson and I worked out a statement of the principles the government was advocating in the case. We reached McCree and read the statement of principles, incorporated some minor changes and then had Adamson type out the principles and hand-deliver a copy to the White House for Eizenstat.

When Adamson stepped off the helicopter with us near Buck Hill Falls, an airman awaited him with a telephone in hand. On the line was Eizenstat, calling from the White House to tell us that the President agreed with the position we had outlined. I instructed Adamson to notify McCree that the brief should be filed with the court settling the matter. There was no issue left open for Mondale to raise.

In the brief that was submitted to the court, the government supported neither Bakke nor the university. Instead, the government argued that more facts were needed before the issue could be resolved, and it urged the justices to send the case back to the lower court to develop the missing facts.

The Supreme Court, in its 5–4 decision, ruled along the lines that McCree had embraced in the first draft.[3] The court held that Bakke must be admitted to the medical school because he had been denied admission by a rigid quota system that worked against whites. At the same time, the court ruled that universities may constitutionally give blacks and minority members special consideration through admission programs that do not employ rigid racial quotas.

The second instance of the Vice-President's intervening in a civil rights matter involved the 1973 killing of Santos Rodriguez, a twelve-year-old Mexican-American in Dallas. Rodriguez was shot to death by Darrell Cain, a Dallas policeman, as the officer questioned the boy, whose hands were manacled behind him as he sat in Cain's squad car. Cain, according to evidence presented at a later state trial, was playing "Russian roulette" with his .357 magnum revolver while questioning the boy about a service station burglary.

The state court convicted Cain of murder with malice, and

the jury sentenced him to five years in prison. Hispanics in Texas and elsewhere in the Southwest protested the sentence as symbolic of the light punishment given policemen who brutalize Mexican-Americans.

The Justice Department's Civil Rights Division looked into the case in 1973, but closed it when Cain was convicted in state court. Department policy at that time barred dual prosecution by federal authorities when a person has been convicted under state law for the same actions.

I changed this policy one month after taking office, being faced with some egregious cases of police brutality that had not been vigorously prosecuted by state officials. The Santos Rodriguez case again came under scrutiny by the Civil Rights Division.

President Carter and Vice-President Mondale then entered the picture. The President, on a June 1978 trip to Texas, was shown color photos of the slain youth by Mexican-American leaders, and the pictures horrified him. He denounced the shooting as "something any American would be ashamed of " and assured the Hispanics that press reports of a tentative Justice Department decision not to prosecute the policeman in federal court were erroneous.

Jody Powell, the President's press secretary, who was on the Texas trip, called me from there to ask how the intense feelings could be resolved. I responded that I would personally review the sensitive case and suggested that the President could tell the Hispanic leaders that. President Carter then gave them that assurance.

I did review the case, and I agreed with the recommendation against federal prosecution by the U.S. attorney in Dallas; by Drew Days, assistant attorney general for civil rights; and by Deputy Attorney General Civiletti. The case simply did not meet the criteria for dual prosecution that we had set in 1977. This was a particularly tough decision because of the senselessness of the crime and the victim's age, but the case fell short of dual prosecution standards because it had been vigorously prosecuted in the state court, even though the jury had decided to sentence the officer to only five years in prison.

There were other barriers to initiating federal prosecution. If we had decided to apply retroactively a new policy to a crime that had occurred five years earlier, the decision could have been challenged as an instance of selective prosecution —that is, prosecuting a case that would not have been pursued if normal criteria had been used. Then, too, the policeman's right to a speedy trial arguably would be violated by trying him five years after the crime. None of these issues flatly ruled out prosecution, but they collectively raised questions of the fairness and wisdom of trying the officer again.

I made the final decision on my way to Australia, where I was going on an official visit, and cabled the result back to the department. A detailed explanation of the decision was issued by the press office.

The reasons failed to mute the outcry from Hispanics. Vilma S. Martinez, president of the Mexican-American Legal Defense and Education Fund, told reporters the decision was "frightening."

Since the President was in Bonn to meet with European leaders on economic problems, Mexican-American groups went to Mondale to protest. He told them he would arrange a meeting for them with Deputy Attorney General Civiletti, who was acting as attorney general in my absence.

Adding to the pressure on Civiletti, President Carter called him and was, as Ben later recalled, "agitated, short and brusque" in telling my deputy that he would have to look at the case again.

During a day of briefings by Civil Rights Division lawyers and meetings with the Mexican-Americans, Civiletti tried unsuccessfully to reach me. He finally called the President and said he could not overrule me because he thought my position was correct. Ben stood up to pressure from the Vice-President and the President for what he thought was right.

President Carter closed the matter in a handwritten note to me on July 20, 1978: "The Rodriguez case was/is very embarrassing to me. I hope you made the right decision. J.C."

The incident involving the FBI charter took place when Mondale was out of the country. For Mondale, asserting or attempting to assert his authority in an intelligence matter must have seemed like a case of doing what came naturally. In the Senate, he had served on the original intelligence committee, which heard testimony of abuses by the FBI and other agencies. Those hearings helped generate the momentum for writing the first detailed FBI charter.

After long, complex negotiations, we had presented to the Senate a draft of that charter. We looked on it as an exhaustive attempt to protect citizens' liberties from unjustified invasions by FBI agents without sacrificing citizens' security by shackling agents so tightly they could not perform their missions. Some senators began to redo sections that had taken months to work out.

Flying back from giving an out-of-town speech, I was asked by a reporter on board the plane about the prospects for adoption of the charter. Here, I thought, was the opportunity to serve notice that the administration had gone as far as it could. I told the reporter, and he wrote in the next day's edition of his newspaper, that if the Senate tinkered too much with the proposal, I would rather have no charter at all and let the FBI operate under guidelines first issued by my predecessor, Attorney General Edward H. Levi.

I heard indirectly from Mondale about the comment at a meeting of the National Security Council, one of the key White House bodies in which a Mondale aide served as the Number 2 man. The deputy, David Aaron, opened the meeting by stating that the Vice-President wanted to know what I had meant to convey by my charter comment.

"I meant exactly what I said," I told Aaron and several others at the meeting. "I work for the President, not the Vice-President, and I checked that out with the President." Aaron sat down without a word and didn't raise the subject again.

When the Carter administration left office, the Senate was still tinkering with the legislation for an FBI charter, and the FBI was operating under the attorney general's guidelines.

These examples of a Vice-President flexing his newly found muscle are cited out of no sense of pique with Walter

Mondale. I have high personal regard for him, and I agree with President Carter's assessment of his skill at helping to govern. Moreover, he was loyal to a fault as President Carter came under increasingly hostile attacks, first from Senator Edward M. Kennedy of his own party, and then from GOP nominee Ronald Reagan. Mondale was an effective point man in the early strategy of reminding voters of the extreme political stances that Ronald Reagan had taken in his political career.

What I am raising here are institutional objections to making the office of Vice-President yet another power center at the White House. There already were four such centers before the Vice-President moved in. One of them, the domestic policy staff, headed by Stuart E. Eizenstat, had more than fifty people when I left Washington. This compared with a peak force of seventy as the staff, then known as the domestic council, operated under President Richard M. Nixon. Under President Gerald R. Ford, the staff dropped to about thirty. More important than the numbers, the domestic policy staff during the Carter administration began to function for the first time as had been envisaged when the unit was formed on July 1, 1970. It was to bring a sense of order to the unstructured and confusing manner in which domestic policy proposals were being funneled to the President and to equip him with the staff resources to handle complex domestic issues, nearly all of which cross departmental lines.

The Office of Management and Budget, another of the centers, is an organization with a name that obscures its sweeping veto authority over substantive policy matters. OMB was the Bureau of the Budget until former President Nixon changed its name in 1970. In the old days—before inflation became runaway—the Bureau of the Budget devoted much of its time to preventing government agencies from stumbling over one another. It would intervene, for example, to stop one department from financing a new highway across a stretch of land that another agency was planning to submerge under ten feet of water. But as holding down spending became a government concern, OMB moved to center stage, finding likely places for the Chief Executive to achieve savings. This budget-cutting became a powerful tool of policy-making.

And the White House Counsel's Office, yet another power center, wields significant power, even when under the stewardship of a relatively unassertive, retiring lawyer like Bob Lipshutz, President Carter's first counsel. The office was established in the early 1940's during the Roosevelt administration. At times, the counsel has been more of a general presidential assistant than a lawyer, but in recent years the job has taken on increasing amounts of legal work. The counsel sometimes serves as a conduit through whom all communications from the attorney general to the President flow. When Lloyd Cutler left his Washington law firm to succeed Lipshutz in the job, the power of the counsel was unmistakable.

One example was the shift in the administration's public stand on whether the Ethics in Government Act of 1978 should be amended. That was a law which I fought hard against but which President Carter backed in the spirit of Watergate reform. The law authorized appointment of a special prosecutor to investigate allegations against any of some 240 persons in the executive branch. These officials are covered by the law even after they leave government as long as the President under whom they served remains in office. They even continue to be subject to investigation by a special prosecutor during the term of the next President if he belongs to the same political party as did the President under whom the ex-officials served.

For more than a year after the law became effective, the Justice Department hierarchy, including my successor, Attorney General Benjamin R. Civiletti, and Philip B. Heymann, assistant attorney general in charge of the Criminal Division, had stated repeatedly that it was too early to push for any changes in it. They acknowledged that the act seemed to suffer from having too much of a hair trigger by requiring appointment of a special prosecutor to investigate government officials for alleged crimes that would not ordinarily be pursued by federal authorities. In conducting a preliminary investigation to decide whether to seek appointment of a special prosecutor, the attorney general is faced with proving a negative. To recommend that a case be dropped under the 1978 law, he must find "that the matter is so unsubstantiated that no further investigation or prosecution is warranted."

Yet on September 18, 1980, Lloyd Cutler, while subjecting himself to that awful tradition of a breakfast session with a group of selected reporters (the "guest" never gets to masticate, let alone digest, his soggy scrambled eggs before being questioned), said he thought the act should be amended. The press did not even mention the Justice Department's oft-stated policy that more time should pass before tinkering with the 1978 law. The President's counsel had spoken, declaring administration policy on a sensitive legal matter.

The next month, Civiletti, in a lecture at Southern Methodist University, spelled out in detail "several changes" that he felt needed to be considered, which gave the impression that he and his beliefs as attorney general were subservient to the statement of the White House counsel.

Illustrative of the tension between the White House Counsel's Office and the attorney general is an incident that took place when the office was created during the administration of Franklin D. Roosevelt.[4] When Roosevelt was governor of New York, Sam Rosenman served him as counsel to the governor. Rosenman became a judge when FDR went to the White House, but the President frequently sought Rosenman's advice. Finally, Roosevelt said: "This is not going to work out at all. I want you to come down and join the staff." They then decided that Rosenman would have a title similar to the one he held when he served under Governor Roosevelt. He would be called counsel to the President. About a week after their decision, President Roosevelt called Rosenman and told him that Attorney General Francis Biddle had objected on the grounds that under the Constitution he was supposed to be the President's counsel and that there was room for no other.

Rosenman said: "I am sorry to hear that. I guess I had better stay up here in New York."

Roosevelt replied: "No. We are going to go ahead with the plan, but with two differences. First, we are going to call you 'special counsel to the President,' instead of counsel, and secondly, I am going to announce it next week when Biddle is in Mexico."

The fourth power center before the Vice-President moved into the White House was the National Security Council, an organization whose influence depends in large part on the person who, as the President's national security adviser, is the chief staff man on the NSC and heads one of its principal subcommittees. During the first term of the Nixon administration, Henry A. Kissinger was such a powerful national security adviser that he eclipsed Secretary of State William P. Rogers and finally moved over to the Department of State to assume the secretary's job in title as well as in fact.

Zbigniew Brzezinski, President Carter's national security adviser, had a similar ascendancy over Secretary of State Cyrus R. Vance. I recall thinking during the administration's first months in office that Vance always seemed to be traveling, and I wondered whether his schedule had been planned by Brzezinski's large staff at the NSC. Brzezinski even had his own press relations man on the staff, which was unusual since Brzezinski was an aide to the President, not an independent policy-maker.

In meetings of the National Security Council, Brzezinski imposed an order on the proceedings that took me by surprise. He would always summarize the sessions, and the six or so points he would glean from the discussions often seemed a highly personal view, especially when it came to resolution of problems. This prevented a free flow of ideas to the President in the national security area.

Despite my having a mandate from the President to run an independent Department of Justice and despite an acquaintance with President Carter that went back to our childhoods in Sumter County, Georgia, I ran into problems with the White House power centers. They tend to fight among themselves, and you have to be careful not to get caught in their crossfire.

One example is the trouble I had recommending federal judges for nomination by the President. Traditionally, this responsibility is exercised by the attorney general, who relies on the FBI for investigating the candidate's background and on such legal organizations as the American Bar Association for an evaluation of the prospect's record and reputation.

The Carter administration made an historical change in the process. President Carter had pledged during the 1976 campaign to pick judges based on merit. We took a major step towards fulfilling that promise by winning the support of Senator James O. Eastland of Mississippi, chairman of the Judiciary Committee, for creating commissions in each of the nation's eleven judicial circuits to recommend candidates for federal appellate judgeships. This was a sharp departure from the past, when senators of the President's party virtually dictated the choice by notifying the White House whom they wanted for a vacancy in their area. If neither of the senators in the state where the judicial vacancy occurred were of the President's party, then a political committee in the state would recommend a nominee whom the President almost always accepted. There was no guarantee that merit would play any role.

For obvious reasons, the recommendation of judicial nominees, a legal matter, flows from the attorney general through the White House counsel to the President. Here we ran into the flak. Bob Lipshutz, as I have noted, is not a combative, overly assertive individual. But he had working on his staff Ms. Margaret McKenna, a lawyer dedicated to protecting and expanding women's rights.

In addition to promising to select judges on the basis of merit, President Carter had pledged to put more women and minorities on the bench. We did this by practicing "affirmative action"—that is, picking women and blacks and Hispanics who were certainly qualified but who might not otherwise win over a white male with longer, more varied experience. So successful were we in placing women on the bench—forty-one women had been nominated and confirmed by the time the Carter administration left office, more than eight times the number on January 20, 1977—that I thought the need for affirmative action in picking federal judges had run its course.

Enter Ms. McKenna. Some women's organizations took issue with our rate of progress, despite our statistics. Unsatisfied by discussions with me and Associate Attorney General Mike Egan, who was in day-to-day charge of judicial selection, the women's groups turned to Margaret McKenna. About this time, the Congress enacted the omnibus judgeship bill, creating 152 new federal judicial posts, which meant that President Carter would be naming more judges at one time than any of his predecessors had. The new judgeships thus upped the stakes in what Ms. McKenna and the women's groups were seeking.

Mr. Lipshutz and Ms. McKenna departed from the historical precedent by attempting to assert White House staff control over the judicial nominations. Their claim was that they were not trying to take over the process but simply were trying to assure that I did not overlook minorities and women in my recommendations. They set themselves up as the keepers of the morality in the area of discrimination, as if I and others at the Justice Department lacked their degree of concern.

The struggle was manageable until I learned that they had applied the option process to judicial nominations. This meant that the name of a prospective judge was circulated to various power groups, which included the domestic policy staff, the Vice-President's Office and the White House lobbyist on Capitol Hill. Each was empowered to vote on whether the prospect that the attorney general had rated as his top recommendation should be selected. The power groups even could add names to the list I had compiled. This system materially altered the relationship between the President and the attorney general. I first realized I had lost control of judicial selection when the President sent me a list of prospects with a longhand notation instructing me to submit someone other than the nominee I had recommended. It was obvious that the document had been submitted to the various power groups in the White House.

This was such an outrageous intrusion into the prerogative of the attorney general and such a politicization of the process of selection that I thought of resigning. Instead, I decided to respond to the move of the White House power centers by calling on my friend, Charles Kirbo, to review the matter and advise the President on what was happening. Kirbo, a confidant of President Carter, is a partner in King & Spalding of Atlanta, the law firm I left to become attorney general and have since rejoined. He first came to know Jimmy Carter by representing him in a crucial election fraud dispute in Carter's 1962 race for the Georgia State Senate. This election victory started Carter on the road that ended in the White House. Kirbo, the slowest talker and best listener I know, intervened to help me block the counsel's power play.

From that point forward, I did take recommendations to a special White House committee, made up of Hamilton Jordan, then-chief White House lobbyist Frank Moore, Lipshutz and, sometimes, Jody Powell. They would consider my recommendations, and I usually prevailed. At my request, the procedure was for me to meet alone with the President in presenting the recommendations.

This proved so debilitating to Lipshutz that I relented out of compassion and allowed him to go into the Oval Office with me. But he played much the part of a silent partner, unless a minority group member or woman was involved. The President came to recognize him as the adviser who always spoke on behalf of minority and women candidates. We were rarely in disagreement.

Another clash with the power centers took place over the snail darter, a three-inch, tannish species of perch that lives in the Little Tennessee River and that was designated an "endangered species" by the secretary of the interior on November 10, 1975. That designation led the Court of Appeals for the Sixth Circuit to block operation of the virtually completed, multimillion-dollar Tellico Dam near where the Little Tennessee flows into the Big Tennessee. The dam would have completely destroyed the snail darter's then only known habitat by turning it into a reservoir, not the kind of water the inedible fish needs to survive.

The Tennessee Valley Authority, builder and would-be operator of the dam, urged the Supreme Court to reverse the lower court's decision, a position the Justice Department supported during the Ford administration. The Supreme Court agreed to hear the appeal. Following the traditional practice of attorneys general to argue a major case before the nation's highest court sometime during their term of office, I picked the snail darter case as my vehicle. My choice produced grins, even chortles, among some Court watchers. Admittedly, I probably fed that humor when on April 18, 1978, I took time from my Court argument to show the justices a snail darter in a test tube, a departure from the usual Supreme Court practice of considering issues of law, not evidentiary fact.

But aside from the question of what Congress intended when it enacted the Endangered Species Act of 1973, there was beneath the surface the issue of who speaks for the government in deciding the law—the attorney general and his "independent" Justice Department, or presidential assistants. The power centers, in this case Messrs. Eizenstat and Lipshutz, had persuaded President Carter to direct me to switch positions and argue against TVA's position in the name of the environment.

I was in a slow burn. The President wanted me to change my position without any change in the law or facts. I wrote him a memorandum pointing out that he had not been shown an earlier memorandum in which I warned of the danger of reversing a legal position the Justice Department had expressed to the court on behalf of the government. The government would be speaking with an unclear, inconsistent voice if it did an about-face in the midst of an appeal.

"A reversal of that position, coming at this juncture, would (sic) not but undermine the respect traditionally accorded the Department [of Justice] and the Office of the Solicitor General by the justices on the Court," I said in the earlier memorandum.

"Second, a reversal of position on the case would well be

publicly perceived as the administration imposing its policy views on the Justice Department despite the department's contrary judgment of the law."

When I met with the President, I told him that ethically I could not do it. He changed his mind and told me to stick with the original position. Nevertheless, I added: "Your staff is not serving you well."

The real reason I argued the snail darter case was to show the White House staff that I objected most strongly to what they had done with an option paper that they had presented to the President on the issue. I was not given the opportunity to answer that paper or even see it before the President made his initial decision. I told the President that if I could write the option papers, I could win every time.

The legal brief we subsequently presented to the Supreme Court included an appendix, in which Secretary of the Interior Cecil D. Andrus, whose department enforces the Endangered Species Act, argued on behalf of the fish. The unusual public conflict, I think, did not escape the justices' notice. In any event, they ruled 6–3 to sustain the court of appeals and block operation of the dam. A year or so later, I learned that Chief Justice Warren E. Burger, who wrote the Court's opinion, had said that I would have won if the case had been reargued, because two justices in the majority had changed their minds.

In 1979, the year after the Supreme Court ruling, Congress in its wisdom exempted the Tellico Dam from the Environmental Species Act, and the dam went into operation. Then, in November of 1980, the Fish and Wildlife Service found fourteen snail darter babies apparently thriving in a creek eighty miles below the dam that had destroyed their critical habitat.

Struggles within an administration over snail darters, civil rights cases and judgeships were not peculiar to President Carter's tenure, of course. But the examples I have cited of power centers vying with one another did contribute to the administration's failure to speak with a clear voice, as well as to the appearance of vacillating, indecisive leadership. There was no sign that the White House staff was implementing a deeply held philosophy of the President, or that he had expressed one to his aides. Instead, the perception and the fact were that the power centers—and the single-interest groups that were so dominant in the centers—struggled to impose their views on the President.

Prime examples of former leaders of single-interest groups continuing to pursue these interests as officials of the Carter administration were Joan Claybrook and Carol Tucker Foreman. Claybrook was an experienced advocate of consumer causes and Ralph Nader's chief lobbyist before she became administrator of the National Highway Traffic Safety Administration. Inside the corporation boardrooms of America's automakers, Administrator Claybrook became known as the Dragon Lady. In 1977, her first year in the job, recalls of automobiles jumped to 12.9 million from 3.4 million in 1976. Foreman was head of the Consumer Federation of America before joining the administration as assistant secretary of agriculture for Food and Consumer Services. The food industry complained bitterly that she never took off her consumer lobbying hat when she moved over to government.

Equally damaging, I think, but errors that President Carter moved to correct, were his early attempts to govern by Cabinet, which resulted in trivializing the presidency; his shunning of the higher-level Washington Establishment; and his overreliance on the lower-level Washington government-in-waiting.

When President Carter took office, he conducted weekly meetings of the Cabinet secretaries at which we would go around the table, each usually mentioning an activity of the past week or something that might be coming up in the immediate future. The discussions were too disjointed, given the range of Cabinet positions, to produce any coherent themes. It was adult Show-and-Tell, and as a result President Carter became entangled in trivial, technical minutiae that occupied too much of his time and attention. For example, he allowed Cabinet officers to persuade him to call large numbers of congressmen about legislative matters that were not important. At other times, he permitted members of the White House staff, people with programs and interests of their own and who seemed to be in business for themselves, to press him about small matters. These staff members would insist that he carry out every campaign promise, no matter how obscure or narrow it was in the larger scheme of government.

The situation was frustrating to watch, and it finally came to a head—of sorts—at a Camp David conference of the Cabinet in May of 1978. In the aftermath, the White House staff assumed more and more power, and the secretaries of most Cabinet departments were relegated to a lower level of authority.

President Carter set the tone of the session with a lengthy observation that the Cabinet officers were not doing a good job in handling their departments, and thus the government. He asked for comment.

Secretary of Commerce Juanita Kreps, supported by Secretary of Energy James Schlesinger, told him the Cabinet meetings as they were being conducted were just not worthwhile. Why should the secretary of defense have to listen to what is wrong with Housing and Urban Development?

I then told the President: "All sorts of people are not being loyal to you. They are loyal first to their particular single interest which brought them into your administration." I urged him to ferret these people out. He thanked me, but did nothing about my suggestion.

The experiment of weekly Cabinet meetings didn't last much beyond President Carter's first year in office. It became clear the sessions were a waste of time when Hamilton Jordan, whose job grew into chief of staff, and White House Press Secretary Jody Powell stopped coming.

Given President Carter's training and experience prior to entering political life, it is not surprising that he would attempt to grasp the fine details of running each Cabinet department. Such details are the lifeblood of engineers. I wasn't totally joking when I remarked to a group of White House Fellows—promising, bright men and women who spend a year sampling government service under White House auspices after rigorous competition for the appointments—that Jimmy Carter was "about as good a President as an engineer could be." I'll concede, however, that in a humorous manner I was continuing a public exchange with the President over his highly negative comments about lawyers. The exchange began when the President, in a speech to an attorneys' group, had sounded nearly as critical of lawyers as Shakespeare had.[5]

The fact is that President Carter has a brilliant mind and unbounded energy. His administration would have differed significantly had he been placed in office simply to govern, and with no opportunity to run for reelection. In the end, it was kowtowing to single-interest groups to hold their loyalty for the next election that prevented him from appearing to have a coherent presidency.

A major reason I do not believe that governing by Cabinet will work is that the Cabinet of today is too large and unwieldy to function as a management tool reporting directly to the President. Such a system would be all right, as it was for President Washington, if we dropped back to four secretaries —treasury, state, defense and justice. The constituencies of these four Cabinet officers are all of America, but the other secretaries represent limited-interest groups, the secretaries of commerce and labor providing clear examples. I know you can argue that they balance each other off and give the Cabinet diversity and breadth, but I believe a more persuasive argument is to reduce the rank of the limited-interest Cabinet officers to agencylike heads.

Of course, if you don't have Cabinet government, you have government by a White House staff that has not been confirmed by the Senate. So you lose one of the checks and balances in our system. Because there is constant friction between the White House staff and the Cabinet secretaries, it is extremely difficult to find quality people to serve as Cabinet heads.

I do think the President was on the right track when he said he was going to have Cabinet government. But the Cabinet he had in mind was too big, and some members tended to set up a government of their own. Cabinet members can't go into business for themselves. They have to be loyal to the President. At the first sign of disloyalty, the Cabinet member should be fired.

President Carter erred in obtaining promises from most Cabinet appointees to serve a full four-year term. Instead, he should probably have asked each of them for an undated resignation, which would have served to put them on notice that none of them, upon moving to Washington, should buy a house unless he or she had very substantial means. A Cabinet officer who would do any more than rent an apartment is a person running too high a risk. You have to be prepared to leave. When the time comes that you are not doing your job right or have a divided loyalty, you should get out.

Some of the trouble that President Carter ran into his first year in office resulted from his anti-Washington campaign theme. He was the outsider who was going to bring a fresh approach to national government. This led him to ignore the Establishment once he was in office, offending potential allies and failing to draw upon experienced individuals.

During the second half of his administration, however, President Carter wooed the Establishment with genuine ardor. He enlisted for the White House staff such Establishment members as Lloyd Cutler, Hedley Donovan of *Time,* Inc., and Alonzo MacDonald, former managing partner of McKenzie & Co., a large management consulting firm. These appointments helped broaden the advice the President was receiving. Unfortunately, by that time the administration was too far down the road for the infusion to work. The fact that Donovan resigned before the election also suggested that President Carter might not have used all the talent as well as he could have.

Any attempt to diagnose what went wrong and caused the people to vote President Carter out of office must touch on style. The United States—and certainly Jimmy Carter—would have been better off if the President had put his feet up on the railing from time to time, taken a drink and chatted with a few friends of broad experience and mature judgment. Such conversations could have helped the President to relax, and perhaps changed his pattern of working so hard on so many matters instead of focusing his energy on the few, truly important problems.

Gentle, but repeated prodding from trusted confidants would have been required to break a work habit that goes back to the President's earliest years. This work habit was used to advantage by the McGovern-Kennedy—and I would add Nader—government-in-waiting that President Carter installed in the middle-level posts at the White House and some Cabinet departments. Their prompting led him to struggle with a mass of minutiae rather than concentrating on the major issues. This deflection of his energies confused the public and weakened the presidency by giving the impression that Jimmy Carter was accomplishing little because he succeeded with so few of the tasks he undertook.

We began our day at the Department of Justice with the kind of informal exchange I am recommending, usually over breakfast and with no agenda. Some eight to twelve personal assistants, assistant attorneys general and the deputy and associate attorney general would gather in the small dining room that adjoins the attorney general's office. No subjects were off-limits, and the free exchange nurtured discussion of matters that would not have been raised in a formal, structured meeting.

President Carter would have lengthy and frequent discussions with his friend, Charlie Kirbo; but the President tended to rely on polls to find out what people around the country were thinking, and Charlie Kirbo followed the same approach. Besides, talking things over with Charlie Kirbo is not the same as uninhibited, daily sessions with aides and colleagues, many of whom are members of your children's generation. That kind of conversation helps prevent you from losing touch with what is on other people's minds.

Such failures and omissions notwithstanding, it is my thesis that a bureaucracy out of control was a chief contributor to President Carter's failure to govern as the people would have preferred.

One doesn't have to reach far back in history to demonstrate this is not a new problem. Somewhat obscured by the attention focused on the Watergate cover-up was the emphasis during his aborted second term that President Nixon and his top aides placed on gaining control of the government. Trusted aides from the White House and the campaign were to be placed in key Cabinet departments to enable the White House staff to stay informed and keep tighter control over these operating arms. We tend to lose sight of how frustrated the Nixon administration became over what it viewed as an inability to make the government respond to the will of the electorate.

It is a problem that knows no party lines, and one that will hamper the performance of all Presidents until the bureaucracy is responsive to elected and appointed managers.

II

CURBING THE BUREAUCRACY

If the Republic is to remain viable, we must find ways to curb, and then to reduce, government by bureaucracy. We must return to government by directly accountable public officials —local, state and federal. The only alternative is to have an increasingly costly and inefficient form of government largely removed from democratic control. When our society is threatened from within by such awesome problems as inflation and poverty, and from without by military aggression and world famine, this ever-growing bureaucracy is more than a painful nuisance. It is a prescription for societal suicide.

When I made my office on the fifth floor of the Department of Justice, I was fond of comparing the problem of the federal bureaucracy that the entire nation faces now with the problem the South faced in Reconstruction. The comparison prompted some to suggest that I was using a hyperbolic attention-getter. But I believe that the bureaucracy is a force more pervasive and more powerful than all the Union armies of the Reconstruction. The federal bureaucracy, by laws and regulations, by orders and printed forms, by a thousand other unseen methods, subjects all of us to some degree of federal scrutiny and control. And it lasts longer than the Reconstruction did.

My gloomy view of the problems of bureaucratic democracy is not a lonely position. Alpheus Thomas Mason, Professor Emeritus of Jurisprudence at Princeton University, has referred to the problem as "the Imperial Bureaucracy."[1] Making the point that a great risk to our system results from one faction of the government or country seeking excessive power at the expense of other parts, Professor Mason wrote:

> The bureaucracy will be peculiarly difficult to stop because it is not one of the traditional parties to our system. It was not foreseen, and therefore not limited, by the Constitution. It does most of its work in secret, it mushrooms out of good intentions—most bureaus exist because of legislation intended to correct some evil or improve the lot of some group—and it pervades the government at all levels, fusing executive, legislative and judicial functions.[2]

The bureaucracy can be so unresponsive to doing something in a new way that more than one President has come to doubt why anyone would describe him as the "leader of the Free World." John F. Kennedy, during his thousand days in the Oval Office, was reported to have complained to a friend that working with the bureaucracy was like dealing with a foreign power. And this from a President known for cutting through bureaucratic delays by picking up the telephone and calling directly to the lower-level official responsible for what the President wanted done.

Sitting as a federal appeals court judge for nearly fifteen years, I thought I had gained real insight into how our national government functions. But I was in for some surprises at the hands of the bureaucracy. If one is to cope, much less prevail, in government, one has to learn the techniques that the bureaucracy uses to survive, control and expand.

Immediately upon taking office, I was hit with a technique I have dubbed the "flooding" principle. Department heads flooded me with lengthy reports, more voluminous than I could absorb, even if I could have read all of them. This created the impression of much work being done. The Antitrust Division and the Justice Department's Office of Management and Finance, which is responsible for housekeeping and budgetary tasks, were the biggest flooders.

So many lengthy reports flowed to me from the Antitrust Division that I was kept off-balance. I had more information than I needed and did not have time for independent thinking. This was a method of control, a means of keeping a new person from controlling. Finally, I told someone to tell the Antitrust Division not to send me such voluminous reports, that I needed no more than three pages to understand things and would advise them if I required more.

As for the Office of Management and Finance, every Cabinet secretary has to decide at the outset whether to concentrate first on nuts-and-bolts problems of running a department or on substantive policy problems. Obviously, the substantive issues are those that elections are fought over and are more challenging than deciding whether the department's print shop needs improved lighting. As a result, the management "experts," career government workers who communicate with one another in fuzzy "managementese," called "bureaucratese" by some, are given fairly free rein. This is a fundamental mistake, because it is in the management divisions, where you have the least turnover, that the perpetuation and expansion of the bureaucracy becomes an end in itself.

A variation of the "flooding" principle is the "travel" principle, also frequently used on newcomers. Keep the supervisor out of his or her office as much as possible. During my first few months as attorney general, I visited, on separate trips, Honolulu, Seattle, San Francisco, Los Angeles and San Diego —and finally caught on to the fact that I was being scheduled out of office. The champion victim was Secretary of State Cyrus Vance, who seemed never to be in Washington.

With the "burying" principle, the bureaucrat assumes authority by burying a proposal deep in the innards of a long report. The sought-for authority will be exercised unless the new fellow in charge is fortunate enough to spot it and call a halt.

The Civil Rights Division of the Department of Justice was a master of the burying technique. Major policy shifts would be buried within a seemingly endless set of proposals. For example, one of the most sensitive laws the division enforces is the Voting Rights Act. Under that law, certain areas of the country, mostly in the South, must ask for the attorney general's approval or go to court in Washington each time they want to change their election law. The areas are those where illegal discrimination against would-be voters has occurred in the past. To be sure, this is not a requirement that local lawmakers enjoy.

The Civil Rights Division one day sent to my office sixty typewritten pages of proposed new regulations for enforcing that politically touchy law. A hawkeye among my special assistants, Nelson Dong, studied the recommended changes, line by line. By careful reading, he found, many pages into the document, that the division was proposing to delegate the authority for approving or disapproving voting law changes from the assistant attorney general for civil rights to a chief of one of the division's sections.

This would have been a major departure. No longer would a high-level official be responsible for deciding the ticklish question of whether a community could change its laws on voting. There was not a trace of a warning flag flying over that proposed change. This is not to suggest that section chiefs, usually career government employees in contrast to the presidentially appointed assistant attorney general, are oafs incapable of decision-making. But that kind of judgment belongs to someone responsible for making administration policy, a presidential appointee who must answer to the man chosen by the people to preside.

A technique that enjoyed immense popularity during the Carter administration and one, I am certain, that President Reagan and his people will come to know is that of "leaking." Now, some members of the press get defensive when you talk about the motivation of government officials in providing them with information that has not been released officially. Reporters like to draw a distinction between information that

comes to them over the transom of their office, with no prob-
ing or invitation by the reporter, and that given to them in
response to timely questions of a news source they have developed.

To me, it matters naught. If the official is providing information that he should not, he is probably doing it for reasons
other than his high regard for the reporter. Often, the leaker
has only part of the story, and the use of this fragmented
information leads to mischief or even harm. I once advised a
meeting of Justice Department employees, not entirely face-
tiously, "If you must leak, at least leak accurately."

Examining the phenomenon of the leak, the Brookings
Institution said in a study:

> Since information is a primary strategic resource in
> Washington, the passing of unauthorized messages out-
> side channels often approaches an art form. There are
> routine leaks to build credit and keep channels open for
> when they are needed, positive leaks to promote some-
> thing, negative leaks to discredit a person or policy and
> counterleaks. There is even the daring reverse leak, an
> unauthorized release of information apparently for one
> reason but actually accomplishing the opposite.[3]

The incoming Cabinet officer can be embarrassed, confused and harassed by constant leaks concerning matters that
have not reached his or her desk. This keeps the newcomer
in the position of playing catch up, rather than being in
charge. You find yourself picking up the morning papers with
more dread than you had in private life.

I think the most vicious use of the technique is the leak to
control a superior's decisions. A good example was the extremely sensitive FBI break-in case which involved what the
FBI calls "surreptitious entries" that agents had conducted in
the New York area as they searched for fugitives of the
Weather Underground terrorist group. The break-ins, conducted at the homes and apartments of friends and relatives
of the fugitives without a court warrant, took place in the early
1970's. They raised the specter of the nation's leading law

enforcement agency itself being involved in illegal activity, violating the constitutional rights of citizens.

I had authorized the indictment of one FBI supervisor in New York who was in charge of FBI Squad 47, which carried out the covert operations. The only reason I did so was that time was running out. The offenses the supervisor allegedly had committed took place nearly five years earlier, and once five years had passed, charges no longer could be brought. Evidence against him was strong, but the question remained whether anyone at that low a level should be indicted. Civil Rights Division prosecutors had recommended the indictment of at least six other FBI veterans, each of them above the supervisor's level. The prosecutor's plan was to move up the ladder of authority, rung by rung. I objected to this approach on grounds that not only was it slow but it showed no inclination to reach the officials ultimately responsible for authorizing the lawbreaking. Time was not as much a factor in deciding whether to move against the six others.

Although it was no secret that I was, for various reasons, leaning against approving the indictments sought by the prosecutors, news stories were published reporting that I would authorize the additional indictments. In the face of these inaccurate stories, which appeared to be Justice Department leaks, I was put in the false position of seeming to change my mind if I rejected the proposed indictments and to have got cold feet about moving against more FBI men.

As it turned out, we dropped the original indictment but then indicted and convicted Edward S. Miller, an assistant FBI director in charge of domestic intelligence, and W. Mark Felt, the former Number 2 man in the agency. We also obtained the indictment of L. Patrick Gray III, former acting FBI director, but the case against him was subsequently dropped, partly for national security reasons but mainly because the evidence was not sufficient to convict. To some extent, Gray was being made a scapegoat by unfounded and vague assertions from within the FBI, many of whose old-timers resented Gray as an outsider.

All but one of the original prosecutors sent me an ultimatum in which they told the attorney general of the United States that he had to authorize the indictments they had proposed or they would resign from the case. They delivered their threat shortly before Christmas of 1977, and I went off for a few days. On returning, I told my staff that the prosecutors' offer was one I couldn't refuse.

They then compounded their extraordinary action by accepting an invitation from Senator Lowell Weicker of Connecticut to testify before a Senate Appropriations Subcommittee that had authority over the Justice Department's budget. Career Justice Department attorneys who had left the case but not the department had agreed to testify in public about a pending criminal matter in which they had refused to accept the decision of the attorney general.

Weicker, then, was gearing up for his later aborted drive for the GOP presidential nomination. This may have led to his distributing a press release as the hearing began—before any testimony was heard—calling for me to resign. As the hearing proceeded, Weicker threatened to hold up the Justice Department's budget if anything were done to punish the rebellious prosecutors.

At this point, I was leaning toward firing the prosecutors to demonstrate that Senator Weicker was not running the Justice Department. But Senator Ernest F. Hollings of South Carolina, the subcommittee chairman, urged me not to do so because it would cause a problem with Senator Patrick J. Leahy of Vermont. Leahy was pushing a whistle-blowers' protection act, a bill that I opposed, and punitive action against the insubordinate lawyers would be viewed in some quarters as a move against whistle-blowers. I took Senator Hollings's advice, and the tempest quickly died. But the episode stands as an example of what can happen when a Cabinet officer imposes his judgment on the bureaucracy. In retrospect, I regret exceedingly that I did not fire the prosecutors. Their action had aspects of hostage-holding and an illegal strike, and I should not have tolerated it for any reason.

The bureaucracy, when it wants to take the decision-making authority in a particular matter away from a superior, can also adopt the "cry politics" technique. It has limitations, however. First, a member of Congress or the White House or some other political person has to inquire about a case being handled by the bureaucrat. Even though 99 percent of such inquiries are proper in a representative form of government, the bureaucrat, concerned that his judgment in the case might not prevail, can cry politics, contending there has been an effort to exert improper influence. More often than not, this will be accomplished by leaking the bureaucrat's version of what transpired to the press. Then the attorney general, or whoever is in ultimate charge of the case, is likely to think twice before rejecting any recommendation made by the bureaucrat.

To be sure, I am not suggesting that every inquiry about a pending investigation by an officeholder or a member of the White House staff is proper. Early in the Carter administration, Midge Costanza, the highest woman appointee on the White House staff, called directly to the Justice Department's Criminal Division to set up an appointment for lawyers representing a New York city councilman then under intense federal investigation. Apparently, word of the President's pledge about an independent Department of Justice had not reached her.

I didn't get too upset about that. I just figured Costanza was ignorant, that she didn't understand the system. What she did was a typical Nixonian approach to government. You get a lot of folks in politics who don't understand our checks and balances, so you have to be understanding.

My rule is to be understanding no more than one time. She never did that anymore. We had a talk about it, and I explained the system and how it operates. It was clear that Costanza would not repeat her error. The councilman, incidentally, was indicted within days of the requested meeting, convicted and sent to prison.

Indeed, I thought the bureaucracy needed some protection from congressmen or White House staff members calling career government employees with inquiries. I must acknowledge that calls from the White House staff were not a problem after the Costanza incident. We issued rules prohibiting that kind of contact from Capitol Hill or the White House. Under the rules, which the Reagan administration has retained, there can, of course, be inquiries. But they must be made of the attorney general, the deputy or associate attorney general or the assistant attorney general in charge of the division handling the matter. This means that there is a buffer between the career attorney and a public official theoretically in a position to exert pressure on the lawyer. Interestingly, after the rules were announced, calls from Capitol Hill on pending matters dropped sharply.

One bureaucratic technique that continually hampers effective management is that of "play it safe." The bureaucrat avoids decision-making by bucking a matter up to his superior without recommendation, knowing full well that it is likely to be bucked down for further study. Or the official one rung further up the authority ladder escapes deciding something by referring a matter back for more study, regardless of whether it came to him with a recommendation.

The play-it-safe technique also results in superiors being unwilling to reverse the recommendation of a subordinate for fear that a subsequent level of authority will decide the subordinate was correct. Under the Voting Rights Act, the Civil Rights Division recommended that I institute suit against a large southern city over changes it had made in its voting district lines. On close examination, we found that the analysis of the underlying case which provided the basis for recommending we take the city officials to court had been done by a paralegal—a nonlawyer who does on-the-job training by assisting lawyers. The analysis was incorrect, but no one in the bureaucracy had questioned whether such a crucial recommendation should be made by an aide who had not yet completed law school. That's the play-it-safe technique at its worst.

As with many truths, real insight into the bureaucracy can be gained through a humorous incident. This one revolved around a deadline my office had set at the Justice Department for submitting some requested information. When one attorney turned in his material two days before the deadline, a member of my staff jokingly told him he would report his action to the Office of Professional Responsibility, which investigates misconduct by department employees.

The attorney responded in kind: "I have been around the department long enough to recognize that no one accepts blame for anything and that there is always a faceless culprit in the bowels of the bureaucracy who bears the ultimate responsibility. This case is no exception.

"After receiving notice of your charge, I immediately checked with my secretary, who explained that in the incredible rush of business she had become confused and inadvertently typed the memorandum before the deadline had passed. However, she believed that she had corrected the error of her ways by placing the memorandum in our outbox, which has gone unsearched by the messengers (perhaps they believe they need a warrant) since my arrival.

"As luck would have it, a new trainee arrived that very day and mistakenly assumed that we wanted the material delivered promptly. You'll be pleased to know that he is no longer with us.

"But there is always a silver lining. Because you were so shocked by the memorandum's arrival two days early, you obviously failed to note an even more egregious breach of department policy. Unlike the usual case, where someone with no constructive comments to add produces a ten-page memorandum to that effect, we had no comments and said so. You may be sure that we will not let either breach occur again."

A major contributor to this sad state of government is the absence of fear—fear of the discipline that one would expect to stop use of the techniques. There is no discipline in the bureaucracy comparable to that in the private sector if these techniques were attempted there. To be sure, some burying and playing-it-safe goes on in the corporate world, but it is not as accepted or widespread.

The harm done to the Republic by a bureaucracy out of control—a major theme of this book—has led to a state of government that is at the center of our current problems. As the bureaucracy flourishes and expands with no real attempt being made to measure its work product—to correlate people hired with work done—it causes government spending to rise, and thus contributes to the scourge of inflation. Paradoxically, this bureaucracy that seems beyond control produces a flood of stultifying federal regulations that seek to control those in private or quasi-private enterprise. The cost of complying with those regulations is mind-numbing.

Perhaps most ominous of all is that the lack of responsiveness of the bureaucracy has much to do with citizen frustration and the belief that we may be unable to govern ourselves.

A major reason that the bureaucracy flourishes as it does is that we have come to accept overregulation, a degree of government interference with private enterprise that has mushroomed in the last fifty years. There is, of course, a history to this, and that is what I want to examine next.

III

ORIGINS OF OVERREGULATION

The United States today is facing a great new challenge in rethinking the methods and scope of regulation of business. At the same time, as the 1980 election revealed, there is increasing public resistance to government's involvement in the lives of individual Americans. Overregulation of the individual by the government takes various forms. A particularly insidious variety is the overregulation of prospective public servants who are considering accepting presidential appointment. The process of Senate confirmation has become a modern-day inquisition that discourages honorable men and women from entering public service, thus injuring the American people by eliminating prospective nominees. A good example is my own experience in accepting President Carter's nomination to be attorney general. And if anyone wants to accuse me of grinding a personal axe, so be it. I'll run the risk in order to illustrate my point.

To appreciate fully what happened to me, you have to remember the circumstances of my appointment. The election of President Carter represented a final healing of the national wound inflicted by the Civil War. But in naming me, a longtime friend who grew up only ten miles away from

Plains, in Americus, Georgia, as attorney general, Jimmy Carter gave the nation one southerner too many.

Interestingly, opponents to my nomination did not stress my long relationship with the President, perhaps because on close examination, a charge of "cronyism" would be difficult to support. Although we had known each other for many years, I was not one of his confidants. I am six years older than Jimmy Carter, and the only family member I am a close friend of is the President's cousin, Don Carter, a senior officer in the Knight-Ridder newspaper chain. I did advise the President on a few legal issues during the campaign, and I assisted in some last-minute fund-raising for the Pennsylvania primary, which turned out to be a crucial contest for him; but my part in the 1976 election campaign did not approach the central role that the Watergate special prosecutor had in mind when, in his final report, he recommended against Presidents naming their campaign managers as attorneys general:

> The President should not nominate and the Senate should not confirm as attorney general, or as any other appointee in high Department of Justice posts, a person who has served as the President's campaign manager or in a similar high-level campaign role. A campaign manager seeks support for his candidate and necessarily incurs obligations to political leaders and other individuals throughout wide geographical areas. If he then takes a high position in the Justice Department, he may take— or appear to take—official actions on the basis of those commitments rather than on appropriate legal and policy grounds.[1]

While I occupied no such role, I was sufficiently mindful of the public perception of my ties to President Carter to know that, in taking the job, I could not serve during a presidential election year. It was largely for that reason that I persuaded the President not to require me, as he had asked his other Cabinet officers, to pledge to remain four years.

Opponents to my nomination considered me suspect because of decisions I had handed down while a member of the

U.S. Court of Appeals for the Fifth Circuit. My nearly fifteen years on the bench spanned most of the civil rights revolution, and no court played as central a role in that tumultuous, constitutionally crucial period as the Fifth Circuit, which runs from Texas through Louisiana, Mississippi, Alabama, Florida and Georgia.

Critics contended I had dragged my feet in civil rights rulings. My service as honorary chief of staff for Governor Ernest Vandiver of Georgia was taken to mean that I shared the segregationist views that he had expressed then. My membership in two country clubs that had no black members—clubs I was persuaded to quit in agreeing to be the President's nominee—was cited as further evidence of my racist character. Yet when Bill Webster, among the best nominees I ever proposed to President Carter, came up for confirmation as FBI director, his membership in a similar club was raised at the Senate hearing. Webster had chosen not to resign and told the Senate Judiciary Committee that he preferred to work from inside to change membership policy. Webster, you see, was from St. Louis, not the Deep South, and the committee accepted his position without a whimper.

The six-day Senate hearing on my nomination as attorney general was pure hell. I encountered flagrant bias toward a southerner. I would have gladly walked out and withdrawn my nomination if such an action would not have been an embarrassment to the President. I didn't need the job and I hadn't sought it, and I resented the demagoguery involved in the proceedings. I was abused by some senators while others were very supportive, but a few were abusing both me and the process in a way no American citizen should have to suffer.

As the hearings rolled on, I stayed in what you could call a low burn. I had tried enough cases in my life to know you can't get anywhere if you get mad. President Kennedy used to say, "Don't get mad. Get even." There's a lot to that.

You're in a fight and your whole reputation for integrity and character is on the line. The interrogators intend to put you to the test. They care so little for your privacy or for your family that you have to wonder why anybody would want to go into government. Fortunately, not everybody who goes through a confirmation hearing is treated that way, but you never know whether you may not be the one. It's like being called before Judge Roy Bean in the law west of the Pecos, where you're just hauled into a saloon somewhere, told to sit down, put under oath and ordered to answer all the questions. The difference is that during a Senate confirmation you've got fifty photographers sitting in front of you; you can't see because the television lights are on; and you haven't any notice about what they are going to ask you.

To prepare for this grilling, I had a group of former law clerks take all my court opinions, all the speeches I had ever made, all the Law Review articles I had ever written, and analyze them. The analysis was recorded in notebooks, and the former clerks grilled me for hours before I went to testify. Thanks to the preparation, I was able to appear without a paper in front of me throughout the examination.

Uniform rules should govern confirmation hearings. A witness should not be sworn unless those who testify against him are also required to take an oath. Some who testified against me would have had to speak differently if they had been under oath and couldn't just engage in rhetoric.

I was the only witness who was sworn. I did not object to that until they called me back on the stand to respond, again under oath, to the unsworn testimony of others. That was a gross denial of due process. These were the people concerned about civil rights, and they were stripping me of my civil rights, right there in public. Instead of worrying so much about how I was going to treat people, they could have started off by treating the nominee for attorney general fairly.

The hearings were televised, and it was great television coverage for the senators. The length of a confirmation hearing, I learned, is closely related to the length of time the cameras remain.

My hearing, however, was carried over into a second week for a reason that had little to do with my qualifications or with television. Senator Robert C. Byrd of West Virginia, then the majority leader and a member of the Judiciary Committee, summoned me to his office and asked that I promise to keep Clarence M. Kelley on as director of the FBI for another two years. I told Byrd I couldn't do this, and that he should take it up with the President-elect. He said, "Then I'm going to hold your hearings over a week." It was during the second week that the critics, including Julian Bond, the Georgia legislator, and Joe Rauh, the former head of Americans for Democratic Action, mobilized and testified against me.

My nomination was confirmed by a Senate vote of 75–21. A good number of those twenty-one later said they had been wrong. They included Senators Robert Dole of Kansas, George McGovern of South Dakota, Jacob Javits of New York and Charles Percy of Illinois, who began a laudatory speech on the Senate floor when I resigned as attorney general: "It is not easy, nor is it a regular occurrence, when an elected official admits that he made a mistake when casting a vote . . ."[2]

Some who had been in the forefront of trying to block my confirmation, such as Clarence Mitchell, said I had done a good job as attorney general after all. Mitchell, now retired, was the highly respected Washington director of the National Association for the Advancement of Colored People.

While my confirmation hearing does serve as an example of the sad state of the process for evaluating a President's Cabinet selections, I must concede that in the long run I benefited tremendously from it. I had to face the senators, fight them off and get used to being on national television. When the hearings were finished, I was a much stronger person than I was when they began. Afterward, I was able to combat Congress on anything.

You have to establish independence. People talk about Cabinet officers being independent of the President, particularly the attorney general. But you must be independent of the Congress, too. If you bow to the Congress, you can do just as much damage as if you're not independent of the White House.

The confirmation hearings provided me with early insight into how the Senate functions. I learned, for example, that youthful aides to senators often are the driving forces behind Senate action and enjoy an influence well beyond their years. In a break during one of the stormiest days of my confirmation ordeal, I overheard an aide to Senator Charles McC. Mathias, Jr., of Maryland suggest to Clarence Mitchell that the NAACP official should have his staff search the Georgia State Archives for material that could be damaging to me. Senator Mathias is among the real thinkers in the Senate, and here was his assistant egging on a critic of mine in hopes of blocking my nomination. I doubt that Senator Mathias was aware of his young staff member's action.

Another senate aide, I learned later, contacted Judge Elbert Tuttle of the Fifth Circuit about testifying against me or possibly providing unfavorable information. Judge Tuttle, regarded as the leading liberal on civil rights questions on the court, turned down the invitation, saying he hoped I would be confirmed. I was gratified later when Judge Tuttle joined the contingent from the South who came to the Department of Justice to witness my swearing in as attorney general.

There were some lighter sides to the Senate confirmation process, too. As assistant attorney general in charge of the Land and Natural Resources Division, we had chosen James W. Moorman. I had a lot of initial doubts about his confirmation, because Jim was general counsel of the Sierra Club Legal Defense Fund, a leading environmental organization, and he had a beard. I thought these two characteristics might do him in with some senators on the Judiciary Committee, particularly the venerable chairman, Senator James O. Eastland of Mississippi, my strongest supporter on the committee and in the Senate—not counting my home-state senators.

Following tradition, I took Moorman to Capitol Hill to meet Senator Eastland before his confirmation hearing was to begin. Looking at the nominee's beard, I approached the task with some trepidation.

The senator's secretary, Jean H. Allen, greeted us: "Go right in," she said. "He has got a group of Mississippi bankers in there. I know they will want to meet you, Judge Bell, and to see Mr. Moorman."

My worry intensified.

Once we entered the office, we found about ten bankers there visiting with Senator Eastland. Would you believe that one of them had a full beard just like Moorman? It was a great thing. My heart picked up. Everyone got along well.

Next, I had to take Moorman around to see Senator Strom Thurmond of South Carolina, then the ranking minority member of the Judiciary Committee and another of my strong supporters. I had the same concerns as we headed for Senator Thurmond's office.

As I explained who Moorman was, the senator walked completely around him, scrutinizing him for what seemed like several minutes, and finally asked: "Did you pick him out? Or did the White House?"

"I picked him out," I replied.

"Okay," Thurmond said, signaling his approval.

Moorman, by the way, turned out to be one of the best people we recruited, a man of great ability and rocklike intellectual honesty. He is an example of a lawyer who had been a vigorous advocate of a single interest but who was able to put that behind him as he carried out his oath to represent all the people.

The President might never have asked me to serve as attorney general if a colleague of mine on the U.S. Fifth Circuit Court of Appeals, then District Judge Reynaldo G. Garza, of Brownsville, Texas, had wanted the position. Soon after the 1976 election, the President-elect assigned me the responsibility of finding someone to be attorney general. He called me in early December of that year and asked that I check the attorney general of Texas, John Hill, as a possibility.

I made two or three calls to people in Texas about Hill, and one of the people I called was Judge Garza, an Hispanic and an outstanding federal judge. I reported to the President-elect that I had made the calls and particularly impressed on him that Judge Garza was very high on John Hill.

The President-elect then began to ask me about Judge Garza and for my assessment of what kind of attorney general I thought he would make. I responded that I was virtually certain Judge Garza would not be interested, but that I would check further if President-elect Carter wished me to do so.

Mr. Carter responded by asking for Judge Garza's phone number, saying he would call him. Judge Garza, never having spoken to the President-elect, thought someone was trying to imitate a Georgia accent and playing a prank on him. In desperation, the incoming leader of the Free World asked me to call the judge and to assure him the offer was bona fide.

Judge Garza told me he was not interested. I then gave him a sales talk about helping his country and suggested that he could return to Brownsville at a later time and go into private practice with his two sons as partners. I also explained the federal pension system to him, emphasizing that he would not suffer a total loss of the retirement benefits he would have as a federal judge if he could serve one year as attorney general. When he seemed to warm up some and it appeared to me that he might take the post, Charlie Kirbo made a few calls checking on him.

But three days later, Judge Garza called me and asked that we not consider him further. He said he simply did not want to leave Brownsville and Texas, and that he could not picture himself as attorney general.

The trend toward converting Senate confirmation hearings into ordeals by fire predated the new cynicism about public officials ushered in by Watergate. The protracted, often acrimonious hearings that were held on the 1967 nomination of Thurgood Marshall to the Supreme Court and the equally rancorous 1969 hearings on the High Court nomination of Judge Clement C. Haynsworth, Jr., were examples of overzealous confirmation proceedings.

But in Senate confirmation hearings, as in much of Washington government, the trauma of Watergate and the overreaction to it distorts the situation. Now, nominees are relentlessly and often rudely grilled about their private lives, and the hostile interrogation is defended on the grounds of maintaining high public ethics.

In evaluating nominees in the past, we required proof of actual wrongdoing before disqualifying a man or woman from public service. Today, we have a new category of disqualification, erroneously referred to as "conflict of interest."

A conflict of interest is not wrongdoing by an individual, but the mere presence of temptation in his or her life. Thus, if a man owns shares of stock in a large oil company, he would have a conflict of interest—or the appearance of one—in making any decision that might affect that particular oil company. Current conventional wisdom goes further and asserts that he is unable to make an objective and unselfish judgment about any oil companies.

According to this reasoning, he is disqualified for any government service relating to that industry. The modern presumption is that no individual, no matter how high his situation or untarnished his reputation, can resist even the lowest form of temptation. A life of rectitude counts for naught. We no longer look to past conduct and a person's reputation for fair dealing. Our system now treats the existence of the slightest apparent conflict of interest as grounds for complete disqualification.

The system has proved costly. For example, in September of 1980, Frank Cary, chairman of International Business Machines Corp., had his name withdrawn from consideration as one of the seven directors of the U.S. Synthetic Fuels Corp. Cary was said to have decided against the part-time job to avoid the public disclosure of his personal finances that was required of him by the Senate Energy Committee. Cary reportedly was willing to give the details to the White House and the Senate committee but balked at releasing the material to the public. Cary's demonstrated management expertise could have helped the government-run corporation in its mission of stimulating development of oil and gas from coal, shale rock and other unconventional sources.

Some prospective appointees of President Reagan—prospective, that is, based on press reports during the transition period—bowed out, citing in part their distaste of exposing themselves to a confirmation grilling. In some cases, the required disclosure of assets, liabilities, income and sources of income apparently tipped the scales against accepting a high-level public job. Part of their reason was concern that publicity about their financial worth would increase the likelihood that they or members of their families would be kidnapped.

Overregulation has turned public service at the Cabinet level into a massive invasion of privacy. My own experience did not end with my resignation as attorney general. I returned to Atlanta after leaving the Department of Justice and rejoined King & Spalding as managing partner. I remarked in humor that I was dedicating myself to becoming one of America's largest taxpayers, but there wasn't much hope because those fifteen years on the bench and three years in the Cabinet gave others too long a head start. Several months later, President Carter called and asked if I would head the U.S. delegation to the Conference on Security and Cooperation in Europe, where human rights were to be the paramount issue. Former Governor William Scranton of Pennsylvania had been heading the U.S. team, but I was told that he had asked to be relieved for reasons of health. No sooner had I agreed to accept the post, then the invasion of my privacy began anew.

I was innundated with forms to complete—from the Department of State, the Senate Foreign Relations Committee and the White House Counsel's Office. They were asking all the questions put to me when I became attorney general, plus a lot more. I simply sent the forms back. I wasn't about to fill them out. I did complete one document in which I gave my Social Security number, my name and two or three things like that—you know, like a prisoner of war giving only his name, rank and serial number.

I refused to submit a personal financial statement. If you give those people a little bit, they keep after you until they find out everything. As head of the delegation, I would have the rank of ambassador. If that meant I had to go through another round with the Senate, I vowed I was not going to do it. The President handled the problem by appointing me a special ambassador, a job I could hold for six months without having to be confirmed by the Senate. Such an appointment is the type of service that has always been rendered in the public interest by the dollar-a-year appointee—Bernard Baruch and

John J. McCloy, for example. But if our trend toward over-regulation continues unabated, these appointees would have to submit to Senate confirmation proceedings as well.

Nor should regulatory harassment in the form of over-regulation of business be allowed to impede national growth, as it has. Federal regulations currently in force cover more than sixty thousand printed pages, plus thousands more in interpretations and guidelines on the regulations. Often, they are written in defiance of the English language. Many of the regulations have retarded our real economic growth by impairing our efforts to improve the productivity of labor and capital.

One virtue of the American system has been the chance for an individual to launch his own small business and see the Horatio Alger dream come true. Excessive government regulation has, in too many cases, helped turn that dream into a nightmare.

A Joint Economic Committee report in 1980 documented the oppressive costs of government regulation for the small businessman:

> Federal paper work is particularly burdensome for smaller business. Small businesses file over 305 million federal forms a year, totaling over 850 million pages and containing over 7.3 billion questions. The average annual cost to each small business is estimated to be about $1,270, a total cost of more than $17 billion.

> The $17 billion figure is large, but it measures only the direct costs of paper-work compliance. Small businesses typically lack the manpower and specialized skills to respond quickly and efficiently to federal data requests. Too often, the time of the owner-operator is spent on paper work at the expense of a careful monitoring of other activities essential to the survival and growth of the small enterprise.[3]

Of course, it is not just small businesses that feel an extra pinch from government regulation. Small organizations of any kind that must comply with government regulations are susceptible. Take a school like Mercer University in Georgia, for example. A study in 1975 found that with a student body of less than three thousand, it was costing Mercer close to two hundred-fifty thousand dollars a year to complete government-required reports.

Experiences like Mercer's caused educators to lobby hard to establish a separate Department of Education, thinking that it would ease their regulatory burden. But they are already learning their hopes were misdirected. Bureaucracies would run out of things to do if they didn't have forms to be completed and processed. It's the forms and regulations that keep people on the payroll.

The Senate Judiciary Subcommittee on Administrative Practice and Procedure spearheaded enactment of a 1980 law to lighten the regulatory burdens on small business, individuals and small government units. In doing so, the subcommittee became a repository of one-liners that illustrate the need for regulatory reform more cogently than complex tales of regulatory disasters.[4]

One told of an Iowa taxpayer who received fifteen government booklets in response to his question on how to fill out one form that the Internal Revenue Service requires small businesses to complete.

In another case, an automobile manufacturer had to attach labels to the batteries in his cars warning the public not to drink their contents because the Consumer Product Safety Commission had classified the batteries as a "household item."

While large businesses are better able to absorb the cost of government regulation, these costs have become a major item on the big corporation's profit and loss statement. A study by Arthur Andersen & Co. found that forty-eight major U.S. corporations in 1977 incurred annual costs of $2.6 billion from complying with the regulations of six federal regulatory agencies.[5]

To appreciate how critical it is that the country rethink the restrictions it places on business, consider the context of overregulation—how we came to be where we are. Until late in the last century, it was the states, not the federal government, that attempted to regulate commerce. State regulation took such forms as monitoring tolls that private owners imposed on travelers using the owners' bridges and similar charges.

But with the end of the Civil War and the start of the great industrial expansion in America, Washington began to intervene in the marketplace. Specific statutory prohibitions were passed, and the first of the regulatory agencies was established. Public indignation over business's exploitation of the consumer almost a century ago led to Congress passing the first two federal landmarks in business regulation—the Act to Regulate Commerce and the Sherman Act.

The Act to Regulate Commerce became law in 1887. It created the Interstate Commerce Commission to watch over railroad fares, rates and business practices, and was passed in response to widespread public resentment over excesses by rail barons. The ICC was the first of the federal regulatory commissions, a concept of governing that the federal government borrowed from the states. Most important, enactment of the law represented a significant shift from a case-by-case supervision of business, which meant very little supervision, to a permanent, continuing regulation by a body that Congress created.

The Sherman Act in 1890 was the United States's first antitrust law. It became law with the impetus of the populist drive against the trusts—railroad, sugar and others—and sought to punish conspiracies for monopoly or rate-fixing.

The Great Depression of the 1930's and the New Deal further spurred regulation by the central government. The period of fastest growth in regulatory activity, however, began in the 1960's as the federal government expanded its role in trying to solve the nation's economic and social problems. As a 1980 joint report of the Senate Committee on Governmental Affairs and Judiciary said of the period: "More than at any other time since the New Deal, the American people looked to the federal government to improve the quality of life."[6]

President John F. Kennedy attempted to reform the regulatory agencies. Before taking office, President Kennedy requested and received a report on them from an expert, James M. Landis, a former Civil Aeronautics Board chairman, SEC member and dean of the Harvard Law School. The Landis Report was highly critical of the agencies, and President Kennedy sought to implement many of its proposed reforms.

Regulatory reform became a backwater issue during President Lyndon B. Johnson's Great Society, although Senator Barry Goldwater's 1964 campaign did urge a return to freer enterprise. In the 1976 and 1980 presidential campaigns, business regulation became an issue whose time had come.

As foreign industries took more and more of what had been America's unchallenged worldwide market, executives of large U.S. corporations complained that pollution control, occupational safety and other regulations imposed by Washington had impaired their ability to compete. Smaller businessmen contended that costs of completing the regulatory forms and other paper work required by the federal government were further reducing their inflation-squeezed profit margins.

When Jimmy Carter campaigned against Washington in 1976, he called for reforming the seemingly mindless variety of regulations often associated with the federal government. In the White House, he made a substantial start in delivering on that campaign promise, but without ever letting the American people know about it. In 1980, candidate Ronald Reagan picked up where Jimmy Carter left off, lumping business regulation with other kinds of federal interference and calling for getting "government off our backs."

A month before President Carter left office, his domestic policy chief, Stuart E. Eizenstat, sounded a new call for restoring balance to government regulation. If, during his four years in the White House, President Carter had been able to implement the reforms Eizenstat was proposing in a swan song address to the National Press Club, he would have won more votes.

"We must reduce government-created constraints in the

free market while still protecting consumers from those who abuse the market and the helpless from the market's negative impacts," Eizenstat said one month after his and my Chief Executive suffered a resounding election defeat. "We must demonstrate a willingness to remove the government from certain sectors of American life."[7]

President Reagan came to office after a decade in which the growth of federal regulations and the staffs to implement them exceeded all other periods. Congress in the 1970–80 decade created seven new regulatory agencies and passed twenty-nine major regulatory laws. Full-time positions in federal regulatory agencies nearly tripled in the 1970's—from 28,000 in 1970 to 81,000 in 1979. The Center for the Study of American Business in St. Louis estimated that budgeted expenditures of the fifty-six agencies with major regulatory functions jumped 400 percent in the decade, reaching about six billion dollars in 1980.[8]

Congress, in creating the ICC as the first regulatory agency, set a pattern which it followed with all of the other so-called alphabet agencies. They would be multimember bodies, the specific number varying from agency to agency. A maximum of one more than half of each panel's members could come from the same political party. Each commission was to be politically independent and expert in the part of commerce it was to regulate.

Congress gave each of the regulatory agencies broadly worded mandates. The Federal Communications Commission, for example, was instructed to award broadcast licenses consistent with the public convenience, interest or necessity. The Federal Trade Commission was told to eliminate unfair and deceptive practices. And the Occupational Safety and Health Administration's instructions were to devise standards that ensure safe and healthful employment and places of employment.

In too many instances, the regulatory agencies have not turned out to be what Congress intended them to be. What Congress was belatedly attempting was to regulate commerce, a mission assigned it by the Constitution but one that it had left to the states until late in the nineteenth century. Yet Congress always has a tendency to ignore problems once it thinks it has dealt with them, and to move on to other issues. The regulatory agencies and the public become victims of this tendency. The lawmakers thought, for example, that the ICC would take care of the problem of the railroads gouging farmers with unconscionable charges. But almost three quarters of a century later, then incoming President John F. Kennedy learned from an expert's study of the regulatory agencies that the ICC had been ineffective in achieving lower rail rates and had become an enemy of rate competition and no friend to the consumer.

Congress has been reluctant to reexamine the functions of any of the regulatory agencies it created. When Congress established the FTC in 1914, the purpose of the commission was to engage in broad-scale economic planning for the entire nation and, particularly, to look into the growing problem of industrial concentration involving the trusts. But over the years, as members of Congress found themselves besieged with consumer complaints from constituents, such as mislabeling of furs, the legislators would dump the matter in the FTC's lap. As a result, the FTC seldom carries out the economic planning Congress originally intended.

To achieve their missions, the agencies were authorized to promulgate rules. These rules are the crux of the problem of overregulation. They are as much the law as if Congress had held hearings and enacted them by statute. Defenders of the present system contend the regulators are doing only what Congress wants, since Congress does not have the time to develop the degree of expertise the regulators have. The agencies, their defenders argue, must answer for their actions to the people, albeit once removed.

Congress's relative disinterest in regulatory activities means that only when an agency does something truly egregious does Congress seriously intervene. This happened in 1980 when an accumulation of business complaints caught up with the Federal Trade Commission, and Congress responded by imposing numerous limitations on the FTC when it appropriated money for the agency. The complaints involved FTC efforts to limit television advertising aimed at young children, to inspect the insurance industry and to establish procedures that industries would have to follow in setting standards for some twenty thousand types of products. Congress either totally barred the FTC's moves or so restricted them that further action became unlikely.

Another sign of Congress's failure to think through its actions in creating regulatory agency authority is the twin antitrust jurisdiction that it has conferred on the Department of Justice and the Federal Trade Commission. Even though there is a working arrangement between the department and the FTC to avoid duplication, businessmen complain that antitrust policy is less clear than it would be if only one agency did the enforcing.

The possibility of such duplication gave me a problem in 1978 when I overruled the Justice Department's Antitrust Division and approved the merger of Lykes Corp. into LTV Corp., creating the nation's third largest steel company. Backed by financial analysts and opposed by Antitrust Division lawyers, I had concluded that Lykes met the test for a failing company, which meant it qualified for an antitrust exemption that would allow it to merge with a healthier firm.

Senator Edward M. Kennedy took issue with my decision and, as chairman of a Senate judiciary subcommittee on monopoly, he urged then FTC Chairman Michael Pertschuk to have his agency take another look at the merger. Kennedy, in a letter to Pertschuk, noted that I had overruled several subordinates in the Antitrust Division, including the assistant attorney general in charge of the division.

"I am informed that every Antitrust Division staff member involved in the decision was of the opinion that for at least twelve different product areas, the merger would result in concentration significantly above that allowed in the department's own merger guidelines," Kennedy wrote Pertschuk.

I responded in a letter to Kennedy: "What you are advocating is that an administrative agency review a decision made by the attorney general during the course of discharging his responsibilities as the nation's chief law enforcement officer.

"If this evidences your concern over my ability to discharge my responsibilities, such an attitude would have unfortunate implications for effective future cooperation between us."

Underscoring the danger of duplicative enforcement, I told Kennedy: "It seems to me that it would be intolerable for the two agencies to undertake a course of action leading to review of each other's enforcement decisions. Not only would that ensure waste and inefficiency, it would also ensure unacceptable confusion and uncertainty in the business community."

Fortunately, Chairman Pertschuk turned down the senator's invitation. But the potential for collision and confusion remains.

In tending to ignore the regulatory agencies, Congress has nurtured the unchecked growth of their rules and regulations. A good example is a case that came before me on the U.S. Court of Appeals for the Fifth Circuit.[9] Pursuant to federal law, the state of Texas had produced a plan to keep smog below the maximum limit set by federal regulations. The Environmental Protection Agency—EPA—disapproved the Texas plan and used its rule-making powers to devise its own plan. The EPA plan incorporated the Texas controls and several other, more stringent requirements.

Texas objected to the EPA plan, pointing out that it was based on standards culled from a study that had been done for the notoriously smoggy Los Angeles area fifteen years earlier. Moreover, there had been breakthroughs in air pollution technology after the Los Angeles study had been completed.

EPA rejected Texas's challenge without any explanation. The case was sent back to EPA for another look. But for our order, the citizens of Texas would be paying for a set of air-quality controls promulgated by Washington bureaucrats, based on out-of-date data that applied to a totally different area. Now, that is rule-making.

A study done for the U.S. Regulatory Council and published in February 1980 gives an insight into the impact of federal and state regulations on a small city, Janesville, Wisconsin.[10] President Carter created the council to try to coordinate often conflicting actions and policies of the regulatory agencies. In the study, the owner-operator of a Janesville bus company founded by his father thirty-two years earlier to provide school transportation and limousine service to bigger city airports said he favored government regulation. But when he thought about the day-to-day impact of regulations on his operation, he remembered a twenty-five-count case initiated against him by an Interstate Commerce Commission inspector that had cost him ten thousand dollars in legal fees. In the end, a judge threw the complaint out of court, but that didn't return the bus owner's ten thousand dollars.

The executive vice-president of a fourteen-employee, twelve-million-dollar neighborhood bank in Janesville said there was "no way" he and an assistant could stay current with the regulations that affect the bank. "I would have to spend sixty percent of my time on regulations alone if I wanted to have a good sense of what was going on," the banker said. "As it is, I just limit myself to those I absolutely must know." And merely that effort, according to the banker, required him to devote as many as four hours a day to reading regulations from the Federal Deposit Insurance Corp. or the Federal Reserve System.

By citing statistics and the examples of overregulation, I am not suggesting that we as a nation should return to the unfettered, laissez-faire economic order that characterized the early nineteenth century. Our world is too complex, the potential dangers to the environment and health and safety of our citizens too great, to exist without regulations. A study by the Center for Policy Alternatives of the Massachusetts Institute of Technology quantified some of the benefits of government regulation: Regulating air pollution from major sources yielded benefits ranging from $5 billion to $58 billion per year. Limitations by the Occupational Safety and Health Administration on worker exposure to asbestos may result in reducing annual deaths from lung cancer and asbestosis by 630 to 2,500 a year. And motor vehicle occupant protection standards adopted between 1966 and 1970 saved more than 28,000 lives between 1966 and 1974.[11] I am not minimizing these achievements when I remain convinced that in too many instances regulation has become an end in itself, thwarting the elected and appointed makers of policy and frustrating the electorate.

The White House has made efforts to bring the regulators under control. President Gerald R. Ford issued executive orders that required regulatory agencies to determine the cost increase that would result from a proposed action and whether there were other, cheaper means of achieving the same end. In 1978, President Carter replaced those orders with one requiring agencies, before they can take an action, to describe in writing the objectives of the action and to list alternative ways of achieving the objectives in a more cost-effective way.

Congress, too, seems to be awakening to public resentment about overregulation. A record number of bills proposing regulatory reform were introduced during the Ninety-sixth Congress. The lawmakers, responding to the pleas of small businesses and local government units, did enact the Regulatory Flexibility Act in 1980, which went a bit farther than the 1978 Carter executive order in trying to protect small business from overregulation. Under the law, every time an agency issues a new rule, it must determine whether the requirement will have a significant impact on the smaller businesses and government entities. If the rule would, the agency must provide alternative ways for small businesses to comply that would be cheaper and involve less paper work.

The clearest sign of reform is Congress's move to deregulate major industries, a trend that was encouraged by the Department of Justice. The Airline Deregulation Act of 1978 became law after Congress established that government regulation had blocked price competition between airlines, resulted in higher fares and restricted the services from which consumers could choose. To measure the impact of that land-

mark legislation, one only has to look at airline advertise-
ments before and after the law took effect. Consumers can
now shop around for the best price—often the best discount
—in flying from one city to another. The Airline Deregulation
Act, in wiping out rate regulations, eliminated costly, paper-
work-generating rate proceedings that could have dragged on
for years, counting the time for appeals.

Less sweeping, but still significant, was the deregulation
that took effect in 1980 in the rail and trucking industries. The
Motor Carrier Act of 1980 opened up that industry to competition by making it easier for truckers to enter markets that
previously were shut to them because of complex ICC application requirements. The legislation also eased ICC restrictions on rate competition. The Staggers Rail Act of 1980
exposed railroads to competition among themselves, but left
substantial regulation intact to safeguard from ruinous rates
those shippers totally dependent on the rails, such as coal and
utilities. Individual shippers now can negotiate contracts with
railroads and truckers. This replaces the bureau's noncom-
petitive-rate practice under which carriers would jointly set
rates, subject to ICC approval.

Deregulation and other recent reforms introduced by the
legislative and executive branches are a beginning. But the
road to lasting reform is a lengthy one, and the tendency is
for reformers to lose their drive once they achieve some success.

Much of the blame for the overregulation of business and
individuals that I have been discussing lies with one branch
of our government—the legislative. When you look closely at
the relationship between the Congress and the regulators, it
is easy to understand why.

IV

CONGRESS—THE ULTIMATE SOURCE OF REGULATORY POWER

To understand the relationship between Congress and the regulators, one must recognize that a Gordian knot binds the subcommittees of the Congress to the regulatory agencies that they are supposed to oversee. The congressional subcommittees—I like to call them baronies or protectorates—nurture the agencies because the agencies are their major source of power. Subcommittees don't take kindly to proposals for cutting back or restricting the agencies, because that action would reduce their own power.

What you have, then, is a large number of protectorates, or baronies, each consisting of a congressional subcommittee and its agency. Sometimes pressure or resistance from those being regulated grows so great that Congress is forced to rein in an agency. But this happens infrequently and only when the regulated victim is sufficiently wealthy or influential.

When I write of the subcommittees of Congress, I'm referring primarily to the chairman of the subcommittee. It is he or she who is truly powerful. The subcommittees are not organized like the Supreme Court, where the Chief Justice is merely the first among equals. The chairman runs the show, and the agencies appreciate that, treating the chairman with more than due deference.

My favorite example of the baronies at work—I was mortified when it occurred—involved the administration's unsuccessful attempt to reorganize a part of the law enforcement bureaucracy. The plan, which I still regard as highly logical, involved transferring the Border Patrol, a unit of the Immigration and Naturalization Service, from the Justice Department to the Treasury Department. This would leave the Immigration and Naturalization Service with its essential, and often neglected, function of helping newcomers overcome their bewilderment and inevitable feeling of loneliness and adapt to the United States. If performed, the Immigration and Naturalization Service's basic function would give meaning to Emma Lazarus's words on the pedestal of the Statue of Liberty: "Give me your tired, your poor, your huddled masses yearning to breathe free . . ."

The Border Patrol agents, in Treasury, could then work harmoniously with the Customs Service, which already is a part of Treasury. The patrol guards the nation's borders to prevent the entry of illegal aliens, while Customs watches the same area to keep out illegal goods. Obviously, the two agencies tend to duplicate one another's duties. Rivalry and lack of cooperation between them has plagued the last several occupants of the White House, as both increased illegal immigration and smuggled narcotics became major headaches.

As part of the same reorganization, agents of the Bureau of Alcohol, Tobacco and Firearms in the Treasury Department were to be moved to Justice. This, it was hoped, would lead to better cooperation and coordination between the ATF agents and the FBI and drug enforcement agents who both were already a part of the Department of Justice.

The reorganization plan ran into immediate difficulty on Capitol Hill. The subcommittees responsible for ATF were unhappy about losing jurisdiction over that bureau. The House Immigration Subcommittee of the Judiciary Committee under Chairman Joshua Eilberg fought to keep the Immigration Service intact, condemning its "service" arm to a continued second-rate existence. Not totally incidentally, minimizing the service function stimulates the need for congressional assistance to constituents. This, in turn, helps assure the congressmen of some indebted voters.

As a result of that kind of opposition from the barons, the protectorates remained protected and the reorganization was shelved.

The doomed reorganization attempt was reminiscent of an earlier effort that floundered on Capitol Hill primarily because of the opposition of sixteen-term Representative Tom Steed of Oklahoma. Congressman Steed, who retired with the end of the Ninety-sixth Congress, was a leading baron in his role as chairman of the subcommittee of the House Appropriations Committee which watches over Treasury and, not incidentally, the budget of the Executive Office of the President. His control over the spending of policymakers in the executive branch gave Mr. Steed a degree of clout envied on Capitol Hill, and he became a special baron among barons.

Legend has it that during the Nixon administration, an associate director of the Office of Management and Budget approved a "Border Management" reorganization that would have combined the functions of the Border Patrol and the Customs Patrol, this time under the umbrella of the Department of Justice. The proposed solution, like the Carter administration's rejected plan, was the logical answer to obvious duplication. However, unlike the Carter administration's proposal, the 1974 OMB plan required no political preclearance. Because Chairman Steed was never consulted, he put so much pressure on Roy Ash, then the director of the Office of Management and Budget, that the hapless associate director responsible for the suggestion had to leave OMB.

The story, which was known within the Executive Office of the President as the "associate directorechtomy," still circulates as a reminder of subcommittee chairmen's powers, particularly of someone in Chairman Steed's position. Perhaps the account is apocryphal. It certainly is embellished. What is important is that some occupants of the Executive Office Building accepted it as gospel, and Chairman Steed's power grew that much more awesome. Certainly one result was that the Carter administration's law enforcement reorganization proposal did not seriously advocate transferring the Law Enforcement Training Center from its illogical placement in the Treasury Department to the Department of Justice. The Federal Law Enforcement Training Center, located at a former naval facility at Brunswick, Georgia, was a special pet of Chairman Steed. When I asked the Justice Department's Legislative Division why, a legislative expert told me, "The center is something he suggested. He goes down there frequently and keeps up with it. He is very proud of the center. He regards it as a personal monument." Only days before Mr. Steed finally left Capitol Hill, the center paid him tribute by naming one of the structures there the Tom Steed Building.

Congress's repeated failure to cut back the Law Enforcement Assistance Administration, a notorious example of pork-barrel politics, is another illustration of an unholy alliance between Congress and an agency. LEAA was created in 1968 by the Omnibus Safe Streets and Crime Control Act. That was a year when urban riots, ignited by such events as the slaying of Dr. Martin Luther King, Jr., combined with mounting violent street crimes to build great public pressure for federal action. The principle that the United States is a federal system and that under that division of power it is the local and state governments that have the main responsibility for countering crime was overlooked.

LEAA, the Department of Justice's first "grant" agency, was to funnel hundreds of millions of federal anticrime dollars to state and local police, courts and prisons. From relatively modest origins—its first fiscal appropriation was $63 million—LEAA became one of the federal government's fastest growing units. By 1975, its annual appropriation had soared to $895 million, though it slipped to $486 million in fiscal 1980.

Even during the Nixon administration, where the slogan of law and order had become nearly all an official needed to justify an outlay, attorneys general, including John N. Mitchell, began to resist Congress's eagerness to pour more and more money through LEAA to states, cities and counties.

There was far too much emphasis on hardware, with the federal government funding helicopters for jurisdictions that found it difficult to justify their use, and armored vehicles for others who feared riots might reoccur. Even eight-hundred-thousand-dollar "miniblimps" to patrol a Los Angeles suburb were under serious consideration by the LEAA grant-givers. The unmanned aircraft would patrol the suburb with a searchlight, a zoom lens camera and a loudspeaker. Fortunately for the federal taxpayer and citizens on the ground, the project was shot down by publicity.

Once the federal spigot had been turned on, Congress seemed unwilling to turn it off. There were very few congressmen who had anything to do with LEAA who did not want to keep it as a source of grants to their constituents.

When I took office, I thought for a time of proposing that LEAA be phased out. It had been operating for eight years, which was certainly sufficient time for the funding of its projects to be taken over by state and local governments. Rumors of my intention produced an outcry of protest that was immediate, unending and not subtle. Congress would have none of it. Instead, we decided on a reorganization program—in the federal government, when you can't eliminate you reorganize —that would sharply reduce LEAA's overhead. Things had got so out of hand that the federal government was financing state agencies whose purpose was to draw up plans for applying for additional LEAA funds.

We did manage to stop that bureaucratic Catch-22 so that states at least had to use their own funds for the planning. But changing the LEAA program was difficult, especially if a change would reduce the amount of money flowing from the agency to a congressman's district or a senator's law enforcement allies back home.

When we would be discussing possible cutbacks in the program with as esteemed a congressman as Rep. Peter J. Rodino, chairman of the House Judiciary Committee, he would frequently remind us that he had helped put together the Law Enforcement Assistance Administration. LEAA was the Department of Justice's only significant grant agency, and

Rodino would tell us it meant funds to Newark, where his constituency lives.

We felt as if we were walking on eggs. A May 24, 1978, memorandum to me from Walter M. Fiederowicz, the Justice Department special assistant who watched over the LEAA program, illustrates the care we took when dealing with the barons about their LEAA protectorate. It read:

"As you know, the current authorization level for the LEAA program is eight hundred million dollars. It is important for maintaining support from Senator Kennedy and Chairman Rodino that we agree to *at least* keep the current authorization level. This does not mean that we will seek appropriations to reach the authorization. It is my understanding that OMB has some misgivings regarding this level of authorization, but that the White House staff is willing to go along with the current level. Primarily for political reasons and for maintaining congressional relations, it is my view . . . that we should not make an issue of the authorization level and that we should go along with the current eight-hundred-million-dollar authorization."

Four months later, Fiederowicz warned in another memo of what would happen to us on Capitol Hill if we stuck with our intention to reduce LEAA's $651 million budget by $114 million to $537 million.

"We are seriously concerned," he said in the September 14, 1978, memorandum, "that a budget reduction of the dimensions proposed by the Budget Review Committee will engender significant congressional opposition and may indeed cause a break in the relationship that the department has developed with Senator Kennedy and Congressman Rodino to bring about badly needed reforms within LEAA.

"There is considerable sentiment within the Congress to increase LEAA's budget, and both Senator Kennedy and Congressman Rodino have intimated that they would be seeking to increase LEAA's authorization above its present level. As a result, it is likely that the primary result of the proposal to reduce LEAA's budget by $114 million for fiscal year 1980 will be an erosion of the Carter administration's credibility with the Congress and state and local constituent groups. This may result in our removal as a major participant in the legislative arena and the takeover of the reauthorization legislation by congressional advocates and LEAA constituents."

The criminal justice system behaves like any other interest group when it finds its congressionally-bred pork being threatened. It prevails on influential congressmen to protect it. The managers of LEAA, being skilled bureaucrats, knew this, and kept the pork going through the federal legislators to safeguard their own power at the agency. Again, the barony principle in operation.

That the Congress was so protective of the dollars flowing to the criminal justice system should come as no surprise. There are powerful members of the Establishment in that system. I can recall meeting with representatives of the American Bar Association to discuss that group's pet project, creation of a National Institute of Justice. The institute would perform many of the functions that LEAA did, but it would be independent of the Department of Justice. In the midst of lobbying for this paragon of independence, a bar association representative had no qualms about reminding me that the association had a grant request of its own pending at LEAA and suggesting that anything I could do to facilitate the award would be appreciated.

Finally, with inflation running out of control, the administration and Congress searched for ways of achieving a balanced budget. Expendable items were eliminated or drastically cut back, and LEAA's follies ranked it as a leader among expendables. It was set to be phased out as President Carter left office.

Hand-in-hand with the barony principle is the rampant self-dealing that I found to be operating on Capitol Hill. By self-dealing I mean a member of Congress attempting to influence a government decision to reward himself indirectly by winning benefits for a valued constituent. Self-dealing is difficult to define or to outlaw because congressmen properly and legitimately serve their constituents by seeking information about matters pending at the agencies. The propriety of such a contact comes into question if it is something more than a neutral request for information.

The best way to define self-dealing is to relate an outrageous example I encountered when the President called me one day to ask that I talk with Vernon Weaver, the administrator of the Small Business Administration. His agency had, among other problems, made a lot of bad loans, and morale there was low. I ended up finding him a new deputy and some other new people, including an inspector general. In the course of this, I ran across something that really puzzled me.

Congressman Joseph P. Addabbo of New York, the chairman of the House Small Business Committee's Subcommittee on Minority Enterprise and General Oversight, had told the SBA to make advances to his constituents under a special program to aid minority firms, and these loans were among the worst the SBA had made. We began to look into the matter officially, and the newspapers reported that the Justice Department was investigating suspicious circumstances surrounding the bad loans.

Congressman Addabbo then called Weaver and said he wanted to see the raw investigative file. Raw files contain all kinds of hearsay, innuendo, unverified allegations and other information that would be harmful to individuals if disseminated outside the investigating agency. The congressman had threatened Weaver about what would happen if the administrator didn't bring the file over to his office. Weaver asked me what to do, and I said he should tell the congressman that I—the attorney general—had the file, and that if he had any questions he ought to call me. He never called.

But subsequently Congressman Addabbo called Weaver again, insisting that the SBA make yet another loan to one of his constituents—a bad loan deal. I told Weaver to tell him the attorney general now was in charge of that and he should call the attorney general. Once again, he never called.

After that experience, I asked the Office of Legal Counsel to look into whether it was a conflict of interest for a congressman to try to get something done for a constituent by taking advantage of an agency over which the congressman had jurisdiction. The answer, contained in an eleven-page memorandum by John M. Harmon, assistant attorney general in charge of the office, pointed up the difficulties of making law in that area.

"The line between proper and improper communications may not always be self-evident," the Harmon memo noted at the outset.

"Without more (to the case), it is not improper for a member of Congress or a congressional aide to attempt to influence a specific administrative decision by the SBA through the submission of facts or arguments or views that go to the merits of the decision," the memo said. But this is "provided the submission is made in a way that is consistent with the agency procedures that govern the decision.

"Nor is it improper for the SBA to receive or to be influenced by such a submission, provided the same condition is met. On the other hand, any deliberate attempt to make the SBA ignore the merits or take irrelevant or extraneous considerations into account in making these decisions is, in our view, contrary to public policy; and any decision based on such considerations may well be defective and subject to judicial or administrative challenge."

The short of it is that it is extremely difficult to draw the line between a congressman simply representing a citizen and using his office improperly to benefit the citizen and/or himself.

Nevertheless, if there were such a job as a career attorney general and I held it, I would try to develop relevant statutes and ethical concepts so that we could reduce significantly the amount of self-dealing that does take place.

The most dangerous aspect of the barony-protectorate relationship is that it has led to government by rule-making, instead of by legislation. The alphabet agencies—the Federal Trade Commission, the Interstate Commerce Commission, the Federal Communications Commission, to name some examples—possess too much unbridled authority. The rule-making has long since evolved into policy-making, and broad questions that should be decided by elected representatives are being resolved by the rule-makers. Nobody elected them. They have no constituents to whom they must answer.

When I call for breaking the Gordian knot, I'm not suggesting the agencies should be removed from congressional supervision. We don't get too much overseeing by the committees, we get too little. Congress, particularly the House, is too close to the agencies it is supposed to oversee to do its job well.

In 1980, after an intense lobbying effort by resentful business groups and some tactical blunders by overzealous Federal Trade commissioners, Congress significantly clipped the wings of the FTC. But this was not an example of the kind of effective supervision I am endorsing. It was a long-overdue response to valid complaints about the FTC overstepping its authority—complaints that would not have built up if the FTC had been properly monitored by congressional watchdog committees.

A frequently proposed solution to excesses by the regulatory agencies—indeed, one that was used by Congress about fifty times during the Carter administration—is the legislative veto. When attached to a government program, the legislative veto requires the President or an administrator of a government agency to hold up on and submit to Congress each decision or regulation adopted under the program. Action on the decision then is delayed for a fixed time—usually sixty congressional working days—while Congress studies it. During that period, a majority of both houses of Congress, either house or, in some cases, even a sole congressional committee can veto the action.

The presumed purpose of the legislative veto is to help Congress improve its overseeing of the federal bureaucracy and to make the "unelected bureaucrats" politically accountable. Laudable objectives, but the legislative veto would defeat, not attain, them. It would add to frustrating delays in agency actions, to lack of accountability on the part of the regulators and to the muscle that special-interest groups are able to flex in the regulatory process.

Most important, legislative vetoes violate the letter and

spirit of our Constitution in two major ways. They infringe upon the President's constitutional duty to faithfully execute the laws. And they authorize congressional action that has the effect of legislation, but without giving the President the opportunity to veto the action, which is guaranteed by Article I, Section 7 of the Constitution.

On Christmas Eve of 1980, the U.S. Ninth Circuit Court of Appeals ruled that a legislative veto exercised in an immigration case violated "the constitutional doctrine of separation because it is a prohibited legislative intrusion upon the executive and judicial branches."[1] The ruling came in the case of Jagdish Rai Chadha, a native of Kenya, who was allowed to remain in the United States by an immigration judge after his student visa expired. The judge was exercising the attorney general's discretion. The judge's action then was vetoed by the House on a private resolution by Rep. Joshua Eilberg of Pennsylvania, which also paved the way for deporting five other persons.

The authority for this legislative veto was contained in a section of the Immigration and Nationality Act, enacted in 1952 over President Harry S Truman's veto. It gave the attorney general discretion to suspend the deportation of aliens who have resided in the United States continuously for seven years, who prove themselves to be of good moral character and whose deportation, in the attorney general's opinion, would cause extreme hardship. The provision states that each time the attorney general suspends a deportation he must submit a "complete and detailed statement" of his action to Congress. If either house of Congress during that session or the next one vetoes the suspension, the attorney general has to order the alien's deportation.

In the case of Chadha, a man of East Indian ancestry, the immigration judge said extreme hardship would result from deporting him. "It would be extremely difficult, if not impossible, to return to Kenya, or to go to Great Britain by reason of his racial derivation,"[2] the judge said.

Congressman Eilberg gave little explanation of why he was challenging the attorney general, saying only that the

House committee which had reviewed the matter felt that Chadha and the five other aliens did not meet the law's requirements, "particularly as it relates to hardships."

After the House veto, Chadha challenged the action as unconstitutional, but the immigration judge, while indicating agreement, said that he lacked authority to decide the issue. Later, the Board of Immigration Appeals said it, too, had no such authority.

Chadha took his case to the U.S. Ninth Circuit Court of Appeals, which ruled in his favor, saying that the Supreme Court has "placed it beyond dispute that the doctrine of separation of powers is vital for constitutional government. . . . Of necessity there will be instances where the proper means for its [the doctrine of separation of powers] enforcement rests with the mutual respect that each branch of government must extend to others."[3]

The court held that separation of powers is violated when one branch of government assumes an "essential function of another, especially on a long-term and routine basis, if that assumption of power is both disruptive and unnecessary to the attainment of a legitimate purpose."[4] By establishing a legislative veto over immigration actions, Congress had invaded the judiciary's power to review deportation orders. "We think this is an interference with a central function of the Judiciary, and that it is an interference which is both disruptive and unnecessary."[5]

The ruling took note of Congress's constitutional power "to make all Laws which shall be necessary and proper for carrying into Execution the foregoing Powers, and all other Powers vested by this Constitution in the Government of the United States, or in any Department or Officer thereof.

"We note that this [constitutional provision] authorizes Congress to 'make all laws,' not to exercise power in any way it deems convenient. That a power is clearly committed to Congress does not sustain an unconstitutional form in the exercise of the power."[6]

President Carter praised the decision, declaring it had "perhaps the most profound significance constitutionally"[7] of any court ruling handed down during his term of office.

A week before President Carter left office, the White House announced that the Justice Department was taking the unusual step of appealing the Ninth Circuit ruling to the Supreme Court, even though the department had argued in favor of the ruling. "The primary reason for appealing the decision to the Supreme Court is to secure a definitive ruling from that Court on an issue which, over the last decade, has created many occasions for confrontation between the executive and legislative branches,"[8] the White House explained. The Supreme Court, in one of the first actions of its 1981–82 term, agreed to hear the Chadha case.

In a June 21, 1978, message to the Congress on legislative vetoes, President Carter made what I think is the central point about relying on them to control the bureaucracy: The vetoes treat symptoms, not causes. The President said:

> The vast effort required to second-guess individual regulatory decisions could impede the crucial task of revising the underlying statutes. Agencies issue regulations because Congress passes laws authorizing them, or —frequently—mandating them. Many of these laws have not been seriously reexamined for years and need change.[9]

There has been a promising means of countering over regulation proposed recently—the Bumpers Amendment— but it is one, I am sorry to say, that the Carter administration opposed.

The amendment, which carries the name of its author, Senator Dale Bumpers of Arkansas, would reverse the presumption that now exists in the courts that an agency's regulation is valid unless a challenger proves otherwise. The burden would be shifted under the amendment so that the government would have to prove the validity of a regulation if it is contested.

To a nonlawyer, the idea of shifting the burden of proof when a citizen is engaged in a legal battle with a government agency might seem just another detail of courtroom procedure. But it can make all the difference in a lawsuit. It can be crucial to whether a plaintiff wins or loses, and shifting the burden from the citizen would help to make the people and the government equal.

President Carter and the Justice Department under my successor, Ben Civiletti, opposed the Bumpers Amendment. Their rationale was that they didn't know the extent of what it might mean, where it might take us. Frankly, I've not known that you take a position on legislation for that reason. I would suppose that laws have been enacted many times when you didn't know the full extent of the effect they would have.

I don't see how in the world you can justify putting a citizen at a disadvantage against the government, which already has more lawyers than any individual can afford. In addition, any regulation some agent—some government worker—now puts out is presumed to be valid. And the citizen has to prove otherwise, a difficult feat to accomplish.

The strongest argument against the Bumpers Amendment is that it would increase litigation and add to the overreliance on the courts in this country that you will find me complaining about later in this book. In adding to litigation, as citizens lost or reduced their fears of taking on the government, the change of legal presumption also would add to costs and delays.

My answer is that this would be true only in the beginning, in the days immediately after the burden is shifted. Very soon, I believe, the agencies, after losing a number of cases, would become more careful about their regulations and take extra care to be sure that they were valid.

So far, I have focused on what's wrong with regulation in our system, a subject I have far from exhausted. But I want now to turn to a delicate form of regulation that was ignored for too long in our history and that I believe the government is handling well.

V

REGULATING INTELLIGENCE AND COUNTERINTELLIGENCE

Much of the life of the attorney general of the United States is spent in an endless chain of meetings, most of them in a stately conference room that adjoins his office. A bust of Oliver Wendell Holmes looks on to instill wisdom. But one night after I had gone home to my apartment in the Watergate—the apartment-condominium part of the same complex which became famous in the Watergate scandal—an aide called to arrange an immediate conference with two FBI agents. We agreed to meet in the Watergate's ornate lobby, and within twenty minutes the aide, Mike Kelly, counselor to the attorney general, and Frederick D. Baron, my assistant who specialized in intelligence matters, arrived with the two agents.

We chose some seats in a corner for the sake of privacy. As residents and their guests bustled across the lobby, the five of us huddled around a table while the agents explained their problem in hushed voices. They had been following a Communist bloc foreign agent, and developments that I still cannot discuss required quickly placing a wiretap on his phone. My aides, Kelly and Baron, reviewed the legal implications of the request. After several minutes of whispered discussion and reflection, I took a document from one of the agents and put my signature on it authorizing installation of the listening device. Later that night, I was told, the foreign operative's phone was tapped and United States counterintelligence added to its knowledge of a potential enemy's espionage attempts.

Although convening in the Watergate lobby was unusual, in other respects the meeting was typical of many that I took part in while in office. The legal issues involved in the secret operations of U.S. intelligence agents were so complex that they inevitably consumed a substantial amount of time; and, to me, the attorney general's involvement in operations conducted within our borders was so delicate that I chose not to delegate this particular responsibility to subordinates.

For the attorney general, intelligence presents three difficult tasks that must be reconciled. First, to provide quasi-judicial overseeing of intelligence operations carried out inside the United States to make sure the rights of American citizens are not abused or ignored and that the vast powers of the intelligence community are not perverted to serve personal or political ends. Second, to provide the overseeing in such a way that the legitimate and vital need for national security intelligence can be served without the intelligence community feeling unduly hampered. Third, to carry out the attorney general's larger role as the nation's chief law enforcement officer by seeing that spies and others guilty of wrongdoing in connection with intelligence—whether the crimes are committed by operatives for foreign powers or by overzealous or unprincipled agents of U.S. intelligence services—are diligently prosecuted. Such prosecution is necessary both as a deterrent to crime by others and as the essence of our system of government by laws, not men. No government agency, regardless of how sensitive its mission, should automatically and as a matter of policy be immune from prosecution.

These tasks can be reconciled, but all three of them present grave and ticklish problems that keep the attorney general continually at odds with the CIA, the National Security Agency, the Defense Intelligence Agency, Pentagon units involved in reconnaissance, the military's intelligence forces, the State Department's Bureau of Intelligence and Research, the FBI, the Treasury Department, the Department of Energy and the Drug Enforcement Administration—all parts of the intelligence community. In almost every instance—viewed from the understandable but inevitably narrow perspective of intelligence work—life for our spies and counterspies would be easier if the attorney general kept his eyes down and his mouth shut. The resulting tensions are, however, unavoidable if the United States is to remain both safe and free.

The revelations of government abuses through investigations by the press and Congress during the mid-1970's demonstrated that there is reason to fear government intelligence activities. It is fair to ask any attorney general how he or she proposes to perform the duties of law enforcer, spy catcher and protector of liberty—and be faithful to each.

Over a hundred years ago, Sir Thomas Erskine May, in his *Constitutional History of England,* described the fear that intelligence agencies can engender:

> Men may be without restraints upon their liberty; they may pass to and fro at pleasure; but if their steps are tracked by spies and informers, their words noted down for crimination, their associates watched as conspirators —who shall say that they are free? Nothing is more revolting to Englishmen than the espionage which forms part of the administrative system of continental despotisms. It haunts men like an evil genius, chills their gaiety, restrains their wit, casts a shadow over their friendships and blights their domestic hearth. The freedom of a country may be measured by its immunity from this baleful agency.[1]

In view of the seriousness of the problems, it is unfortunate that the Justice Department's regulation of intelligence agencies is a matter the American people seem unconcerned and unfamiliar with, particularly since the headlines about FBI and CIA excesses have moved off page one of the nation's newspapers. Perhaps because the regulation of intelligence is

an infant endeavor and has not had time to take on the inefficiency and unresponsiveness of the more seasoned bureaucracies, it is among the more effective controls operating in
Washington.

That assessment is something most citizens must take on
faith, because the regulatory process is so secret that my ap-
praisal of its efficiency is difficult to challenge. The Senate and
House committees that oversee intelligence work, the Justice
Department unit that advises the attorney general on intelligence matters and the Foreign Intelligence Surveillance
Court, established in 1978 to consider requests for electronic
eavesdropping in national security investigations, do virtually
all their work in secret. This secrecy, while necessary, no
doubt contributes to the public tendency to ignore the control system—and lack of public scrutiny can of course open
the way to a recurrence of intelligence abuses.

In 1975, the Rockefeller Commission (set up by President
Ford to investigate intelligence agencies' abuses that had
come to light through press accounts) found that in 1954 the
Department of Justice and the CIA reached an important, but
secret, agreement: If an agent were suspected of wrongdoing,
the CIA alone would decide whether referral of the matter to
the Justice Department and the ensuing publicity would damage national security. If no referral were made, the incident
would remain a CIA secret.

In 1976, the Senate Select Committee to Study Government Operations with Respect to Intelligence Activities,
headed by Senator Frank Church of Idaho, provided details
of the agreement by citing a "memorandum for the record"
sent in 1954 by CIA General Counsel Lawrence R. Houston
to Deputy Attorney General William P. Rogers. On at least
two subsequent occasions—January 6, 1960, and June 10,
1964—the CIA reviewed and reconfirmed the arrangement.

The Rogers-Houston agreement was an outgrowth of
contradictions in the National Security Act of 1947. As the
Senate Intelligence Committee pointed out, the act made the
director of Central Intelligence responsible for protecting the
sources and methods that the CIA used in collecting and

analyzing intelligence, but it also forbade the agency from "exercising law enforcement and police powers and 'internal security functions.' "[2] The committee added that "the CIA never went to Congress for a clarification of this ambiguity, nor did it seek interpretation from the chief legal officer of the United States—the attorney general—except on the rarest of occasions."[3]

Both the Rockefeller Commission and the Senate Intelligence Committee found that the Justice Department had abdicated its responsibility by allowing the CIA to decide for itself which wrongdoings should be referred to the Justice Department and which should remain locked away in the secret files. The agreement illustrates how strong the impulse is within an intelligence agency to be a law unto itself, to avoid exposing itself to monitoring by outside officials in the name of preserving secrecy. Human nature being what it is, of course, the personal ambition and natural self-protectiveness of intelligence officials would inevitably tempt them to use self-policing to hide errors and embarrassments rather than solely to maintain necessary secrecy. And the record of recent years contains abundant evidence of officials who yielded to just such temptation.

The mid-1970's disclosures of abuses by the intelligence agencies led to dissolving the Rogers-Houston agreement. Abuses that had already occurred included the CIA's Operation CHAOS, in which the agency, from 1967 to 1973, compiled computerized files on thousands of American dissidents. The CIA's effort was in response to demands by two Presidents—Lyndon B. Johnson and Richard M. Nixon—that the agency determine what role foreign powers had in domestic unrest, but much of the information in the files went far afield from that question.

Another clear abuse was the CIA's opening and photographing thousands of letters a year between Americans and persons in Communist countries from the 1950's through the early 1970's. This operation was conducted in knowing violation of federal statutes that outlaw opening the mail. During the long span of its operations, the CIA briefed only one attorney general, John N. Mitchell, on them, and he reportedly concurred in their value.

From 1975 through 1977, the intelligence community worked on developing methods for referring possible violations of the law within their agencies to the Department of Justice. The going was slow. Their general counsels are not experienced in either constitutional law or prosecution, but instead have usually come up through the agencies' ranks. Because they think operationally rather than analytically, they're often not sensitive to serious constitutional problems that arise in intelligence work. Their primary concern is to protect their clients.

But in the long run the clients will not be protected if their constitutional violations are treated as dirty linen that should be hidden from the public; for when such violations are revealed by congressional hearings or, as happened in the mid-1970's, by press accounts, the stain of guilt spreads throughout the agency. Similarly, in the long run neither the CIA nor the public at large is well served by hiding cases of successful spying against U.S. agencies—no matter how embarrassing disclosure may immediately be.

On February 18, 1976, President Gerald R. Ford issued Executive Order 11905 on United States Foreign Intelligence Activities, introducing the intelligence community to the world of checks and balances. The order required senior intelligence officials to "report to the attorney general that information which relates to detection or prevention of possible violations of law by any person, including an employee of the senior official's department or agency."[4]

Chief among the FBI's abuses was its COINTELPRO effort—Counterintelligence Programs—during the 1960's. The programs were not directed at obtaining evidence to use in possible criminal prosecutions in line with the FBI's mission. Instead, COINTELPRO resorted to improper acts to disrupt or neutralize the activities of groups and individuals selected by the FBI on the basis of loosely drawn criteria. Targets of the operations were identified not as criminals or criminal suspects, but in such vague terms as "rabble-rouser" or "key black extremists."

The disclosures of COINTELPRO led to guidelines, for the first time, by the attorney general on dos and don'ts for the FBI in domestic intelligence work. These guidelines were hammered out by a team of Justice Department lawyers and FBI officials and issued by my predecessor, Attorney General Edward H. Levi, who estimated that intelligence work occupied about 70 percent of his time in office. Later, classified restrictions were created for the FBI's foreign intelligence and counterintelligence work.

Nearly two years after President Ford's groundbreaking order, President Carter issued Executive Order 12036 on United States intelligence activities, which made even clearer the fact that the agencies were no longer the sole judges of their possible misdeeds. One element of the order deserves special mention because of its emphasis on the safeguarding of civil liberties. In setting forth the conditions for using intrusive intelligence-gathering techniques, such as electronic surveillance, television monitoring and mail surveillance, EO 12036 required that the heads of intelligence agencies establish procedures subject to the approval of the attorney general: "Those procedures shall protect constitutional rights and privacy, ensure that information is gathered by the least intrusive means possible, and limit use of such information to lawful governmental purposes."[5]

As far-reaching and significant as the Carter order was, for a while it seemed it would never be issued. Justice Department lawyers had to work with teams of experts from the government organizations that had a stake in its provisions. Their first draft left President Carter unhappy. The President, who frequently reveled in his nonlawyer status, especially when he was working with lawyers, told the Justice Department that its work was incomprehensible, redundant, wordy and full of intelligence jargon wrapped in legalisms. The second draft did not do it for the Chief Executive either. Finally, the third draft, a completely reorganized order one-third shorter than the earlier attempts, satisfied the President.

The order did not end all conflict between the law enforcers and the intelligence agencies. Intelligence officials, ever-mindful of the need to protect at virtually all costs their "sources and methods"—a phrase they use repeatedly and in near-reverent tones—warily regard an attorney general who declares he intends to prosecute spies. And that is what I did in 1977 as soon as I felt I had a grasp of the problem. Expanding on a policy that had begun under the Ford administration, I made it clear that we would stop shying away from sensitive espionage prosecutions for fear of revealing too much about our own intelligence apparatus. I had decided that it would no longer be national policy to frequently limit our response to declaring persona non grata foreign diplomats caught in the act of spying or assisting spies and shipping them home unpunished.

The units of the federal government involved with intelligence missions look on espionage prosecutions as potential minefields for them, even though they are directed against the other side. They see the hazards of prosecution as far greater than any benefits that could result. For one thing, prosecutions can require testimony from CIA sources who have been operating under cover, a surfacing that ends or severely limits their future value. For another, a public trial might reveal too many details of U.S. intelligence and counterintelligence capabilities or, just as damaging, tell a potential enemy the extent of our knowledge about their knowledge. And there is the problem of possible retaliation against U.S. intelligence operatives in the country whose spies we are prosecuting. We do not know how many of our agents or sources in foreign lands are under suspicion, so we are unable to assess precisely what our decision to prosecute may cost.

Important as all these considerations are, in our system of government having an effective intelligence operation is only one of the country's requirements. It is not a be-all and end-all. We cannot suspend the normal operations of our legal and prosecutorial system for the convenience of a single agency, no matter how important its work.

One reason for our intelligence agencies' lack of enthusiasm for prosecutions was especially galling to me. That was their belief that federal judges could not be trusted to handle sensitive national security information. In an espionage prosecution, the judge is more crucial than in a standard criminal case because so many rulings on what prosecutors have to disclose and whether evidence is admissible are made *in camera*—in a closed hearing—before only the judge.

There is no record of judges leaking information given them. Yet the intelligence community has a deep-seated distrust of the judiciary. One manifestation of this lack of trust emerged when we were in the process of establishing the Foreign Intelligence Surveillance Court, which would extend to Americans suspected of spying for foreign powers the same kind of constitutional protections used in standard criminal investigations. In such instances, investigators are required to obtain an order from a federal judge to conduct wiretapping or bugging. The Surveillance Court meets in an off-limits section on the sixth floor of the Department of Justice Building in closed session at unannounced times.

To help arrange the procedures for this panel, CIA Director Stansfield Turner and I went to the Supreme Court to consult Chief Justice Warren E. Burger. The meeting took place in the justices' conference room, where the nine members of the Court hold secret sessions without any aide or other outsider present to cast votes on cases and decide which issues the court will consider. We sat on couches at the end of the spacious room, opposite the imposing conference table with the nine empty chairs around it. Tea was brought in and poured from a handsome silver service. I found myself spending some of the session persuading the Chief Justice to reject Turner's proposals for requiring the seven judges on the secret panel to submit to polygraph examination by the CIA. Admiral Turner also wanted the CIA to investigate and clear the judges. Fortunately, the Chief Justice agreed with me that the Foreign Intelligence Court would lose all credibility if it subjected itself to being declared fit by those whose requests for wiretapping and bugging it was judging. In any event, we convinced Admiral Turner that federal judges were not people who would be guilty of breaching security.

Our decision and that of the Ford administration to prosecute spies is reflected in the total number of espionage cases that the Justice Department brought from 1975 to 1980. During that five-year span, thirteen individuals were indicted, as opposed to only two people in the nine-year period from 1966 to 1975. This difference is even more meaningful when you remember that in the 1966–75 years the FBI did not operate under restrictive guidelines drawn up by the attorney general.

The thirteen persons publicly charged with spying from 1975 through 1980 were only a small percentage of the number of espionage agents questioned by the FBI during that time. Some fled the country, others were declared persona non grata and sent home, while still others became double agents. Some cases were also under investigation by the counterintelligence agencies of Canada and Britain and were disposed of by those nations.

If security permitted full disclosure, I am certain that I could convince even the most skeptical that our intelligence operations flourished at the same time as prosecutions and public disclosures took place. One example that I can cite concerns a Soviet spy who had been turned into a double agent by the FBI, Colonel Rudolph Albert Herrmann, a so-called illegal intelligence officer. An illegal agent is different from a "legal" operative, who is part of the foreign diplomatic corps or a news correspondent based in the United States. An illegal enters the country where he will operate by illegal means and assumes an identity usually unrelated to his actual homeland and does work that is unconnected to his true mission. If, in the case of the United States and Russia, diplomatic relations were ever severed, all the legal operatives would be expelled, and espionage activities would be carried on by the illegals so long as they remained undetected.

In 1980, the FBI, realizing that the Soviets knew Herrmann had gone over to the U.S. side, decided that he could perform one more task for America before he and his family took on another identity and went into hiding. Col. Herrmann —a pseudonym—appeared at an unusual press conference at FBI headquarters that was held to make Americans aware of the kind of espionage activities being conducted in this country. Herrmann spoke to reporters from behind a frosted glass screen in a heavily accented voice disguised by a modulator, describing in detail what he had done on behalf of Soviet intelligence while working as an illegal agent.

Herrmann had spent eleven years in the United States on behalf of the Soviet KGB, collecting political intelligence, arranging exchanges of information with other operatives and making an unsuccessful attempt to interfere with a U.S. space shot. He and his family had entered the United States from Canada, and Herrmann worked as a free-lance photographer in a suburb of New York City. Each weekend, he set aside time to listen to coded messages transmitted from Moscow. His assignments included performing services for other Soviet agents and setting up "dead drops," or hiding places, throughout the country that were used by the KGB to provide money for operatives and to pass and receive messages.

Herrmann was detected by U.S. counterintelligence agents when a Communist spy operating under diplomatic cover—a legal—was followed to a dead drop site and Herrmann showed up a short time later. The FBI turned him into a double agent, a conversion which was facilitated by the KGB's insistence over Herrmann's repeated objections that his teenage son return to Moscow for spy training.

Herrmann was a big fish among illegal intelligence officers. He provided the FBI with valuable information on the KGB's methods of communicating with its agents here and elsewhere in the world, including the cipher systems they used to encode messages. He told of accommodation, or front, addresses in Europe, seemingly legitimate places of business where KGB agents go to send information to Moscow with little risk of detection. Herrmann's double agent role ended in the fall of 1979 when the Soviets became suspicious and brought home several of their intelligence operatives who had been in contact with, or otherwise known to, Herrmann.

John L. Martin, a Justice Department lawyer who has spent much of his career trying to wage a legal fight against espionage, likes to tell of the occasion when he finally came to realize that I was serious about my decision to prosecute spies. The incident occurred during my first year in office when John was briefing me on the investigation of Truong Dinh Hung or, as he became known in America, David Truong.

David Truong was the son of a Vietnamese political figure who ran against South Vietnamese President Nguyen Van Thieu on a peace ticket in 1967 and was jailed for his effort by the strongman incumbent. The younger Truong moved to the United States. As an anti-Vietnam War activist, he asked Dung Krall, the Vietnamese-American wife of a U.S. naval officer, to carry packages between him and representatives of the North Vietnamese government in Paris. The naval wife agreed, but unknown to Truong, his courier was an informant for American intelligence. When it was discovered that Truong's packages contained copies of diplomatic cables and other classified government papers dealing with Southeast Asia, the key question became how Truong was acquiring the classified material.

It was at this stage of the investigation that John Martin was briefing me. He was especially vexed by the CIA's opposition to letting the courier-informant testify in court if the case turned into a prosecution.

"Don't worry, John," I counseled him. "I want you to get out there and do a good job. As attorney general, I always wanted to catch me a spy." John later told me that from that time on he knew he had the backing of the attorney general.

The Truong case is an excellent example of opposition from the intelligence community to our policy of prosecuting spies. It also illustrates the trade-offs and difficult choices involved. The CIA's resistance came from its wish not to reveal that its informant was Dung Krall, whose father had served as the North Vietnamese ambassador to Moscow. With extensive contacts among the Vietnamese community in Paris, she had been invaluable in supplying the CIA with useful information on the Vietnamese government.

My predecessor, Attorney General Edward H. Levi, had turned down the FBI's request to open two of Truong's packages without first obtaining a search warrant from a federal court, and the FBI feared that the warrant would jeopardize security if the warrant papers became public.

The courier service was still going on when I came to office in 1977, and the FBI sought my permission to open another package the bureau had been told of by Mrs. Krall. While I felt I did not have the power to authorize the search, I thought President Carter did, since the courts and Congress have maintained consistently that the President has such powers as part of his responsibility for protecting the national security of the United States. This is the "foreign intelligence" exception to the requirement of the Fourth Amendment to the Constitution that no search be conducted without obtaining judicial authority.

On May 12, 1977, President Carter gave written approval to inspect the Truong packages for a ninety-day period. The search immediately hit pay dirt. One of the first packages opened contained classified information about Vietnamese designs on Thailand, American prisoners of war in Indochina and American military material that had fallen into the hands of the Vietnamese government.

We still did not know the source of the classified documents, so I gave the FBI permission to wiretap Truong's phone and, later, to place a hidden microphone in his apartment. In less than a month, the phone tap picked up Truong arranging a meeting at his apartment with a man who identified himself only as Ron. There was a problem, however, in trying to pin down whether Ron was Truong's government source. Don Marsland, and FBI agent assigned to the case, had been instructed not to conduct a physical surveillance of Truong because of indications that Truong suspected the government was onto him.

Marsland was not to be put off. He took his wife to dinner at a restaurant in Truong's neighborhood the night of the meeting and then suggested they take an after-dinner walk. Strolling by Truong's apartment building at the appointed hour, they observed a white male entering and then leaving after only a few minutes. The Marslands followed the man to the headquarters for the United States Information Agency at the corner of Eighteenth Street and Pennsylvania Avenue, two blocks from the White House.

Marsland watched as the man signed the building log and rode the elevator to the seventh floor. The agent checked the log and found that the man had signed in as "R. Humphrey." The agency, now known as the International Communications Agency, is the State Department's propaganda arm. Armed with this new information from Marsland, we returned to the President for written authority to place a closed-circuit television monitor in Ronald L. Humphrey's office, the communications room where he was a night-watch officer. We soon had irrefutable evidence that Humphrey was supplying Truong with copies of classified documents.

It was relatively simple for the State Department to plug its security leak by removing Humphrey. Prosecution was trickier. Despite the documentary evidence, it was clear that we could not win and sustain convictions in court unless Dung Krall testified and we could establish the legality of the package searches and the electronic surveillance. Otherwise, we probably could do no more than ship Truong back to Vietnam or Paris and discharge Humphrey, making certain he never again had access to classified material. This would have set back my policy of prosecuting spies wherever possible.

Defending the legality of the surveillance, despite the fact that it established precedent, turned out to be a simple chore compared to obtaining the courier-informant's testimony. Mrs. Krall had told an FBI agent that if the time ever came when she would be asked to testify, she might be willing. The CIA, however, said she would not be available, that Mrs. Krall wanted to remain operational. John Martin came to me about the apparent contradiction and urged that she be asked again about testifying, this time in front of both CIA and FBI agents.

Meantime, CIA resistance came from the top. Director Turner wrote me that Mrs. Krall would not be able to testify. I responded that the FBI had said she might be willing, a response that I'm told angered Turner. Apparently, he realized that his own people had misled him about her willingness to surface publicly.

At this point, I told Martin to go to London to see Mrs. Krall. Accompanying him would be William Fleshman, Jr., her FBI "handler," as an agent responsible for an informant is known, and the CIA case officer. Turner's general counsel at CIA headquarters, Anthony Lapham, joined the party, saying he wanted to keep an eye on Martin. But even this high-level delegation didn't settle the problem. Mrs. Krall told the delegation that she wanted to think more about testifying. But the CIA officer then returned to her London apartment, this time on his own, and urged her not to take the witness stand. We learned of his visit almost immediately. When Martin returned to Washington, he and I went to the CIA's headquarters across the Potomac River in Virginia, and I exercised my authority to regulate the intelligence community. I told Admiral Turner that his officer was to have no more contact with Mrs. Krall. Finally, some months later, with the United States government paying $11,800 for her relocation and protection, in addition to her $1,200-a-month informant fee, Mrs. Krall testified.

She was crucial to the conviction of Truong and Humphrey and to the expulsion of Vietnam's ambassador to the United Nations, Dinh Ba Thi, with whom she had had contact in New York. He had been named an unindicted coconspirator by the federal grand jury that indicted Truong and Humphrey.

CIA foot-dragging in the Humphrey-Truong prosecution didn't end when the agency failed to prevent Mrs. Krall from testifying. Judge Albert V. Bryan, Jr., who presided over the trial, charged that "somebody in the CIA was being cute"[6] when the agency delayed turning over to defense lawyers material on Krall that was in its files. Under the Jencks Act, the government is obliged, well before the trial begins, to give the defense information in its files bearing on prosecution witnesses. The material, in this case, consisted of reports by Krall's CIA case officer on conversations he had held with her.

But this delay had no effect on the outcome. In the face

of overwhelming evidence, Humphrey acknowledged copying the documents and giving them to Truong. He maintained he did so to improve U.S.-Vietnamese relations, an improvement that he thought would help reunite him with a Vietnamese woman he called his common-law wife and her family. The woman and her children did manage to leave Vietnam and enter the United States. But the reunion did not last long; Humphrey and Truong each were sentenced to fifteen years in prison in the only espionage trial related to the United States's anguished involvement in Vietnam.

Prosecuting spies is not without its costs, as I learned in the Humphrey-Truong case. Michael E. Tigar, an attorney for Truong, accused me of violating the law in authorizing surveillance of his client. Drawing very selectively from a ruling by Judge Bryan which barred from admission as evidence some information that had been picked up by the surveillance, Tigar wrote Earl J. Silbert, U.S. attorney for the District of Columbia, on April 3, 1978: "The attached order, entered by United States District Judge Bryan in Alexandria, indicates that a number of federal crimes were committed in the District of Columbia in 1977. . . . It appears that those violating these statutes include Griffin Bell, FBI Agent William Fleshman, Jr., and other persons named in the attached opinion. . . ."

Silbert wrote Tigar in reply: "As I am certain you agree, the fact that a judge in a criminal case determines that evidence was obtained by law enforcement officers in violation of the Fourth Amendment does not 'indicate' that there was a violation of the criminal law by those persons who obtained or participated in obtaining the evidence involved. Indeed, the mere fact that evidence was obtained in violation of a person's Fourth Amendment rights does not even establish civil liability of the officers determined to have violated those rights, since the law is clear that these officers have at the very minimum a defense of good faith. To establish criminal responsibility for a violation of law would require the more onerous burden of proving a criminal intent."

But Tigar persisted, and in a May 12, 1978, letter he wrote

Silbert: ". . . You should know that a senior Justice Department official advised the attorney general in August 1977 that the continuation of the warrantless tap was, in his view, unlawful. I do not know whether this will have any effect on your views, but I bring it to your attention."

Silbert replied that he had discussed the matter with the senior official who told him that he "never stated that 'continuation of the warrantless tap was unlawful.' " He added that while there was "a possible difference of opinion about the need for judicial authorization of continued electronic surveillance, there is nothing to indicate that the continuation of electronic surveillance without a warrant was undertaken without complete good faith, let alone criminal intent. Accordingly, this office has concluded that the matter does not warrant criminal investigation."

The conviction of Humphrey and Truong was a powerful object lesson to others who might have been tempted to steal documents from the State Department and give them to an adversary of the United States. The chief argument against prosecuting them was that it meant surfacing Mrs. Krall as an intelligence informant. With the choice being to let Humphrey and Truong go free or blow Mrs. Krall's cover, the CIA didn't offer any really good reason not to give her up, and our decision was not a difficult one.

A few months later, we made an even sharper break with the old nonprosecution policy in a case involving two Soviet men employed by the United Nations in New York. The officials were Rudolf P. Chernyayev, a UN personnel officer, and Vladik A. Enger, an assistant to the undersecretary general.

FBI agents took them into custody in May 1978 in a Woodbridge, New Jersey, shopping center, along with Vladimir P. Zinyakin, as the three were attempting to retrieve an orange juice carton that contained microfilm of antisubmarine warfare equipment. Zinyakin, as an attaché at the Soviet UN mission, enjoyed diplomatic immunity from prosecution, but Chernyayev and Enger did not. Zinyakin left the country at the request of the United States.

Enger and Chernyayev, over strenuous objections from

the State Department and the CIA, became the highest ranking Soviet officials to be tried in this country on espionage
charges. Col. Rudolf Abel, the spy we traded for U-2 pilot
Gary Powers, was higher up the ladder of KGB authority, but
he was an "illegal," who had entered the United States without the official UN status of Enger and Chernyayev.

Enger, Chernyayev and Zinyakin were caught in what the
FBI calls a dangle operation. In this case, an American naval
officer was dangled to lure a Soviet spy ring that operated
both on land and aboard a Soviet-owned pleasure ship in the
Caribbean, the MS *Kazakhstan*. The project was code-named
"Lemonaid." The officer, selected by a friend of his in naval
intelligence, was Lt. Commander Arthur Lindberg. Lindberg,
a supply officer who purchased goods for the naval base at
Lakehurst, New Jersey, planned to retire from the service, and
this made him ideal bait.

The FBI wanted someone the Soviets would regard as
vulnerable, and Lindberg presented himself as a frustrated
officer living beyond his means who was going no further in
the navy. In the summer of 1977, he prepared to board the
Kazakhstan at New York for a week-long cruise to Bermuda.
FBI agents told Lindberg to be careful, reminding him that
someone once had fallen overboard from the ship and
drowned. At sea, Lindberg found the crew aloof, uninterested
in any contact with passengers. As the days passed, Lindberg's mission seemed to be failing. As a last resort, the night
before the ship was to dock in New York, Lindberg—following the FBI's instructions—wrote a note. "I am interested in
making additional money prior to my retirement and can
provide you with information which may be of interest to you
. . . If you are interested, telephone me at (201) 922-9724 at
11:45 A.M. Aug. 30, 1977. Ask for Ed."

Lindberg placed the note in an envelope addressed to the
Soviet ambassador. As he was heading for the covered gang-
way to leave the ship, Lindberg handed the envelope to a
ship's officer as if he were leaving a tip.

The Soviets took the bait immediately, calling for "Ed" at
the diner pay phone number Lindberg had left. The next nine

months became a turnpike odyssey, with Lindberg driving up and down the Garden State Parkway and the New Jersey Turnpike to wait by phone booths the Soviets would designate for contact and to pull off the road at "drop sites" to leave secret papers and pick up his pay.

The Soviets asked Lindberg for U.S. antisubmarine-warfare secrets that involved underwater acoustics and detection systems. After naval intelligence made certain that the documents were no more than minimally helpful to the Soviets, Lindberg placed copies in empty orange juice cartons and radiator hoses at preselected sites near busy roads. The Soviets paid him more than twenty thousand dollars in amounts ranging from two thousand to five thousand dollars, and once gave him "a Christmas bonus" of one thousand dollars.

Lindberg was able to identify Chernyayev as the man tailing him on one of the drop-off missions, and the FBI videotaped Chernyayev and Enger at drop sites and in pay phones as they communicated with Lindberg. Despite the solid evidence, the State Department and CIA vigorously opposed prosecution of the two Soviets. The State Department argued that the prosecution would damage detente, and the CIA warned that the Soviets would retaliate against Americans in the USSR. We countered that if Soviet counterintelligence were onto some of our agents, they might as well be declared persona non grata, because their usefulness would have been impaired.

President Carter finally had to resolve the argument. CIA Director Turner and my deputy, Ben Civiletti, presented their positions in the Oval Office. I'm told that when Admiral Turner pressed the point of potential harm to our agents if we prosecuted, the President responded that, based on the quality of information he had been receiving, he was surprised we had anyone working inside the Soviet Union. The notion of prosecuting spies caught in the act of stealing naval secrets appealed to President Carter, and he authorized the prosecutions.

At one point, I urged the establishment of a spy detente. Both sides would agree to use as spies only their people with diplomatic immunity. If they were caught, the most that could be done would be to send them home. Anyone else caught spying would be prosecuted to the full extent of the law. It was to be a form of intelligence parity. I was told that it was innovative but impractical. Nevertheless, the prosecutions of Enger and Chernyayev represented a step in that right direction.

In addition to the objections of the CIA and the State Department, the Pentagon expressed concern about disclosing classified materials during the trial. As a result, prosecutors tried but failed to bar the public and press from the proceedings during testimony about the sensitive documents. U.S. District Court Judge Frederick Lacey ruled that the accused Soviet spies' right to a fair trial "must prevail over the government's claim to secrecy and to protect itself.

"If we cannot say at the close of these proceedings that the defendants have had a fair trial, then the United States and the court have fallen short of what's required of all of us,"[7] the judge said.

Enger and Chernyayev were convicted and sentenced to fifty years each in prison. Judge Lacey said he imposed that long a sentence to prevent the Soviet Union from doing "what one of their leaders once said he would do—bury us."[8]

The Soviets retaliated in two ways. Three weeks after the FBI arrested Enger and Chernyayev, on June 11, 1978, Soviet militiamen surrounded the station wagon of Francis Jay Crawford at a stoplight on a Moscow street and hauled Crawford off to Lefertovo Prison. Crawford had been working for nearly two years as service manager in the Soviet capital for the International Harvester Co. of Chicago—"a tractor man," as his associates called him.

Crawford was charged with buying twenty thousand rubles on the black market at one-fourth the official exchange rate. After his arrest, the State Department and the CIA intensified the pressure to drop the charges against Enger and Chernyayev. Our policy of prosecuting spies was at stake, and I would not give in. "I'm not about to trade two KGBers for any tractor salesman," I told my staff.

Three months later, about a month before Enger and Chernyayev were to be tried, Crawford was convicted and given a five-year suspended sentence. Three Russian codefendants who, unlike Crawford, pleaded guilty were sent to prison for four-to-five-year terms. Crawford and the Soviet defendants were denounced as "hooligans and criminals" by the state prosecutor. I felt relieved when Crawford was allowed to leave the Soviet Union on September 8.

The Soviets dropped their second shoe of retaliation only a week after Enger and Chernyayev formally pleaded innocent to espionage charges in federal court in Newark, New Jersey. The government newspaper *Izvestia* exposed a sensational spy case involving an American diplomat, which the Kremlin had been sitting on for nearly a year. The usual practice of both sides had been to give little or no publicity to the expulsion of persons protected by diplomatic immunity who were caught spying.

The spy was Martha A. Peterson, a vice-consul in the U.S. embassy in Moscow. According to *Izvestia*—and U.S. authorities made no effort to challenge the account—Ms. Peterson, on July 15, 1977, was caught in the act of filling a dead drop with cameras, gold, Russian currency, instructions and ampules of poison for one of her operatives, known as Trigon. The dead drop site was a niche in a bridge over the Moscow River near the Luzhniki sports stadium.

Izvestia used the apprehension of Ms. Peterson to support its most sensational charge: that she earlier had been an accessory to the murder of a Soviet citizen who had stood in the way of CIA-backed espionage operations. The newspaper said she had supplied ampules of poison to an unidentified male accomplice, who used them to eliminate the innocent Soviet citizen.

Ms. Peterson was allowed to leave the Soviet Union the day after her arrest, but not before the Soviets photographed her sitting at a table alongside Clifford Gress, the U.S. Embassy counselor, as she was being interrogated by Soviet security agents. Her espionage paraphernalia was displayed prominently on the table.

Moscow made clear that the belated announcement of Ms. Peterson's apprehension and expulsion from the Soviet Union was in response to the arrest of Enger and Chernyayev, which *Izvestia* referred to as "the new campaign over Soviet espionage that has been launched in the U.S.A."[9]

I did try to accommodate the prosecution of the two Soviet spies to our foreign policy. After their arrest, Secretary of State Vance called to relay Soviet Ambassador Dobrynin's personal request that the two men be released on bail. Noting that our policy was not to free spies on bond, I asked if the Soviets would do anything for us in return. Vance said they had mentioned nothing specific but urged me to go along, contending that then the Soviets would owe us a favor. I was willing, but Robert Del Tufo, the United States attorney in Newark and the chief prosecutor in the case, resisted. Only after much persuasion did he agree, and they were released pending trial.

After their conviction, Vance asked that they be released while their case was appealed. This time I opposed him, but Vance kept underlining the importance to our foreign policy of temporarily freeing them. I called Del Tufo, and he refused. He finally agreed to ask Judge Lacey to release them, but only after I said he could make clear that he opposed the move and was reluctantly following orders. Enger and Chernyayev spent little time behind bars, despite their fifty-year sentences. While their convictions were being appealed, the two spies were traded to the Soviet Union for five Russian dissidents who were allowed to emigrate and for other considerations I cannot discuss.

Nevertheless, we had made our point. The arrest, prosecution and conviction of the two KGB men who were using UN employment as a cover for spying put the Soviet Union on notice that the United States would no longer tolerate such actions as necessary evils of international relations. Judge Lacey put it well when he sentenced the two UN employees: "I ask myself how many FBI agents have to be assigned to representatives of the Iron Curtain countries to make sure our hospitality is not undermined."[10]

The CIA was vigorous in trying to block the Enger-Chernyayev prosecutions, a move that if successful would have thwarted effective regulation of intelligence. But that CIA effort did not approach the intensity or imagination of the Pentagon's campaign against the public trial of William Peter Kampiles. Kampiles was a twenty-three-year-old, low-level CIA employee who handed the Soviets a major intelligence coup. His case is an example of espionage that probably would not have come to public notice had the 1954 Justice Department-CIA agreement been in force, because the prosecution revealed significant breaches in the CIA's own security.

Kampiles worked as a trainee at CIA headquarters in Langley, Virginia, from March through November 1977. He served as a watch officer in the agency's operations center, where he monitored incoming intelligence reports from around the world and routed them inside the agency. For use in the operations center, a technical manual on the top-secret KH-11 spy satellite was kept in a file near the watch officer's work station. *The New York Times* reported in its coverage of the trial that the KH-11 is so sophisticated that "it can produce legible photographs of billboards from hundreds of miles in space."[11] Unlike earlier spy-in-the-sky satellites, whose gleanings had to be recovered by search planes as they were parachuted periodically back to earth, the KH-11 transmits its pictures in coded signals.

Kampiles, according to his confession, which he later sought to recant, and to other court evidence, sold a copy of the KH-11 manual to Michael Zavali, a military attaché at the Soviet embassy in Athens. He was paid a paltry three thousand dollars for the priceless document. *Los Angeles Times* correspondent Robert C. Toth reported that it was priceless because once the Soviets had the manual, they realized they had been tricked into believing that the KH-11 was electronically dead by U.S. technicians who made it seem silent. Instead of transmitting its TV-like pictures down to earth as other advanced satellites do, the KH-11 radioed its pictures up into space—to a communications satellite that relayed them to a U.S. intelligence station halfway around the world. Toth reported that American intelligence was confident that the ruse was working because when the KH-11 passed over the Uzbekistan missile center in the Soviet Union, it was able to photograph an aerospace glider that had been left out in plain view. Yet only a few hours earlier, when the KH-9, a U.S. spy satellite that transmits its pictures directly to earth, flew over the same missile center, the Soviets had carefully hidden the space glider and other objects of interest.[12] The KH-11's photograph of the glider gave the United States its first evidence that the Soviets were making a craft similar to the U.S. space shuttle. But after Kampiles delivered the manual, the Soviets would undoubtedly hide anything of possible interest every time the KH-11 passed over Uzbekistan, just as they had been doing for the KH-9's overflights.

Publicly trying Kampiles for his crime stood to embarrass the CIA for what kindly could be called lax security procedures. As Admiral Turner said in a July 2, 1978, memorandum to all CIA employees—a memo that eventually was read into the court record by Kampiles's lawyers: "In recent months, evidence has mounted that many employees are removing agency documents from their office environment and taking them home for work-related purposes. This practice is a flagrant and deliberate violation of agency security regulations and must be stopped immediately."[13]

The CIA's early handling of the Kampiles investigation was another embarrassment. Kampiles met the Soviet military attaché in Athens shortly after leaving the CIA, and then returned to the agency and tried to tell a former colleague there a self-serving story about his adventure. Kampiles's tale stopped short of revealing that he had turned over the KH-11 manual to the Soviets. Nevertheless, his ex-colleague, who worked in the CIA's office of legislative counsel, listened for only a short time as the two men sat on a bench outside CIA headquarters before deciding that Kampiles should be talking with one of the agency's Soviet bloc experts.

The former colleague then went into the headquarters building, leaving Kampiles waiting outside, and attempted to bring an expert back with him. But the expert refused, according to testimony at the trial, saying that under the President's executive order on intelligence it might be improper for him to be dealing directly with an American—a gross exaggeration of the order. The expert finally agreed that Kampiles could write the agency setting out his dealings with the Soviet intelligence agent. Kampiles did write the letter, but it remained unopened for two months at the CIA.

Finally, CIA officials read Kampiles's letter and asked the ex-employee to come to Washington for an interview. Eventually, Kampiles failed polygraph examinations and confessed that he had sold the satellite manual to the Soviet agent. This was nearly four months after the CIA had the first inkling that its former watch officer had been dealing with the Soviets. Agency critics could cite the passage of so much time as evidence that the CIA's internal security procedures were too loose.

Eventually, the CIA cooperated fully with attorneys at the Department of Justice in the prosecution of Kampiles, but the Department of Defense protested. The problem arose over our obligation—if we proceeded with the prosecution of Kampiles—to introduce the KH-11 manual as evidence at the trial in a way that would keep its contents secret. The CIA, after an exchange of memoranda between me and Admiral Turner, agreed with our plan of presentation, and the CIA—not the Pentagon—was the agency involved, for the CIA had written the manual and, much to the agency's chagrin, had seen the system compromised by a former employee.

Nevertheless, one month after Kampiles's arrest and a scant six weeks before the trial was to begin, lawyers from the Department of Defense objected to the procedures that the Justice Department and CIA had worked out. They contended that the government could not acknowledge at the trial that the United States was conducting overhead reconnaissance of the Soviet Union, a means of intelligence-gathering regularly reported as fact by the press. We all knew at the time that President Carter was planning a major policy speech on October 1, 1978—less than two weeks away—in which he would acknowledge the United States's overhead reconnaissance program.

The Pentagon lawyers also argued that we could not refer in the courtroom to the existence of the Office for the Collection of Specialized Intelligence through Reconnaissance Programs, a little-known organization that oversees the satellite program and related efforts. What no one present realized was that the CIA already had authorized the publication of a book by its former director, William Colby, in which he discussed both the overhead reconnaissance effort and the existence of the specialized intelligence office.

The Pentagon lawyers presented four "theories" that the prosecutors could choose from at the trial to avoid revealing the program or the office. They were that the KH-11 documents actually had never been given to the Soviets; that the KH-11 system had been proposed but never implemented; that the satellite system had been constructed but never launched; or that the system had been launched but never placed in operation. One problem with any of the falsehoods was that Kampiles knew the Soviets had the manual in their hands and that the KH-11 was an operational system. The Pentagon approach showed no respect for the integrity of our criminal justice system. All of the proposals would have required making material misrepresentations to the court in violation of Section 1621 of Title 18 of the U.S. Criminal Code and several provisions of the Code of Professional Responsibility of the American Bar Association.

When John Martin of our prosecution team made these points in a meeting with the Pentagon lawyers, they replied that "conversations are now taking place at higher levels" and that the prosecutors would be "receiving instructions." The next day, when Martin and others on the team told me that the Defense Department was exerting extreme pressure, I reaffirmed that Justice, not the Pentagon, was in charge of the case.

The instructions from higher levels never came, but the Pentagon lawyers did propose that we solve the problem by conducting a closed trial. Our prosecutors responded that the

Sixth Amendment to the Constitution provides: "In all criminal prosecutions, the accused shall enjoy the right to a speedy and public trial . . ."

There were two elements of evidence that we had to keep from being made public at the trial. One was the KH-11 manual itself, the release of which would have told the world about the capabilities and workings of our extremely advanced satellite. The other was the method we used in establishing that the KH-11 system actually had been compromised.

The trial judge, the late Phil M. McNagny, Jr., solved the first problem by ruling that only the attorneys, jury and expert witnesses could see the manual, and that the document would be kept out of the official public record of the proceedings. The problem of not revealing how we first learned that the KH-11 was no longer a secure system required a closed hearing before the judge, in which the government presented sensitive material that included national security information. Judge McNagny helped preserve the secrecy of the investigation by instructing defense lawyers not to ask in open court how the government came by this knowledge.

After an eight-day trial, the jury convicted Kampiles of all eight espionage counts that he had been charged with. Judge McNagny sentenced him to forty years in prison, and the U.S. Seventh Circuit Court of Appeals affirmed the conviction. The Kampiles investigation and prosecution illustrated how an extremely delicate spy case can be tried under the open American judicial system without giving away national secrets. His conviction served as a deterrent to espionage, but it did not end the controversy inside the government over my policy of prosecuting spies.

After Kampiles's conviction was upheld by the appellate court, Richard J. Stone, the Pentagon's deputy assistant general counsel for intelligence, international and investigative programs, excoriated the prosecution in a letter to Philip B. Heymann, assistant attorney general in charge of the Criminal Division. Stone contended that many of the government's problems in sensitive national security prosecutions "stem from a curious perspective evidently entertained by lawyers of the Criminal Division's Internal Security Branch that the Defense Department and CIA were not 'clients,' but 'victims.' " He said the prosecutors should be instructed to establish a lawyer-client relationship with government agencies in espionage cases.

But the duty of government prosecutors in criminal cases transcends representing as house counsel the bureaucratic interests of a particular agency. The prosecutor is an officer of the court and also the agent of the President in performing his constitutional duty to take care that the laws be faithfully executed. In espionage cases, this means that the government prosecutor must consider not only the genuine needs of national security but also the constitutional rights of defendants and the ethical constraints imposed on him or her as a lawyer.

The successful prosecution of espionage cases requires that government attorneys establish and maintain credibility with the federal district judges of this nation. The judges know that our recent history is marred by improprieties committed at the highest levels of government in the name of national security. That same history demonstrates that the intelligence, military and diplomatic communities share a willingness to overprotect their activities. Prosecutors in espionage cases cannot accept at face value representations about what is important and what can be disclosed from government agencies whose security has been breached. If Justice Department lawyers allow themselves to be misled by the agencies, the lawyers may be guilty of misrepresentation in the courtroom and may jeopardize the protection of genuine national security matters.

Maintaining independence and integrity under relentless, resourceful pressure from the government bureaucracy can be difficult. But to observe the Constitution and the laws of the United States, the Department of Justice must make prosecutive decisions. Article II, Section 3, of the Constitution states that the President shall "take care that the laws be faithfully executed." Section 516 of Title 28 of the U.S. Code provides that "the conduct of litigation in which the United

States . . . is a party . . . is reserved to officers of the Department of Justice."

During the administration of President Gerald R. Ford, the Justice Department reacted to disclosure of intelligence abuses by moving to restore balance in the relationship between national security and the administration of justice. An October 22, 1975, memorandum from Deputy Attorney General Harold R. Tyler, Jr., told assistant attorneys general who were stymied by the refusal of government departments and agencies to produce evidence that "it is the responsibility of the Department of Justice to enforce the law vigorously and it cannot abdicate this duty . . ."

During the Carter administration, the position expressed by the Tyler memorandum was accepted by the CIA. In 1978, CIA Director Turner told a House subcommittee that was assessing the use of classified information in litigation: "It is the attorney general who has the discretion to exercise, the power to act and, therefore, the authority to decide whether a prosecution is warranted and on what basis to go forward."[14]

But the CIA director's acceptance of the principle that the attorney general is preeminent in prosecuting violations of law involving intelligence did not end the interagency tensions produced by applying that principle. The prosecution of David H. Barnett illustrates that point. Barnett was a turncoat former CIA agent who sold the Soviets secrets on America's intelligence operations that, among other horrors, identified to the KGB thirty U.S. operatives who had worked overseas.

Prosecuting Barnett represented a substantial embarrassment to the CIA, and could have revealed intelligence secrets that would have told the Soviets how much we knew that they knew. I learned that CIA officials had urged John Martin to settle the case quickly without a public trial, by obtaining a quick and unrevealing indictment and bargaining a guilty plea with Barnett. Martin refused and was backed by Attorney General Civiletti, who instructed him in a May 1980 memorandum that there was to be no indictment unless the case could be prosecuted successfully.

Carrying out those instructions, Justice Department lawyers plodded through CIA's relevant files, interviewed witnesses and built a solid case against a traitor. Barnett confessed to accepting $92,600 from Soviet KGB agents for information on a highly successful covert CIA operation, code-named HABRINK, and for trying to infiltrate three organizations, the Senate and House Intelligence Committees and the U.S. Intelligence Oversight Board.

HABRINK was an operation that collected information on weapons the Soviets had provided to Indonesia in the 1960's. The information, which was used by the United States military to develop countermeasures, described the workings of the Soviet SA-2 surface-to-air missile, the Soviet *Styx* naval cruise missile and the Soviet W-class submarine. As an example of the program's value, HABRINK, by revealing how the guidance system for the SA-2 functioned, enabled the United States to jam radio frequencies directing the missile during the Vietnam war, thereby saving the lives of many bomber crews flying over North Vietnam.

By disclosing the HABRINK operation to the Soviets, Barnett told them what we knew about some of their weapons, how we gathered information from Third World countries to whom the USSR was supplying arms and the identities of the agents involved.

The case against Barnett was so strong that he chose to plead guilty—and not because the government had settled for the quick and unrevealing indictment and the bargained guilty plea. In the prosecution statement, the government said that other secrets Barnett allegedly had sold the Soviets would have formed the basis for additional charges if the case had gone to trial. The evidence was given under seal to the trial judge, thus keeping disclosure to what prosecutors regarded as the minimum, and he sentenced Barnett to an eighteen-year prison term. Thus the Barnett case became a further deterrent to the threat to national security from a potentially hostile state—and without compromising the nation's intelligence agencies.

VI

TOUGH CASES AND THE FUTURE OF INTELLIGENCE REGULATION

The delicate business of regulating intelligence does not always cause problems between the Justice Department and the intelligence agencies. Stansfield Turner, when he was CIA director, told me that the Justice Department's handling of the Frank Snepp case did more to lift the sagging morale of the CIA than any other single incident he could recall. With the Snepp case, we won from the Supreme Court a ruling that upheld the validity of the contracts that employees of the CIA and other government agencies sign in which they promise not to publish or otherwise reveal information about their agency without first submitting it to the agency for clearance.

Frank W. Snepp III was a CIA intelligence analyst in Saigon until Americans fled the capital in 1975. He charged in his 1977 book, *Decent Interval,* that the American evacuation had abandoned thousands of the CIA's Vietnamese employees and collaborators, exposing them to retaliation by the North Vietnamese. Snepp maintained that high U.S. officials had ignored CIA-gathered intelligence showing that the North Vietnamese would attack Saigon and, as a result, had failed to plan the evacuation properly.

By the time Snepp's book appeared, legal precedent had

127

established that government agencies can require employees to obtain clearance for classified material that they intend to publish. The case in point occurred when the CIA sought to censor portions of a book, *The CIA and the Cult of Intelligence,* by one of its former agents, Victor L. Marchetti, and by John D. Marks, an ex-State Department official. Marchetti and Marks did submit their material in advance of publication, and then engaged in extensive arguments in and out of court over what in their book was classified or should have been. The book finally was published with deletions mandated by the CIA.

Snepp's was a different case. The government made no claim that his material was classified—only that he had signed a secrecy oath which constituted a contract and had then refused to abide by its requirement that he submit his book for clearance. Stansfield Turner urged us to take Snepp to court to demonstrate that such agreements are enforceable. The CIA was then thirty years old, and a substantial number of men who had spent their careers with the agency were retiring. Several hundred other agents recently had been discharged in a purge of the CIA's clandestine service, following the disclosures and recommendations of the Rockefeller Commission and the Senate and House Intelligence Committees. If Snepp were allowed to flout the secrecy provision, other ex-agents were likely to follow his lead and agency secrets could be compromised.

Turner said Snepp's refusal to abide by the contract had raised "a fundamental issue for our society. If the society cannot trust the judgment of its public servants regarding what should or should not be withheld from the public, then the society can in fact have no secrets at all."[1]

But even more was at stake than the CIA's secrecy oath. Other agencies that require employees to sign similar contracts include the FBI, the Department of State, the National Security Agency, some units of the Treasury Department, the Department of Defense, the Nuclear Regulatory Commission and the Department of Energy. Yet to go to court, I virtually had to order the Justice Department's Civil Division to file the suit. Its lawyers kept warning that the press would attack me on grounds that I was eroding the First Amendment's guarantee of a free press. I told them that the suit concerned breach of contract and had nothing to do with the First Amendment or censorship. If Snepp did not want to work for an employer who required him to obtain clearance for what he wrote about his employment, he didn't have to take the job. There's no longer involuntary servitude in this country.

The press, as the Civil Division lawyers predicted, did attack me for the suit. When I stood my ground and emphasized that the suit was for breach of contract, the media began to report the government's case more favorably. The experience taught me that the press, even when an interest to which it gives great priority is involved, can distinguish between the genuine and the phony and will not be taken in by a critic of government who simply broke a contract and then tried to wrap himself in the flag of the Constitution.

Snepp's two-day trial was acrimonious. U.S. District Judge Oren R. Lewis ruled that Snepp had "willfully, deliberately and surreptitiously breached his position of trust with the CIA."[2] Judge Lewis ordered Snepp to turn over his "ill-gotten gains" to the government and barred him from seeking to publish any other material about the CIA or intelligence activities that he obtained while a CIA employee without first clearing it with the agency.[3]

The judge brushed aside Snepp's undisputed argument that his book contained no classified information, holding that Snepp "is not the judge of what portions, if any, of CIA's intelligence may be made public."[4] The publication of *Decent Interval* without clearance by the CIA "caused the United States irreparable harm and loss," Judge Lewis said. "It has impaired the CIA's ability to gather and protect intelligence relating to the security of the United States of America."[5]

The U.S. Fourth Circuit Court of Appeals, reviewing the case, softened the decision against Snepp by ruling that instead of forfeiting all profits from the book, as Judge Lewis had ordered, he should be required to pay only those damages that a court, through a trial, determined had actually resulted.[6]

When both the government and Snepp appealed, the Supreme Court reinstated the hard line, noting that Snepp had breached not merely a contract but a position of trust. That kind of violation, the Court said, merited a punishment beyond the usual one for breach of contract. Over the dissent of three justices, the Supreme Court held that Snepp must pay the government all present and future profits from the book.[7] The three dissenters argued that the contract Snepp had signed could not reasonably cover more than classified material and that extending it further might be a violation of the First Amendment's free press guarantee.[8]

The Supreme Court decision gave the government a means of deterring those who would violate contractual guarantees of secrecy without having to prosecute the violators on espionage charges. CIA Director Turner threw a champagne reception for the government lawyers immediately after the trial, and in December 1980 the Department of Justice, relying on the authority of the Snepp decision, adopted guidelines for enforcing secrecy contracts.

The balancing of constitutional guarantees is never more delicate than when the First Amendment's right of free press and expression is on the scale. While not a genuine issue in the Snepp case, the free-press guarantee was central to *The Progressive* magazine's plan to publish an article on the workings of the hydrogen bomb, another case that produced a struggle inside the Department of Justice. In *The Progressive* case, what weighted the scale against normal freedom to publish were the imperatives of national security.

The Progressive has a long tradition of political muckraking. It was founded in 1909 by Senator Robert M. La Follette of Wisconsin, who later ran for President on the Progressive party's ticket and was a leading opponent of U.S. participation in World War I. The magazine sought to publish the H-bomb article to advocate unilateral nuclear disarmament. To this day, I do not understand how technical details on the workings of the thermonuclear weapon facilitate understanding or debate of the issue of disarmament.

Howard Morland, the free-lance author who wrote the H-bomb article, argued that the government uses secrecy about the weapon as a means to stifle public debate over producing and stockpiling it. He suggested that similar secrecy about the workings of the internal combustion engine would chill debate "on the contribution of the internal combustion engine to air pollution, to the fuel crisis, to whether we have mass transit or build more highways."[9] Before publication, *The Progressive*'s editors sent a copy of the Morland article to the Department of Energy for verification of the material's technical accuracy.

The Department of Energy, then headed by Secretary James R. Schlesinger, not a man to mince words, said Morland's article would publicly disclose data that the Atomic Energy Act of 1954 required be held restricted. Schlesinger also stated that releasing the data could help foreign governments shorten the time needed to develop thermonuclear weapons. No Cabinet secretary in my tenure ever pushed us harder to move in court against a defendant—in this instance, to seek an injunction to block publication of Morland's article. At one point, Schlesinger came to my office for a meeting about what he saw as a lack of vigor in the government's legal tactics. On the way through the reception area that leads to the attorney general's suite of offices, Schlesinger paused at the desk of my secretary, Fay Cain, and picked up a sign Mrs. Cain has displayed for years. The sign was a quote from Shakespeare: "Let's kill all the lawyers." Schlesinger joined me and four Justice Department attorneys and placed the sign in the center of the conference table without a word or smile.

I needed no prodding to pursue *The Progressive* suit, although some of my colleagues did. To me, the issue was clear. As the case evolved, we had to acknowledge that in the twenty-five years since development of the bomb, numerous bits and pieces of information pertaining to thermonuclear weapon design had been declassified or had seeped into publications that carried no security classification. The Morland article differed because it would put more of the information in one place and in easy-to-digest form than any of the earlier publications.

The essential secret involves how to couple the fission

atomic trigger in an H-bomb to its thermonuclear or fusion fuel of deuterium and tritium, the two heavy isotopes of hydrogen. Published accounts at the time said numerous design concepts will permit an H-bomb's fusion fuel to burn, but only one means of coupling the fission explosive to the hydrogen fuel works in a practical way. Other governments in possession of nuclear weapons have needed from two to nine years to find that one superior way. But once they have discovered it, it has taken them only a matter of months to make it work. We were convinced that Morland's article provided a map and a shortcut to the right road.

President Carter supported our decision to seek an injunction against publication of the material if we failed to persuade *The Progressive*'s editors to change their minds. In a March 2, 1979, memorandum to the President, I concluded: ". . . while we cannot assure you that we will prevail in this suit, the potentially grave consequences to the security of the U.S. and the world itself resulting from disclosure of the data are obvious and frightening." The President wrote his response in longhand: "Good move. Proceed. J"

But restraining a publication from publishing—so-called prior restraint—is a rarity in America. Chief Justice Warren E. Burger, dissenting from the Supreme Court's refusal in 1971 to restrain *The New York Times* in the Pentagon Papers case, made reference to the strong presumption against the validity of imposing prior restraints. "So clear are the constitutional limitations on prior restraints against expression," Burger said, "we've had little occasion to be concerned with cases involving prior restraints against news reporting on matters of public interest. There is, therefore, little variation among the members of the Court in terms of resistance to prior restraints against publication."[10]

But the Chief Justice's reasoning on why he was dissenting from the Court's refusal in the 1971 case to impose prior restraint applied with more force to *The Progressive*. When "the imperative of a free and unfettered press comes into collision with another imperative," Burger said in his 1971 dissent, deciding the case is simple or easy only for "those who view the First Amendment as an absolute in all circumstances."[11]

On March 26, 1979, U.S. District Court Judge Robert H. Warren issued a preliminary injunction against *The Progressive.* He characterized his action as "the first instance of prior restraint against a publication in this fashion in the history of the country."[12] The judge indicated that he viewed the case as the kind of clash of imperatives that Chief Justice Burger cited in his Pentagon Papers dissent. "The court can find no plausible reason why the public needs to know the technical details about hydrogen bomb construction to carry on an informed debate on this issue. . . . What is involved here is information dealing with the most destructive weapon in the history of mankind, information of sufficient destructive potential to nullify the right to free speech and to endanger the right to life itself."[13]

Lawyers for the magazine and its editors immediately appealed Judge Warren's decision, and five weeks later, the government's case took a turn for the worse. A volunteer researcher for the American Civil Liberties Union, which represented *The Progressive*'s editors, found a copy of a government document containing details of the H-bomb's triggering device that had been mistakenly declassified and placed on shelves open to the public at the Los Alamos Scientific Library. Authorities closed the library to the public, but then another document containing three concepts which the government described as "the essential secret of the H-bomb" was found to have been declassified improperly in December 1973. These discoveries tended to support Morland's contention that his article was based wholly on material available to the public.

At this point, the entire team of Justice Department lawyers assigned to *The Progressive* matter, with the backing of Deputy Attorney General Civiletti, recommended in a memorandum that we drop the case. I responded in longhand on the margin of the memorandum, trying to implant backbone in our legal team: ". . . Our case is now weakened, but we should not dismiss. We must state frankly the changes in facts but go forward on the following basis: First Amend. not absolute; thus some disclosure does not mandate full disclosure—rather, the public interest and At. Energy Act require that we do our best; to do less is to submit to the coyotes of the media when the vast majority are so responsible as not to publish a national secret of the kind involved. By going forward, even if we lose, we support the national security, the law (i.e., the Atomic Energy Act), and we enhance the First Amendment by keeping it from being used as a suicide provision—as the great majority of the media recognize. There is sometimes honor in taking a weak position. Nevertheless, pin DOE [Department of Energy] down on representation; be completely candid with the court—and do your best. Our position is not groundless, GBB 6/3/79."

Within days after we argued in support of Judge Warren's decision before the U.S. Court of Appeals for the Seventh Circuit, the case took on the appearance of the little Dutch boy and the leaking dike. The government was fast running out of fingers to plug the holes.

First, *The Daily Californian,* the student-run newspaper at the University of California in Berkeley, attempted to publish a copy of a letter from Charles R. Hansen describing the construction of a hydrogen bomb. In his eighteen-page letter, Hansen, a computer programmer, disclosed more to the public about the principles underlying thermonuclear weapons than anyone else ever had. Describing himself as an amateur scientist, he said he had been interested in nuclear weapons for eight years. He maintained he was "a very conservative Republican" and that he "didn't think any U.S. government agency has the right to dictate what people say or think."[14]

The government quickly obtained an injunction barring *The Daily Californian* from publishing the letter. But Hansen, who had sent the original to Senator Charles Percy of Illinois, had mailed copies to other publications. The Madison (Wisc.) *Press Connection,* a tabloid with a circulation of twelve thousand, published the Hansen letter in a special section on September 16, 1979.

Eventually, it was established that at least twenty-two

documents relating to H-bomb construction had been improperly declassified and placed on open shelves in government libraries. I took the position that this did not necessarily mean that foreign powers had obtained the critical information. Schlesinger agreed, comparing the situation to a *Chicago Tribune* story during World War II that could have revealed to the Japanese—but didn't—that the United States had broken the code they were using for their military communications. But in the case of the H-bomb formula, the printing of the Hansen letter by one publication, an action that was reported throughout the world, made pointless any effort to restrain publication by others.

Thus ended that attempt to safeguard intelligence. Although I don't know whether any nations already have used the shortcut to produce an H-bomb, I fail to see that publishing the letter buttressed in any way the First Amendment guarantee of a free press. The ragtags of the press took it upon themselves to judge what was in the public interest, a dangerous precedent and one that in the future could well lead to censorship. If we become involved in even a highly limited war, with *The Progressive* case as precedent, censorship would be very likely.

Taking other espionage cases to court raised different problems. As a former federal judge and long-practicing lawyer, I found one problem particularly appalling—graymail, a legal tactic that falls just short of blackmail. Under our American system of jurisprudence, which places a high premium on the rights of defendants, an accused person can obtain information about himself that is in government files. This process is called "discovery."

Lawyers for defendants in sensitive espionage cases can, through discovery, gather material that they claim to need to defend their clients. But often the disclosure in the public courtroom of the material they seek would jeopardize national security. However, if prosecutors objected to turning over the material on grounds that it is not relevant to a defendant's case, the dispute would be thrashed out in open court anyway, thus breaching the security that government lawyers sought to maintain. The cost of possibly disclosing national secrets in order to apply legal sanctions might become too high.

Proceeding case by case, we sought to fashion a remedy. We tried, for example, to restrict to closed hearings before a judge the argument over what matters involving national security matters the defense could raise. But not all judges were willing to go along with us. We had to drop the prosecution of two International Telephone & Telegraph Corporation executives for allegedly testifying falsely about helping the CIA in Chile because a judge balked at accepting a proposed government protective order on national security material.

Public confidence in the administration of justice would suffer if government officials and others with access to military or technological secrets could not be prosecuted for crimes. As a result, the Carter administration proposed—and the Congress enacted—graymail legislation that was patterned after the remedy we had tried with uneven results to work out in court.

The graymail law provides for closed hearings before a case goes to trial on whether classified information would be relevant, material and admissible as evidence. If it is judged to be, the court can consider alternatives to disclosing the sensitive information. If the judge decides the material should be admitted, the law gives the government the right to appeal instead of having to decide then whether to permit disclosure of the evidence or to drop the prosecution. This means that foreign intelligence prosecutions are not nearly as susceptible to the pressure of graymail as they used to be. Although it has been law for only a short time, the new procedure seems to work well—another illustration that regulating intelligence activities in a democracy is possible.

Critics of my controversial decision to plea bargain with —rather than prosecute—Richard Helms, the former director of Central Intelligence, have contended that what motivated me was the fear of graymail. Helms had failed to answer truthfully the questions of a Senate committee about the CIA's covert involvement in Chile in trying to block the election of Salvador Allende. If the government had prosecuted Helms for perjury, so the argument went, this former keeper of the deepest of national secrets would use graymail to force prosecutors to drop the case against him. Not so.

That argument fails to appreciate either the patriotism of Helms or the close questions involved in the regulation of intelligence. Considerable pressures were brought against prosecuting Helms, and a good many people of influence attempted to put in a good word with me and the President for the former CIA director. The campaign for Helms began after it became known that we were reviewing a referral by the Senate Foreign Relations Committee of his testimony for possible prosecution. Averell Harriman, the Democratic senior statesman, Eric Sevareid of CBS Television and Zbigniew Brzezinski, President Carter's national security adviser, were among those urging that we not prosecute Helms. The strongest plea was made by James Schlesinger, then my colleague in the Cabinet but previously director of the CIA.

After the pressure reached the Oval Office, the President summoned me to say that Schlesinger and Brzezinski had told him that my prosecuting Helms would give away many of the nation's great secrets. I replied that we might avoid the danger if the President would authorize me merely to conduct plea-bargaining discussions with Helms's counsel, Edward Bennett Williams, one of Washington's most respected criminal defense attorneys.

Williams had arranged to meet with my predecessor, Attorney General Levi, if Helms should be indicted, so that he could present his client's defense personally to the attorney general. The case involving Helms then was his authorizing CIA security agents to break into the apartment of an agency employee in Fairfax, Virginia, to determine if she had been compromised by Cuban intelligence. Such an action involved the agency in domestic operations, an area it was forbidden by law from entering. The law at that time, however, was muddy enough so that no prosecution was brought.

Helms's Senate testimony was a different matter. It was indisputable that Helms had not told the Senate committee the truth, but it was equally clear to me that he had lied to prevent divulging an agency secret—in line with the oath he had taken as director of Central Intelligence.

I place Helms among the most honorable men I encountered in Washington, so I did not think graymail was the problem. A man would hardly lie to the Senate to keep from divulging his agency's secret and then divulge other secrets to avoid being prosecuted. I mentioned this view to Williams.

"You've touched on a problem," Williams said.

"Having touched on it," I said, "let's solve it."

The solution was to apply an obscure statute that former Attorney General Richard G. Kleindienst had pleaded guilty to, making it a misdemeanor offense not to testify "fully and accurately." Helms, however, refused to plead guilty and would only enter a plea of nolo contendere, or no contest, to the charges. The legal distinction is minimal, and U.S. District Court Judge Barrington Parker treated Helms as a guilty defendant in accepting his plea and delivered a blistering tongue-lashing to the former CIA director.

"You dishonored your oath and you now stand before this court in disgrace and shame," Judge Parker told Helms as he fined him two thousand dollars and gave him a suspended two-year prison sentence. "If public officials embark deliberately on a course to disobey and ignore the laws of our land because of some misguided and ill-conceived notion and believe that there are earlier commitments and considerations which they must first observe, the future of the country is in jeopardy."[15]

Edward Bennett Williams had pleaded for leniency, saying that Helms would bear "the scar of a conviction for the rest of his days."[16] But minutes later, talking with reporters outside the federal courthouse, Williams and Helms got in the last word. Apparently angered by the judge's rebuke, Helms and his lawyer said Helms would "wear this conviction like a badge of honor."[17]

After the sentencing, about four hundred retired CIA employees gathered at the Kenwood Country Club in Bethesda, Maryland, and on the spot raised more than enough to pay

Helms's two-thousand-dollar fine. They put two wastebaskets atop a piano and tossed in checks and money to cover the fine. When Helms appeared at the meeting, they gave their former boss a standing ovation.

During the first months of the Reagan administration, it became evident that the struggle over regulating intelligence would intensify. The Heritage Foundation, an ultraconservative think tank with influence in the administration, proposed undoing virtually all intelligence reform measures. The intelligence proposals were among the more controversial in a 1,093-page volume published by the foundation and entitled, *Mandate for Leadership: Policy Management in a Conservative Administration.*

Among other things, the foundation called for revoking the attorney general's guidelines governing FBI investigations, rules that had been formulated by Attorney General Levi during the Ford administration. Directors of the CIA and FBI "ought to declare that investigations will be initiated and pursued according to the best judgment of professional counterintelligence officers, limited only by the letter of applicable statutes,"[18] the foundation report said.

It called, too, for doing away with the Foreign Intelligence Surveillance Court. The court reported in 1980 that during its first year of operation it had approved 207 uses of wiretapping and microphones that the director of the FBI and the attorney general had certified were needed, and had not denied or modified a single application. The figures are not surprising, because the FBI director and attorney general review each proposed surveillance before certifying it to the special court.

Despite the court's record of giving intelligence agents the tools they seek, the Heritage Foundation denounced the tribunal as "constitutionally repugnant and a judicial aberration."[19] Rather than being monitored by judges, the report said, intelligence investigators should "be accountable to the Congressional Select Committee after the fact."[20] The foundation acknowledged the need for regulating the uses to which counterintelligence is put, but not the means employed to conduct counterintelligence. "Legal sanctions have a definite role in shielding the public from possible abuses of counterintelligence. But by its nature, the law cannot restrict executive activity a priori without smothering or perverting it —especially investigative activity. The law can and should place stern penalties on anyone who misuses the products of counterintelligence activities."[21]

The foundation's proposals for relaxing controls on intelligence agencies found receptive ears in the Reagan administration. In March 1981, *The New York Times* received a leak of a draft of a presidential order that would have cut back sharply on President Carter's Executive Order 12036 tightening regulation of intelligence-gathering. Under the draft order, the attorney general's role in monitoring intelligence activities and curbing abuses would be limited; the Carter order's requirement that information be collected by the "least intrusive means possible" would be eliminated; and the CIA again would be allowed to engage in electronic surveillance in the United States to assist or coordinate with other intelligence agencies. The Carter order had banned such domestic operations by the CIA.

The proposed changes drew immediate criticism from civil liberties groups, congressmen and others. Administration leaders including Attorney General William French Smith and Presidential Counselor Edwin Meese III found it necessary to back away from the draft document. The CIA conducted a rare on-the-record briefing for reporters to calm fears that the agency wanted to regain powers that earlier had led to abuses of civil liberties. One of the intelligence community's most respected professionals, Vice-Admiral Bobby Inman, deputy director of the CIA and former director of the National Security Agency, told newsmen at CIA headquarters that he did not favor some changes proposed in the draft. He gave the Senate Intelligence Committee similar assurances and dismissed the draft as a "third-level working-staff paper."[22]

But no one denied that the new administration planned to relax restrictions on intelligence-gathering. The early exposure of the draft and the resulting uproar meant only that the Reagan administration would need more time than it initially seemed to think in which to ease the regulatory controls of the intelligence community. The role and well-being of the intelligence agencies—especially the CIA—is too important for tinkering with the executive order. The self-gratification that the tinkerers might enjoy is not worth the damage it would do to the perception of whether intelligence agencies function in a legal manner.

VII

CONTROLLING CRIME

In 1969, The National Commission on the Causes and Prevention of Violence observed that violence in the United States had risen to alarmingly high levels. It pointed to the ominous drift of American society and offered this apocalyptic warning of what the nation's cities might become:

- Central business districts in the heart of the city, surrounded by mixed areas of accelerating deterioration, will be partially protected by large numbers of people shopping or working in commercial buildings during daytime hours, plus a substantial police presence, and will be largely deserted except for police patrols during nighttime hours.

- High-rise apartment buildings and residential compounds protected by private guards and security devices will be fortified cells for upper-middle and high-income populations living at prime locations in the city.

- Suburban neighborhoods, geographically far removed from the central city, will be protected mainly by economic homogeneity and by distance from population groups with the highest propensities to commit crimes.

• Lacking a sharp change in federal and state policies, ownership of guns will be almost universal in the suburbs, homes will be fortified by an array of devices from window grills to electronic surveillance equipment, armed citizen volunteers in cars will supplement inadequate police patrols in neighborhoods closer to the central city and extreme left-wing and right-wing groups will have tremendous armories of weapons which could be brought into play with or without any provocation.

• High-speed, patrolled expressways will be sanitized corridors, connecting safe areas, and private automobiles, taxicabs and commercial vehicles will be routinely equipped with unbreakable glass, light armor and other security features. Inside garages or valet parking will be available at safe buildings in or near the central city. Armed guards will "ride shotgun" on all forms of public transportation.

• Streets and residential neighborhoods in the central city will be unsafe in differing degrees, and the ghetto slum neighborhoods will be places of terror with widespread crime, perhaps entirely out of police control during nighttime hours. Armed guards will protect all public facilities such as schools, libraries and playgrounds in these areas.

• Between the unsafe, deteriorating central city on the one hand and the network of safe, prosperous areas and sanitized corridors on the other, there will be, not unnaturally, intensifying hatred and deepening division. Violence will increase further, and the defensive response of the affluent will become still more elaborate.[1]

Just twelve years later, the commission's dire predictions read like a dispassionate portrait of everyday reality for most of urban America. The fear of violent crime, especially street crime, has become a fundamental emotion of national life. Pollsters find that crime ranks just behind the pocketbook issues of inflation and the state of the economy as subjects of public concern. Politicians, from the lowliest local official to aspirants for the highest office in the land, declaim against the menace and offer up their rhetorical solutions.

Yet there is something curious about the crime problem. Americans say they are terrified of crime; but all across the country police departments are being cut back. Americans say they want vicious criminals kept away from society; yet voters routinely refuse to expand the nation's overflowing prisons. Law enforcement officials are urged to crack down on habitual offenders; but the tools necessary merely to identify these hard-core offenders are seldom made available. Presidents and other federal officials are applauded for declaring war on crime; yet federal aid is being cut off for some of the more promising new anticrime programs that have been developed by state and local governments.

The explanation for these contradictions is rooted deep in America's history and character. Citizens of a rich and spacious land, we have indulged ourselves in a tendency to skirt around hard choices between conflicting viewpoints and to avoid realities that clash with what we want to believe.

The plain facts about crime are relatively simple:

- There are bad people in all countries, including America, and the tiny fraction of bad people in the population accounts for a very large portion of the violent crime being committed in the United States.

- Rehabilitation is a noble concept, and an appealing one in a nation that likes ideals best when they have a practical, efficient ring to them. But in most cases, it just doesn't work.

- No one really knows what the root causes of crime are, but we can't wait until the answers are found. We must begin protecting society now.

- Illicit narcotics breed crime in the United States—both in the trafficking in drugs and in illegal acts by users to support their habits. Narcotics, then, is one root cause we have identified, and one that any strategy to control crime must seek to reduce significantly.

- To control crime, both liberals and conservatives must drop their debating games and begin to work together on realistic solutions. Conservatives, for example, have to stop trying to fight crime by attacking Miranda warnings, the insanity defense and exclusionary rules; liberals instinctively fight back in the name of civil liberties; the result is always a stalemate, one that diverts attention from more fruitful anticrime measures. Similarly, liberals have got to stop advocating gun control as a panacea; far-reaching gun control is politically impossible now; squabbling over it may feel good to liberals, but in the meantime potentially useful alternatives go unexplored. And everyone has got to stop ducking the embarrassing but obvious connection between crime and race.

- Finally, we have got to recognize what our most serious crime problems really are and then make tough-minded decisions about priorities so that we target our limited resources where they will do the most good.

Too many Americans, particularly the opinion-makers, do not like to face the fact that we have bad people in this country. We cringe from the reality, perhaps because of the inherent optimism that goes with the territory that is America. This optimism makes many of us believers in the perfectibility of man, unwilling to accept reality.

It is beyond challenge, however, that a tiny percentage of people—less than one quarter of one percent—terrorize the

99.75 percent of the rest of us. They are the violent criminals, and we must adjust our system of criminal justice to concentrate on them. The problem, of course, is how to identify this hard core. Historically, Americans have rejected the idea of attaching permanent labels to people and making lifetime judgments about them. Such labeling would smack too much of the European caste system which our forefathers left behind or of the Communist system of today. These philosophical concerns do us credit as a people, but they need not prevent us from dealing effectively with criminals. We have managed to put aside philosophical concerns to govern effectively in other areas. For example, while we cherish individual liberty, we recognize the need to impose quarantines to halt the spread of infectious disease. In the same way, when an offender has multiple convictions for rape, society must conclude he is dangerous and prevent him from being free to repeat the act. Our resources should be concentrated on identifying recidivists, prosecuting them speedily and segregating them—perhaps permanently. I'll concede that adopting my strategy will make it tougher to be a prison warden, but the alternative is continuing to release the multiple offenders at great cost to society.

A barrier to taking the hard-line approach is our belief in rehabilitation, a faith that has almost no basis in fact. In 1974, one of my predecessors, Attorney General William B. Saxbe, sparked a controversy when he declared that rehabilitation is a myth. The same observation today would not stimulate a serious debate. Prison rehabilitation is a failure. For 150 years, we have been trying unsuccessfully to implement the Quaker theory that it would be better to use prisons for rehabilitation than for inflicting punishment. The time has come to abandon that notion and to concentrate on the real reasons for putting criminals in prison. Imprisonment is for punishment, for deterring and preventing additional criminal conduct, and thus for protecting the law-abiding part of the public.

A very small percentage of prisoners are rehabilitated just by virtue of being in a different environment. Prisons ought to educate the illiterate and try to teach inmates some sort of useful trade so that those who do emerge have some chance of coping with life without breaking the law. Beyond that, the point of imprisoning criminals who do *not* belong to the ir- redeemable hard core is to punish them and to deter future criminal conduct. The notion that prisons can rehabilitate criminals the way garage mechanics fix cars appeals to our natures. But the number of prisoners who can be reformed by imprisonment is so small that rehabilitation should not be a major consideration in sentencing.

The national confusion over the reasons for building and maintaining prisons also reflects the American guilt complex. We constantly feel the need to explain to ourselves why we have certain institutions, and the concept of rehabilitation softens the ugliness of maintaining prisons. The truth is that state and local prisons and jails, with a population of 508,385, have run out of space, and our ambivalence about why we have prisons at all adds to the difficulty of establishing a sensible policy on who should be in what kind of prison and for how long. Prisons and jails are operating at 17 percent above their rated capacity, and two thirds of the inmates are kept in spaces below acceptable standards of square footage for each prisoner. On June 30, 1981, there were 25,733 con- victs in federal prisons, an increase of 1,370 inmates during the first six months of the year, reversing a trend that had produced a 25 percent decline in the federal prison popula- tion since 1978.

Federal authorities attributed the reversal to "more ag- gressive law enforcement and to a more conservative federal parole policy,"[2] even though the FBI now leaves most single- instance auto theft cases to local authorities and involves itself in fewer and fewer bank robberies. The federal prison popu- lation has also risen, despite a Justice Department policy of recommending community-based treatment, instead of incar- ceration, for more nondangerous criminals.

State officials, trying to cope with the surge in their own prison populations, have had to resort to such steps as hous- ing prisoners in tents and prefabricated buildings, double-bunking them in cells built for one inmate and releasing prisoners before they have served their terms or would normally qualify for parole. Some states have had to keep prisoners in local jails that were designed only as temporary holding facilities while trials were conducted or while prisoners were awaiting transportation to the prison where they were supposed to serve their sentences.

Seventy percent of America's prisons are high-security institutions, with supposedly impregnable walls, guard towers and other costly features. But the National Institute of Corrections recently estimated that no more than 15 percent of the inmates need to be housed under high-security conditions, indicating that state prison authorities would be well advised to follow the lead of the federal government in relying more on minimal supervision settings. The institute reported that about half of those in prison today in America could be placed instead in community treatment centers or set free under good probation supervision. We are keeping the wrong people in the wrong kind of prison. In deciding whether a first offender should be sent to prison, authorities should weigh such factors as whether the crime was violent and whether the lawbreaker appears to be a violent person. For those with previous convictions, the choice between prison or lesser punishment can be based on the offender's track record as well as on the nature of the latest criminal act.

Because the prisons are unmanageably overcrowded, another major element in the criminal justice process is breaking down. The parole system, which is supposed to supervise and facilitate the reintegration into society of prisoners who are capable of straightening themselves out, has, instead, become a kind of overflow drain for overcrowded prisons. All too often, parole is now being used to vacate prison cells indiscriminately to make room for the hordes of new prisoners who are being held in local jails after their convictions. The inevitable result is that prisoners are set free who are not ready to become law-abiding citizens, and overburdened probation officers cannot keep track of the ex-prisoners they are theoretically responsible for.

An illustration of the misuse of parole took place in Georgia during 1980, when nearly five thousand prisoners were released solely to ease overcrowding of the prisons. "We realize we have released a bunch of habitual offenders,"[3] James T. Morris, chairman of the Georgia Board of Prisons and Paroles, said. Describing some of those released early as "bad actors," he admitted they did not deserve parole under normal conditions. But the alternative would be worse, he maintained, because overcrowded prisons create the potential for deadly violence. "We don't like what we're doing necessarily," Morris said, "but we believe we're addressing the situation in a responsible way. And we're the only body authorized to do this."[4]

Instead of dealing with overcrowded prisons by perverting the parole system, we should insist that prosecutors and judges send to prison—especially high-security institutions—only those hard-core violators who need such treatment. There must be greater coordination of the efforts of police, prosecutors, prison administrators and parole and probation authorities. And prosecutors must use the very wide discretion they possess in ways that help the whole system function effectively. It surprises many laymen that there is such a thing as prosecutorial discretion. Because certain conduct is a violation of law does not mean that a prosecutor must file charges and seek to convict and punish the violator. Traditionally, in deciding whether the interests of society would be served by prosecuting a given case, prosecutors have considered such factors as their offices' resources and workloads, the seriousness of the criminal act, whether it is a first offense and whether the violator is regretful or defiant. Today, prosecutors and judges faced with decisions on how to deal with defendants also need to consider the impact of their decisions on the prison and parole systems. Perhaps embezzlers, for example, should not be sent to the penitentiary, because the result would be that violent criminals had to be paroled to make room for nonviolent offenders.

If prosecutors are to exercise their discretion effectively, they will need certain kinds of information that most do not have now. The prosecutor should know, for example, what kinds of offenses are being handled by judges with probation and what kinds with prison sentences. He should know how many of the cases are being settled by bargained pleas rather than by courtroom trial. And he should especially know the full criminal record of an individual being prosecuted. In fact, however, it was not until the mid-1970's that prosecutors began to collect and analyze such information. The key to these efforts was using the computer as a management tool. Adopting a system devised by the Institute for Law and Social Research in Washington, district attorneys in the District of Columbia; Cobb County, Georgia; New Orleans; Los Angeles; and New York initiated a computer-based effort that eventually became known as "career criminal" programs. The programs seek to pick out, from the mass of cases passing through the prosecutor's office, those violators who have made a career out of crime—the recidivists, or criminals who repeatedly break the law.

In beginning this discussion of controlling crime, I cited a 1969 forecast by the National Commission on the Causes and Prevention of Violence of what life would be like in America. While its predictions have proved uncomfortably close to the mark, I do not think there is anything very helpful in the commission's conclusion that the root of violent crime is "an enormous deficit of unsatisfied needs and aspirations," particularly "in our crime-plagued metropolitan areas."[5]

What causes crime is a complex, unresolved question, subject to great dispute. I don't know the ultimate causes; neither does anyone else. What I do know is that we have not been well served by the so-called liberal approach to dealing with crime, which is to try to identify and then to root out and eliminate the underlying causes, thereby reducing the commission of criminal acts. If we wait to take meaningful action until there is no poverty and no unemployment, until all the guns have been collected or registered and until we understand the deepest wellsprings of antisocial conduct, then crime will be utterly beyond control and some of our most cherished principles may be counted among its victims.

Part of our difficulty is that we do not know the true extent of crime in America. We know more about it than we did in 1930, when the FBI took over from the International Association of Chiefs of Police the task of collecting figures on the number of serious crimes reported to law enforcement agencies around the country. The result was the FBI's Uniform Crime Reports, quarterly and annual compilations of reported crimes supplied voluntarily by more than fifteen thousand state and local law enforcement agencies.

But these reports tell us nothing about what are sometimes called the dark statistics of crime—criminal acts that are not reported to police. The best estimates we have indicate that the police in this country are not notified of as many as two thirds of the criminal acts that take place. In recent years, we have sought to assess the volume of this unreported crime by surveying a large, randomly selected national sample. Twice a year the Bureau of the Census interviews members of 60,000 representative households. The approximately 260,000 interviews that have been conducted annually since 1975 make up the nation's first criminal victimization surveys.

In addition to showing that a large amount of crime is going unreported, the National Crime Survey, as the poll has become known, appears to contradict some of the trends in crime rates shown by the FBI's Uniform Crime Reports. In some cases, the contradictions are so gross that they cast doubt on our ability to answer the rudimentary question of whether the incidence of crime is or is not growing. For example, the FBI's compilation of police data reveals that violent crime increased 4 percent from 1977 to 1978[6]; but the National Crime Survey indicates that violent crime dropped 4 percent from 1977 to 1978.[7] For the next year—1978 as against 1979—both measures showed that violent crime increased, but the FBI's Uniform Crime Reports recorded an 11 percent jump, while the National Crime Survey showed only a 4 percent rise.[8]

Each of the two reports has its defenders who question the other's methodology. Advocates of the FBI's report point out that the National Crime Survey was based on what people said had happened to them some days, weeks or months after an event, rather than on what they told police immediately after the incident, when they are less likely to exaggerate or embellish. Backers of the survey method counter that data collected by police can be manipulated for political purposes. If a police chief is seeking public support for a larger budget, he can point to statistics indicating a crime wave as justification, but if he is trying to prove to a critical city council that his performance is exemplary, a drop in the crime rate could be helpful. Mindful of the temptation to manipulate the figures, the FBI has tried to ensure the integrity of the voluntarily supplied data, but critics contend the protective steps fall short of being foolproof.

Partly to end the confusion, we formed a Bureau of Justice Statistics during the Carter administration, which was to include both measures of crime, as well as other figures on civil and criminal justice. Since then, I've noticed that neither side in the debate over crime statistics scoffs openly at the other, preferring instead to emphasize that each measures different things—crime reported to police and crime victimization regardless of whether it was reported to law enforcement authorities. But I'm afraid the steps we took were not lasting ones. During the early days of the Reagan administration, it became clear that collecting and validating data on criminal justice would not receive the emphasis or funding we had planned.

Despite the lessening of disagreement between advocates of the two measures of crime, I still cannot understand how one can show that crime is up while the other reports it is down. The official explanation is that the National Crime Survey records so many more incidents of crime than those reported to police that there is room for contradiction; but even so, I think the explanation defies common sense. Such a contradiction would not be tolerated in an area of public policy like national defense. But crime has never been given the sustained, coherent attention that national defense receives.

The Law Enforcement Assistance Administration (LEAA),

already discussed in Chapter IV, is a good example of our sporadic, illogical response to the threat of crime. LEAA was phased out early in the Reagan administration, despite intensive lobbying by those groups that had grown accustomed to relying on the federal funds it provided. It was estimated that its abolition would lead to the loss of between thirty thousand and forty thousand jobs in criminal justice around the country. Rather than abruptly cutting off those hundreds of millions of dollars of LEAA grants for state and local criminal justice operations, we should have phased them out more gradually, perhaps at the rate of 10 percent a year. The "cold turkey" approach means that cities and counties, under intense budget pressure already, will simply abandon these federally funded programs, regardless of their merit.

Although I was more critical than any other attorney general of LEAA's record of waste, of financing the routine rather than the innovative and of spawning a large, unneeded bureaucracy to award and administer its grants, I must acknowledge that the agency developed or funded some meritorious programs. The efforts of some local prosecutors to identify and concentrate on convicting so-called career criminals with the aid of LEAA funds should be replicated in the offices of prosecutors throughout the nation. From 1975 to 1981, LEAA financed fifty of these programs. More than 11,800 recidivists were identified, and 92.8 percent of them were subsequently convicted of the crime for which they were apprehended. That unusually high rate of conviction reflected the emphasis prosecutors put on priority cases. The career criminals drew sentences that averaged thirteen years and eight months in prison, terms significantly longer than those that would otherwise have been imposed.

Another of LEAA's success stories was the STING programs that the agency financed in forty-seven cities, beginning in 1975. Police officers, by pretending to be fences who were eager to pay good money for stolen property, drew into their net truckloads of stolen goods. The ninety-three STING operations led to the arrest of nearly nine hundred persons, 90 percent of whom were convicted. Stolen property valued at three hundred million dollars was recovered, and authorities were able to return 90 percent of the items to their original owners.

Regardless of the success of these and other LEAA programs, I seriously doubt that the keepers of state and local treasuries will fill the void created by the federal pullout. In the wake of across-the-board federal budget cuts, local and state taxpayers seem unwilling to pick up the slack. Their refusal to do so reflects Americans' naive assumption that we can solve the problem of crime without spending a great deal more money than we do now. When our citizens go into their local election booths or when their legislators reflect their will in the statehouse or city council chamber, the fear of crime they express in public opinion polls is left behind. They often reject proposals for hiring more police or building prisons, even when the expenditures are to be financed by one-time means such as a special sales tax. Crime has not been reduced in Los Angeles, Miami and New York; yet their police departments are smaller than they were five years ago. Political leaders fail to educate the electorate when they talk out of both sides of their mouths by denouncing crime in emotional speeches and then seek public approval by cutting the money needed for programs to reduce crime.

The blame for refusing to provide sufficient funds must be shared by the national, state and local governments, although under our system fighting crime is primarily the responsibility of state and local authorities. For years, Washington has misled the people by constantly throwing money to local units of government to solve problems that were viewed as national because one or more other localities experienced the same or similar problems. It is going to take a while to straighten out the people on this point. Federalism is a fine form of government, as long as each unit of the federal structure is willing to do its job. The idea of burdening all of a nation's taxpayers with the cost of services, such as police protection, that benefit only the citizens in a small part of the nation is not the way the federal system is supposed to work. Local and state taxpayers should realize that the federal government really is almost the only government in our nation that is going broke. Most of our state governments operate under fiscal systems that prohibit them from spending more than they take in and from amassing huge deficits.

And the dole provided state and local governments by Washington does not always take the form of money. The FBI, for example, is quicker to make available its excellent crime laboratory to states that do not have the capacity for lab work than to states that have invested in law enforcement laboratories. While this policy may make sense for solving a particular crime, over the longer term it has the effect of rewarding states that don't spend their own taxpayer dollars and punishing states that do make an effort to help themselves.

Confusion over which of our governments is responsible for fighting crime is compounded by America's acceptance of violence as an inevitable by-product of an urban civilization. When a youth gang in a barrio or ghetto slays members of a rival organization or a citizen who has mistakenly wandered onto its turf, our reaction is not to urge a police crackdown on the wrongdoers but to install improved deadbolt locks on our doors or otherwise tighten the security of our residence or place of work. Inevitably, when a public figure is assassinated or wounded, there is talk of how sick and violent our society has become. The diagnosis misses the point. The sickness is not that the nation's citizens have become violent; the sickness is that our citizens have grown excessively tolerant of the few among us who are violent.

Our unwillingness to do something meaningful about crime has hampered effective government action for years. I encountered it during the first major crisis I experienced as attorney general—the seizure of buildings and the taking of hostages in the District of Columbia by Hanafi Muslim terrorists. Most of the hostages were held in the Washington office of the B'nai B'rith, about a mile from the White House. One of our options was to storm the building, using flak-vested, helmeted District of Columbia police officers. To improve their chances of success, the officers needed concussion grenades to neutralize the heavily armed Hanafis. The grenades were not a part of the metropolitan police department's arsenal, so I turned to the Pentagon for help.

Secretary of Defense Harold Brown and Jack Watson, secretary to the Cabinet, turned me down, citing posse comitatus, a federal law that bars military involvement in civilian law enforcement. The law was enacted during Reconstruction to bar the federal government from sending troops into the South, but the military has used it frequently to avoid any involvement in civilian affairs. The provision of special grenades to save the lives of hostages and police officers is a far cry from military intrusion in civilian matters. The crisis was resolved when foreign ambassadors lent their services and persuaded the Muslims to release the hostages and throw down their arms. I later learned that Maurice Cullinane, then chief of the metropolitan police, had made private arrangements with military officials to obtain the grenades. Cullinane, a highly respected police officer, had worked with the military a few years earlier in enforcing the law during antiwar demonstrations. But we cannot depend on a special relationship between one police chief and the military to save us during a crisis. We have to rely on the regular institutions of government, administered wisely.

After the crisis was over, I told President Carter about it and warned that if he didn't do something to rectify the attitude of the Pentagon, we could have a situation in which law enforcement people were killed because the military and White House staff were hiding behind a Reconstruction Era statute. He said I should have brought the matter to his attention and he would have ordered Brown to give us the grenades.

While combating crime under our system of federalism is primarily a state and local responsibility, there are violations of law that the federal government is uniquely able to counter. Thus, during the Carter administration, we attempted to focus the Department of Justice's priorities on attacking organized crime, white-collar crime—particularly corruption by public officials—and narcotics, areas where we thought that federal law enforcement agencies had special expertise and resources.

We altered the allocation of investigative and prosecutive resources to comply with these new priorities. Among other things, this meant the FBI reduced its efforts against bank robberies. As FBI Director William H. Webster pointed out, much more money was leaving banks by the back door because of fraud than through the front door because of holdups. In addition, local authorities had a greater chance of success in apprehending and convicting bank robbers than they did in making significant inroads against organized crime, which only a national attack has a chance of defeating, or at least curbing, since crime syndicates operate across state borders and have massive resources to draw on to defend themselves. Our shift of priorities caused unhappiness among local police and prosecutors, bankers and some agents inside the FBI who looked on bank robberies as a means of building up impressive statistics on how much money the bureau had recovered and returned to its rightful owners—impressive propaganda fodder for congressional appropriations hearings.

In the fight against organized crime, we abandoned the earlier federal strategy of pursuing organized criminals on a case-by-case or attrition basis, under which the government sought to win enough convictions to deplete the ranks of syndicated crime. It had become clear that the federal government would run out of resources before that strategy worked. At the same time, we found that organized crime had expanded beyond prostitution, extortion and gambling—its traditional sources of income—into legitimate businesses such as banks and pension funds and hotel service companies.

We targeted for investigation and prosecution enterprises in which management and labor had been taken over by organized crime and we sought to drive out the infiltrators. The prime example of this approach was the prosecution and conviction of labor leaders and their cohorts in management who had turned key Atlantic and Gulf Coast ports into highly illegal operations where under-the-table payoffs and coercive violence were routine business-labor practices. The complex investigation, which carried the FBI code name of UNIRAC for union racketeering, resulted in the conviction of more than one hundred labor officials and waterfront businessmen, including Anthony Scotto, a general organizer for the International Longshoremen's Association and president of its largest local, Brooklyn Local 1814. Scotto drew a five-year sentence of imprisonment and a $75,000 fine.

As a result of the new strategy, the FBI and federal prosecutors reached further up the rungs of organized crime's ladder than ever before, destroying the myth that the really powerful members of organized crime were beyond the reach of law enforcement.

Along with attacking organized crime, Washington has a central role to play in cutting off the flow of illicit narcotics. The drug trade should be given high priority in our anticrime strategy for several reasons. First, the incredible amount of tax-free money it generates is irresistible for organized crime. Second, the high cost of feeding a drug habit causes addicts to turn to crime, much of it violent. Finally, the impact of the drugs themselves on our young people is often catastrophic. Washington's role is crucial because the drug trade involves our international relations with the countries where fields of opium poppies, coca (from which cocaine is made) and marijuana have become major cash crops.

The conclusion that drug addiction and trafficking are central to America's crime problem is supported by statistics. One third of the twenty-six thousand men and women now in federal prisons were narcotics addicts at the time they were arrested, and one fourth of cases pending in the offices of the nation's ninety-four U.S. attorneys involve drug offenses. The theory that a massive campaign against illicit drugs in the United States would be the best way to halt the rise in crime gained major support in 1981, as federal authorities in the executive branch and on Capitol Hill focused on the clear evidence presented by a study made in Baltimore by a team of Temple University and Johns Hopkins University experts which found that 237 addicts committed more than 500,000 crimes during an 11-year period in which they were out of jail and using heroin.[9] The study went beyond earlier investigations by indicating that "it is opiate use itself which is the principal cause of high crime rates among addicts. . . ."[10] Once addiction ceases, crime rates drop markedly. This notable decrease in criminality—an overall 84 percent decline— occurs for all types of offenders throughout the risk years (the period addicts are not incarcerated).

"It is apparent, then, that a major means of reducing the amount of crime committed by opiate addicts is within sight. If we can control addiction, it is evident that we will reduce criminality appreciably."[11]

In measuring the criminality of heroin addicts, the investigators introduced the concept of "crime days"—with one crime day being a twenty-four-hour period during which one or more crimes are committed by an individual. Interviews with 243 male opiate addicts revealed their crime days averaged 248 a year when they were on the drug and only 48 when they were not using it regularly. Six of the addicts committed no crimes during their "years at risk," which the study defined as the period they were on the street and thus able to use heroin. For two thirds of the remaining 237, theft was their principal crime.[12] The study did not tabulate as crime the use or possession of drugs.

The findings prompted the study's four authors to depart from the cautious style of comment and interpretation usually found in such reports. They concluded, ". . . it is time to get on with the task at hand and not be sidetracked by irrelevant ideological, scholastic or methodological arguments.

"Existing knowledge and methodology is sufficient to address the problem at hand. We know that criminality is rampant among heroin addicts. We know that addiction markedly increases this criminality. And we know that addiction can be impacted through treatment and control measures."[13]

The Baltimore study provided objective support for a judgment that a special agent in charge of one of the FBI's field offices in a major American city relayed to me when I was attorney general. He said that at least half of the bank robberies in his city were drug-related.

Early in their terms of office, both the Carter and Reagan administrations considered reorganizing the Federal Drug Enforcement Administration in order to sharpen the attack on illicit narcotics. After studying the possibility of merging the Drug Enforcement Administration with the FBI, I rejected the idea but did give a go-ahead to joint efforts by the FBI and DEA in three pilot cities. The pilot programs produced only mixed results.

The study of the feasibility of an FBI-DEA merger was conducted by Richard H. Ash, an assistant FBI director whom Director Clarence Kelley regarded as one of the bureau's top investigators. His study took note of sharp differences between the DEA and the FBI that would have to be overcome before a combination could succeed. For one thing, the FBI's educational and training requirements were substantially higher than the DEA's, and DEA agents were harder to discipline because of civil service protection which did not cover FBI agents. This meant that any full-scale merger under which all DEA agents would automatically become FBI agents was out of the question.

Another major difference was the agencies' investigative tactics, particularly their handling of informants. The DEA generally used informants to meet the specific needs of a drug "bust"; the FBI developed long-term relationships with its informants so that they supplied information on a continuing basis about a variety of investigations. DEA had what is known in law enforcement as a "street-wise" approach, knowledgeable in the customs and practices of low-level drug pushers, much as the narcotics squad of a local police department would be. But this approach did not often lead them to the high echelons of drug traffickers.

Four years later, the nature of the drug threat and the capabilities of the two investigative agencies had changed enough for the Reagan administration to decide to install a twenty-year FBI veteran, Francis M. Mullen, Jr., as administrator of the DEA and to involve the FBI directly in the war on drugs. Three factors prompted the latter decision. The FBI had gained experience in conducting long-term undercover operations, enabling them to climb higher up the ladder of the drug underworld; it maintained substantially better records than DEA; and it had developed the capability of tracing funds that sophisticated criminals tried to launder through legitimate enterprises.

But no matter how knowledgeable or vigorous domestic drug investigations become, their efforts will prove futile unless combating drugs attains priority status in our foreign policy operations. We have demonstrated—in Turkey during the Nixon administration and in Mexico during the Carter years—that eradicating drug crops in the ground through offsetting cash payments to farmers and the use of herbicides such as Paraquat is the most effective means of reducing the drug threat.

Those who make and implement foreign policy, however, seldom see the control of drugs as a major element in their mission. The Ash study cited the lack of a hard-line U.S. policy toward drug-source countries as a prime reason why the FBI should avoid getting involved in the drive against narcotics. We have even gone so far as to ban the use of foreign aid funds for Paraquat—on the flimsiest of evidence that it would have damaging side effects—while allowing Florida to spray 61,000 pounds of it on its food crops in 1980.

In saying that we must control crime now, I am not arguing that we should abandon all efforts to understand why America is so violent.

Comparisons of degrees of violence in industrial democracies are difficult. Nonetheless, a recent study, based on 1976 data, of reported crime in the United States, Japan and England-Wales found that the United States had 8.8 homicides per 100,000 of its population in 1976; in Japan, 1.75 per 100,000; and England and Wales, 1.1. The rate of reported robberies in the United States was seventeen times that of Japan and eight times that of England and Wales. For rape, again per 100,000 of population, the U.S. rate was 26; the Japanese, 3; and for England and Wales, 2.[14]

Why is America so violent? Part of the answer could be that we are a diverse people whose different racial and ethnic origins produce tensions. Difficulty of adjustment could, in part, explain why the rate of violence among American blacks is so much higher than that among whites. The proportion of black prisoners serving terms in our federal and state prisons is 46 percent of the total prison population.[15] That is four times the percentage of blacks in the U.S. population. But just mentioning this disturbing fact can draw suggestions that you're taking a racist approach to our crime problem. Nevertheless, the reason for there being such a disproportionate number of blacks in our prisons cries out for an answer. The prisons are filled with people of lower intellect and educational attainment than those outside prison. Liberals would contend that this reflects the fact that those people have been mistreated, but I think that explanation is too simple.

The theory that American violence goes back to the country's frontier experience doesn't impress me either. Most of our people never had anything to do with the frontier. I believe that lack of discipline is the largest single factor in our high rate of violence, and that this lack of discipline stems directly from the breakdown of the home and the school as the traditional institutions where young people learn basic values.

Gun control advocates often tie America's high rate of violent crime to the freedom to possess firearms, concluding that nothing can be done about reducing crime without controlling guns. I would agree that there is a need to tighten existing laws and to introduce new controls, such as requiring that in the future a record must be made of all handgun sales —private transfers as well as over-the-counter sales. Gun control should not, however, be considered a panacea for controlling crime. The estimated fifty million handguns now in the possession of Americans cannot be confiscated for reasons of constitutional law and good political sense. Stiffer gun controls, then, would affect only the legal transfer of existing weapons and the distribution of new handguns.

The best evidence of how unrealistic the demands for

tighter controls are comes from an incident during the Carter administration's second year in office. Jimmy Carter had run for President on a pledge to ban cheap handguns and to require registration and "appropriate" licensing for handgun ownership and a waiting period before the sale of a handgun to determine that the buyer was not mentally incompetent or a convicted felon.

In a move considerably more modest than the pledge, the Department of the Treasury proposed in March 1978 a series of regulations to facilitate tracing weapons used in crime. Under the plan, all new firearms would have to carry a single, readily identifiable serial number. Previously, the same number was often inscribed on several guns, and several different numbers could appear on one firearm. Importers, wholesalers and manufacturers would be required to report quarterly to the Treasury Department the names and addresses of all retail outlets to whom they distributed guns and the serial numbers of the firearms. The makers, distributors and licensed dealers would have to report within twenty-four hours to the Treasury any firearms that had been lost or stolen. The resulting centralized files would have replaced a laborious system under which the Treasury Department, seeking to identify the owner of a weapon used in a crime, had to contact the manufacturer, who would then search through his reports for the name of the wholesaler and, eventually, the dealer, who was already required to keep the names and addresses of gun purchasers. The centralized data, stored in computers, would speed the tracing process from days to a matter of minutes or even seconds.

In announcing the proposed regulations, Treasury Department officials emphasized that the data bank would not constitute a national registration of firearms because no central register of individual gun owners would be maintained in Washington. The National Rifle Association, one of Washington's most effective lobbying groups, regards registration as the first step toward confiscation of guns by federal authorities.

Despite Treasury's disclaimer, the NRA rebelled and unleashed its lobbying campaign, contending that Treasury was trying an end run around Congress to accomplish by regulation what it could not achieve by law. The Treasury Department, which had asked for comment on the proposed regulations within sixty days, received two hundred thousand letters protesting the rules. At the same time, a heavily lobbied Congress dropped the $4.2 million from Treasury's fiscal 1979 budget earmarked for implementing the new rules. The idea was shelved, and that marked the Carter administration's last attempt to deliver on the gun control promise.

Despite the opposition it would face, I think a computerized register of serial numbers of handguns purchased after the registration law took effect and the names and addresses of those who bought them from a dealer or private party is mandatory for law enforcement. Given the mobility of our society, the record would have to be maintained by federal authorities to achieve the speed needed for tracing the gun after a crime has been committed. The computerized register should be authorized by Congress, not by the executive branch through regulation, to avoid the charge that another end run was being attempted. The only hope of pushing such a bill through Congress would be a massive lobbying campaign supported by law enforcement agencies throughout the nation. Perhaps examples of cases where a data bank would have saved lives and helped convict criminals who otherwise were freed for lack of evidence might offset the NRA's likely opposition.

Closing loopholes in existing gun control laws also would help. For example, federal law forbids the purchase of handguns by felons, persons under criminal indictment, illegal aliens, persons adjudicated mentally incompetent and drug addicts. But the buyer simply is required to complete a form at the time of purchase stating that he does not fall into any of the proscribed categories. There now is no reasonable way to hold a dealer responsible for establishing that the buyer told the truth in completing the form. If, however, Congress were to amend the law to require a substantial waiting period between the time the form is completed and the handgun is turned over to the purchaser, local or federal authorities could establish the purchaser's identity and ascertain that he is not precluded from owning the weapon. If we attempted to impose the waiting period by state legislation rather than by federal, those states that did not go along could still sell handguns to any purchaser who came along.

The ban that Congress placed on importing into the United States small, inexpensive handguns—so-called Saturday night specials—should be broadened to include the parts for such a weapon. As matters now stand, the supply of Saturday night specials can be maintained by assembling cheap, foreign-made parts in the United States.

Vigorous enforcement of firearms laws already on the books in cities, counties and states would further help discourage the use of guns in crimes. One example of lax enforcement can be shown by my reply to Mayor Maynard Jackson of Atlanta after he asked me for advice on controlling crime upon my return from Washington to Georgia in 1979. In my letter to the mayor, I told him of the casual attitude often exhibited by the municipal court in handling firearms violations. "Small fines were imposed in some instances where a person had discharged a firearm in the city limits or had committed other violations of firearms ordinances and this attitude, as reported to me, stood in sharp contrast to the need for more careful regulation of firearms in our city." There is reason to believe that the attitude of other cities is just as relaxed as that of Atlanta, and that the indiscriminate use of weapons is thereby encouraged.

One gun control measure has drawn widespread support because it does not ask anything of legitimate firearms owners. It is a law requiring that persons convicted of felonies while carrying a gun go to prison for a term of years in addition to the time imposed on them for the felony conviction. However, as cochairman of Attorney General William French Smith's Task Force on Violent Crime, I discovered that the mandatory sentence approach would make little difference. My conclusion came from an evaluation of a 1977 Michigan

law mandating an extra two years in prison for persons convicted of felonies while carrying a gun. Until this analysis by
Colin Loftin, a University of Michigan sociology professor,
the Michigan law had been credited with sharply reducing
violent crime in Detroit. But Loftin found that the decline in
Detroit's homicides, robberies and aggravated assaults began
five months before the gun law took effect in January 1977,
and four months before the initiation of a publicity campaign
for the new law. The study also found that robberies committed both with and without a gun declined equally, and that
there had been "no significant change in gun assaults."[16]

Loftin, explaining his research to the federal task force,
said: "These patterns are quite different from what one would
expect if the gun law had any discernible deterrent or in-
capacitative effects on violent crime." If Michigan's Felony
Firearm Law had reduced offenses committed with a gun,
"there would be cause for celebration," he added. But, "the
evidence suggests a harsher reality. The costs of reducing gun
violence will be greater, perhaps much greater, than we might
have hoped."[17]

While we redirected and restructured the federal attack on
crime and renewed the FBI during the Carter years, we did
not respond to the widespread public concern over violent
crime in the way the Reagan administration has. Our failure
to do so partly reflected the fact that we already had a full
plate to deal with. But it also resulted from differences of
opinion and approach between the policy-proposers in the
Department of Justice and the liberal policy-analysts on the
President's domestic policy staff.

In September of 1977, during President Carter's first year
in office, he asked me to outline an administration program
to improve the investigation and prosecution of crime. The
goal, as he explained in a memorandum to me and the secretaries of the four other Cabinet departments that would be
directly affected by an anticrime program—the Departments
of Treasury, Commerce, Labor, and Health, Education and
Welfare—was to submit a formal crime message to Congress
early in 1978. Because of a lack of a sense of urgency and

conflict with the White House staff, the message was not delivered that year—or any year that Jimmy Carter was in office.

We did draw up the outline, with Ben Civiletti, then assistant attorney general in charge of the Justice Department's Criminal Division, directing the effort. But sending crime memos to the President was like sending something to sea in a bottle. You were lucky to ever see them again. By the time the different groups in the White House finished trying to agree on what should go to the President, there wasn't much left of the original. The staff was especially sensitive about doing anything that they thought might hurt politically. Their judgment on not hurting politically was to avoid upsetting anyone on the ultra left—the 5 percent or 10 percent of the people who are on the far left—instead of making a decision that would suit Middle America, the people who suffer from crime. Of course, blacks and people in poverty suffer most from crime, but there was nothing to benefit them in the program that was toned down by those trying to satisfy the ultra left. The far leftist would say of any crime program, "You want to lock everybody up." It just infuriates them to have someone like me say, "We have bad people in this country, and they ought to be locked up." You can't run the country for that small a fringe. That is where the Carter group went wrong, trying to be all things to all people.

On October 13, 1977, we circulated within the administration a list of ten general principles of the crime program. Heading the list was a statement on violent street crime, the area that Attorney General William French Smith chose to emphasize during the Reagan administration's first year. "Violent predatory street crime is our chief criminal justice problem—a problem which plagues our cities, suburbs and rural communities. The federal criminal justice system is limited in directly combating violent street crime by the Constitution and statutes, by case history and by resources. Nontheless, the federal system must improve its support of the primary law enforcement effort against violent crime by state and local governments."[18]

On May 1, 1978, President Carter delivered in Los Angeles a Law Day speech that was to have served as the medium for announcing the crime program. But instead of focusing sharply on crime, the speech was expanded at the suggestion of the domestic council to cover the administration's program for improvements in the civil justice system as well. Neither subject, however, received much attention, because the President chose to incorporate in his remarks a broad-gauged attack on lawyers and the legal profession—and that made the news.

VIII

TOO MUCH LAW

In no country, perhaps, in the world is the law so general a study. The profession itself is numerous and powerful, and in most provinces it takes the lead. The greater number of the deputies sent to the Congress were lawyers. But all who read, and most do read, endeavor to obtain some smattering in that science. I have been told by an eminent bookseller, that in no branch of his business, after tracts of popular devotion, were so many books as those on the law exported to the plantations. The colonists have now fallen into the way of printing them for their own use. I hear that they have sold nearly as many of Blackstone's *Commentaries* (on the law) in America as in England.[1]

—EDMUND BURKE

Scarcely any political question arises in the United States that is not resolved, sooner or later, into a judicial question. . . . The lawyers of the United States form a party which . . . extends over the whole community and penetrates into all the classes which compose it; it acts upon the country imperceptibly, but finally fashions it to suit its own purposes.[2]

—ALEXIS DE TOCQUEVILLE

We Americans are, as these early commentators on our society indicated, a litigious lot. To borrow from an observation common in my youth, we want to make a federal case out of every dispute. In recent years, however, the American trait of relying on the law to solve our problems has gone too far. As *Newsweek* magazine said about the time the Carter administration took office: ". . . if Americans want to prevent their system of government from being changed in a fundamental

169

manner, they will have to find ways in which to prevent every buck from being passed to a judge and every problem from being turned over to a lawyer."[3]

Unquestionably, we have created the best legal system in the world, one of our country's accomplishments that we can be most proud of. It makes a substantial degree of justice available to more people more of the time than any comparable system in history. Unhappily, we have made too much of a good thing. Our society has turned over to our judicial and quasi-judicial proceedings too many questions of public policy that timorous politicians are unwilling to handle. This shifting of burdens has heightened the danger that the whole legal structure will collapse. Its costs are too great. In too many instances, it operates so that justice delayed is justice denied. Too often, victory goes to the party that can financially afford to wage protracted court battles rather than to the party with the most meritorious claim or defense.

The ailing condition of the nation's legal system fosters the belief that the whole American system of government has begun to fail. That view, which seeps down to every level of society, is the ultimate poison for a democracy. During the Carter years, we tried to contain the legal explosion and increase the sense that justice was being done, but the steps we took were only the beginning. A bolder drive must be undertaken.

The phenomenon of overreliance on the courts goes hand-in-hand with that of excessive government regulation. Even in pre-Revolutionary days, the colonists developed the habit of turning to the courts and government councils to arbitrate disputes. As the nation grew, it was natural for people to resort to the courts and Congress to solve broader problems. And when these problems became too technical and time-consuming for Congress and the courts, Congress created the independent regulatory agencies.

Government and its bureaucracy have not spewed forth rules and regulations on their own. They have done so in response to demands of special groups, but even so people are often unhappy with the results. The whole process has gone too far—creating such a jungle of rules and litigation that both the government and the private sector have at times been nearly paralyzed. Businesses press enthusiastically for subsidies and other considerations but then complain when the government aid leads to paper work and controls. Environmentalists lobby for strict regulations to restore clean air but don't like it when an equally "activist" government encourages oil and mineral exploration. And neither the businessman nor the environmentalist recognizes his own role in creating the problem.

Ironically, government regulations spur citizens to turn to the courts in search of relief, adding considerably to the cost and complexity of American life. As if this were not bad enough, the explosion of legalism has aggravated our problem with crime. Judges lack time to spend on criminal matters because they—and the rest of the court machinery—are enmeshed in too many civil cases that have no business in the courthouse. Prosecutors plea bargain with criminal defendants and sometimes settle for penalties far short of what should have been meted out because the courts cannot possibly conduct a full-scale trial for every case. The civil side of the law is hurt as well. Many of the civil cases that do belong in court often take years to resolve when they should be settled in months. We make a hollow promise when we provide citizens with ready access to the courts but then deny them prompt disposition of the issues they are raising. Once on the court calendar, cases drag on endlessly as attorneys use every wrinkle to bend court procedures for their clients' benefit. No decision seems final when attorneys file appeal after appeal.

In addition to the deep-rooted tendencies noted by Burke and de Tocqueville, several features of twentieth-century America have combined to produce our present degree of overreliance on the nation's legal system. The affluence generated by the industrial and technological revolutions is one reason. As Jethro K. Lieberman wrote in *The Litigious Society:*

Pockmarked beggars, weak with hunger and half-blind, wandering the byways of an overpopulated land that cannot yield a subsistence to most of its inhabitants, do not file lawsuits when they trip in an unpaved street. But in our affluent society, the window shopper with an eye on a jewelry display may seek recompense for a bruised knee, anguish and loss of services, caused by a stumble on a cracked sidewalk. . . .

. . . . .

We reject harm and ill-being as the natural estate of the species. We live in a cocoon of health and happiness. Who is unhappy is ill: Mental depression is something to be cured; economic depression something to be guarded against. For a vast part of the American populace, daily life is outside nature, no longer subject to the old vagaries. The common enemies of man—war, famine, disease and poverty—are vanquished, or ought to be. When they occur they are viewed as anomalies, perturbations of the social order, obstacles that need quick removal to restore the norm.[4]

The shift from a rural to an urban society has also played a part. Crowded living conditions have created serious trouble out of what had once been simple realities. Tension and conflict were inevitable by-products of the new life, and people turned to the courts for help. In the old days, Americans would go to the justice of the peace for relief. My grandfather, William Sampson Bell, was a justice of the peace for Sumter County, Georgia, and people came to him—not the high court, which is what the trial court was called—unless they had a problem of considerable weight. Unfortunately, the justices of the peace didn't join the migration to the cities, so the people lost an effective means of resolving disputes.

A series of Supreme Court decisions refurbishing the Constitution further encouraged citizens to use the courts. Fundamental new rights were perceived in criminal law, in civil liberties—ranging from voting to schools to employment —and in the protection of the heretofore seldom-heard-from, such as prisoners and the mentally ill. At the behest of plaintiff groups that had grown weary of state and federal legislators' unwillingness to deal with long-festering ills, judges stepped in to fill the void, acting on the basis of constitutional guarantees of equal protection and due process. Their rulings encouraged others to seek redress in similar fashion. Congress, even though some of its members complained about the imperial judiciary's overreaching, increased the number and scope of government programs, which in turn led to disputes that produced more business for the courts.

The legal explosion has also damaged the quality of justice. More and more judges, especially on the appellate level, are relying heavily on law clerks to cope with caseloads. In the process, the judges become staff administrators rather than jurists, and relatively inexperienced student lawyers write the law. Unless the pressure is eased, what lies ahead seems worse.

The deteriorating performance of the judicial system directly affects millions of Americans. Delays in trials or other resolutions of cases involving defendants freed on bail may result in their committing additional crimes. The same danger arises when there are delays in resolving appeals by convicted violators who are not yet behind bars. Business controversies may go unresolved for years because of the jammed dockets, with far-reaching economic consequences. A penniless plaintiff with a clearly meritorious claim may go unpaid—and suffer irreversible damage, and citizens regularly lose the benefit of important legal rights because there is no practical means of securing them.

The federal government itself needlessly adds to the volume of litigation and speaks in a legal voice that confuses rather than clarifies. The government does so largely because of its failure to recognize the Department of Justice as the government's principal and controlling branch on legal matters. Instead, a Balkanization of authority has taken place as general counsels for various agencies constantly seek to conduct their own litigation, often losing sight of the larger picture by focusing on the parochial. This problem of a divided legal authority is not a new one, and Presidents of such stature as William Howard Taft, Woodrow Wilson and Franklin D. Roosevelt have tried unsuccessfully to solve it.

If each agency develops its own legal voice, the agency bureaucrats will be freer to chart a course without interference by the President's lawyer, the attorney general. To appreciate the scope and seriousness of the challenge, consider how many lawyers work in the central government and where they work. Shortly after I became attorney general, President Carter asked me to determine the total number of lawyers in government and their functions, information that had not been gathered for several years.

Our inventory of every department and agency found 19,-479 lawyers performing lawyerlike functions—litigating, preparing memoranda, giving advice and drafting statutes, rules and regulations. We found more lawyers in the Defense Department and the military services than in the Department of Justice—5,247 to 3,806—and about one half of the Justice Department's total worked not in Washington but out of the ninety-four U.S. attorneys' offices around the nation. Although the attorney general is thought of as the executive branch's chief legal officer, he has virtually no control over the lawyers outside the Justice Department.

The lack of control is no accident. It is rooted in an historic fear of a strong attorney general. This country's Founding Fathers knew the tyranny that could result from strong central enforcement of laws, and they hesitated to create machinery in the executive branch that could lead to oppression. Reflecting their concern, the Judiciary Act of 1789—the first bill introduced in the first Senate of the United States—created the office of the attorney general but gave him no role in penal law or representation of the government in civil trials.

Edmund Randolph, the first attorney general, had served as an aide to General George Washington and had become his close friend as well as his lawyer. But the relationship won him no special treatment from Congress. He was to do nothing more than represent the United States before the Supreme Court and, upon request, to give opinions on matters of law to the President and heads of departments. Congress clearly ranked him below the heads of the three departments—War,

Foreign Affairs and Treasury—in terms of succession and protocol. While the salary for the heads of the departments was set at $3,500, that of the attorney general was only $1,500. While the department heads were given staff and quarters, the attorney general received nothing more than his salary—no funds for office rent, hiring clerks, stationery, postage, candles, lamp oil or coal for a heating stove. These expenses had to come from his own pocket.

The 1789 law did create thirteen United States attorneys, or district attorneys as they were called then, to represent the United States in the lower federal courts. In so doing, it established the precedent for the decentralization of legal authority we are experiencing now, since no provision was made for these lawyers to answer to the attorney general or to be supervised by him in any way.

In 1791, Randolph, in his first report to President Washington as attorney general, sought to remove some of the restraints that Congress had imposed on his office. He asked for authority to participate in cases before the lower courts so that he could have some influence over disputes that he eventually would have to argue in the Supreme Court. He sought to supervise the district attorneys, who already had shown tendencies to enforce the laws unevenly. And Randolph requested a clerk to help with the mechanical chores of his office. President Washington endorsed his attorney general's three requests and transmitted them to Congress. They were all ignored.

Congress's snub set a pattern that lasted for decades. Randolph had been succeeded by seven attorneys general before Congress, in 1818, finally appropriated funds to hire a clerk for his office. Presidents Jackson, Polk and Pierce each asked Congress to give the attorney general some authority over the district attorneys, but it was not until 1861 that Congress went along. Fear of strengthening the attorney general persisted for much of the nineteenth century, despite the growth of the federal government's legal business.

Not until 1870 was the Department of Justice created. The debates in Congress at the time pointed up the concern over the government's speaking with more than one voice on legal matters. Senator Jenckes of Rhode Island attacked the folly of allowing several solicitors to enunciate U.S. legal policy.

> ... we have found that there has been a most unfortunate result from this separation of law powers. We find one interpretation of the laws of the United States in one department and another interpretation in another department. . . . It is for the purpose of having a unity of decision, a unity of jurisprudence, if I may use that expression, in the executive law of the United States, that this bill proposes that all the law officers therein provided for shall be subordinate to one head.[5]

Despite Senator Jenckes's good intentions, Congress continued to grant independent litigious authority to individual agencies and has kept on doing so right up to the present day. Witness the Consumer Product Safety Commission, the Commodities Futures Trading Commission and the International Trade Commission, as well as the Environmental Protection Agency. Today, thirty-one separate units of the federal government have authority to conduct at least some of their own litigation.

Professor John Davis has aptly summarized the situation as:

> ... a continuing effort by attorneys general to centralize responsibility for all government litigation in Justice, a continuing effort by many agencies to escape from that control with respect to civil litigation, and a practice by Congress of accepting the positions of the attorney general in principle and then cutting them to pieces by exception."[6]

Some grants of separate litigating authority seem to have been enacted simply because of loud and persistent complaints from the agencies seeking the authority. Others seem designed to increase the control of particular congressional committees or subcommittees over particular agencies or programs. Neither a congressional committee which works closely with an agency, nor the agency itself, wants the Justice Department making decisions counter to its desires. Fiefdoms have been created, and the Justice Department's efforts to ensure uniformity in governmental litigation can constitute a real threat to them.

While recognizing that Congress intended some regulatory agencies to be independent of the executive branch and the President, I do not think this independence should extend to legal matters. The price is too high. It can and sometimes does result in two sets of government lawyers opposing each other at taxpayer expense. And it often permits interagency disputes to be carried to the judicial branch instead of being resolved through the Department of Justice, which could handle them more efficiently. These disputes are questions of government policy, which our country's Founding Fathers did not envision judges deciding. The independence of the regulatory agencies could still be preserved if the Justice Department represented them on legal matters. The department would merely be bringing uniformity to government legal positions, and it would still recognize the independence of the regulatory agencies' enforcement efforts.

To get an idea of how far we are from achieving centralized authority, consider the steps we felt forced to take to assert some measure of control when I was attorney general. Michael Egan, my associate attorney general, who came to Washington from an Atlanta law practice, conceived the idea that the Justice Department should operate like a private law firm. Somehow, we had to convince all the government departments that they ought to use our services—that we were good lawyers who would not charge anything for representing them. Mike met with all the general counsels in government departments once a month, but his determined sales effort had limited success.

There is another way to approach the problem, one that I now advocate. The President should say to his Cabinet: "On any issue involving legal matters where there is substantial doubt, I want you to get a legal opinion from the attorney general, just as I do."

There is one area of Justice Department legal representation where centralized authority has been little challenged: the work of the solicitor general. That office is a role model for the kind of governmentwide law office that I am advocating. The solicitor general represents all the executive departments and the independent regulatory agencies before the Supreme Court.

The solicitor general's screening function is one of the few things helping ease the pressure that the explosion of law has created for the Supreme Court. In 1971, Chief Justice Warren E. Burger expressed the sentiments of a unanimous court in telling Congress that the Securities and Exchange Commission should not be empowered to conduct Supreme Court litigation independently of the Solicitor General's Office. The Chief Justice, citing the solicitor general's "highly important role in the selection of cases to be brought here," predicted that diluting his authority would very likely increase the workload of the Supreme Court.[7]

Beyond this direct contribution to Supreme Court efficiency, the solicitor general, as counsel for the entire federal government, is responsible for presenting cases before the Court in the manner that will best serve the overall interests of the United States. He alone decides whether lower court decisions adverse to the government should be appealed and whether the government should file amicus curiae, or friend-of-the-court, briefs in cases to which it is not a party but might wish to express its views. Over the last ten years, the Court reviewed only between 6 percent and 10 percent of all the cases presented to it, but 60 percent to 70 percent of the cases that the solicitor general asked it to consider on behalf of the government. The solicitor general's high rate of success reflects his careful screening of cases and his skill in presenting the government's views. If the legal activities of all government agencies—local as well as federal—were subjected to that kind of professional screening, the government's contribution to "too much lawyering" would be cut substantially.

Moreover, the quality of the government's legal activity would improve. The solicitor general vigilantly avoids inconsistencies in the government's positions. Because he has a responsibility to the entire government, he is careful, when litigating a significant legal issue with governmentwide impact, not to pick a case that would be a poor vehicle because of its factual or procedural context. An individual agency, whether federal or local, often does not see this broader picture. To its lawyers, vindication in the pending case is more important than the long-range interests of the United States. Former Solicitor General Erwin Griswold said of the office's field of vision:

> The solicitor general's client in a particular case cannot be properly represented before the Supreme Court except from a broad point of view, taking into account all of the factors which affect sound government and the proper formulation and development of the law. In providing for the solicitor general, subject to the direction of the attorney general, to attend to the "interests of the United States" in litigating, the statutes have always been understood to mean the long-range interests of the United States, not simply in terms of its fisc, or its success in the particular litigation, but as a government, as a people."[8]

Instead of helping the Solicitor General's Office, Congress has sometimes authorized agencies to file independent petitions for a writ of certiorari (asking for Supreme Court review). Fortunately, such separate petitions have been relatively infrequent, averaging one or two a year during my tenure as attorney general. One reason for this may be that solicitors general have almost always remembered that control over the government's litigation should not be used to transform the Department of Justice into a superagency sitting in judgment on the policy decisions of other departments.

I have stressed the Solicitor General's Office as a role model because I believe that all 3,800 lawyers in the Justice Department can perform as effectively as the 20 attorneys in the Solicitor General's Office. And what is true of the federal government is true of state and local governments, not to mention the legal departments of private business corporations. The nation can take a large step toward solving its legal ills if responsible executives insist that decisions about litigation be made in a rational, coordinated and selective way—with proper regard for their cumulative effect.

If officials at the policy-making level have a role to play in reducing the burden of too much law, so do individual attorneys. And here, too, what is true for government is true for those in the private sector. One thing I did as attorney general was to advocate vigorous enforcement of Rule 11 of the Federal Rules of Civil Procedure, which I felt was often violated. The rule states: "The signature of an attorney constitutes a certificate by him that he has read the pleading; that to the best of his knowledge, information and belief, there is good ground to support it; and that it is not interposed for delay."

Each day, lawyers exercise tremendous discretionary power over the affairs of their clients. Whether the clients are the government or a private individual or entity, they must depend upon the lawyer to file such papers as he or she deems appropriate. Rule 11 is too frequently ignored in the interest of advocacy. How often does a lawyer stop to reflect on the presence or absence of the "good ground" for the filing? How many motions are filed and discovery proceedings attempted not to seek the truth but merely to delay—sometimes for tactical reasons and sometimes for delay's own sake? How many appeals are taken by lawyers who know there is no "good ground" for appeal?

Abuse of Rule 11 does more than add to the judicial system's burdens. It undermines the principle of fundamental fairness to the client, to the opposing party and to the courts that is basic to our system; it erodes the people's confidence in the law by fostering the impression that lawyers undertake unnecessary litigation for their own interests; it diverts judicial resources from consideration of meritorious filings; and it obviously increases the costs of resolving disputes. We don't have sufficient safeguards against the filing of frivolous cases by lawyers. Rule 11 ought to be applied in every court

—federal and state, on the appellate as well as on the trial level. If it were, we would have time in the courts to handle more serious matters.

As attorney general, I announced a policy of holding each lawyer in the Justice Department responsible for pleadings and positions taken orally in court. If a lawyer knowingly violated Rule 11, we were prepared to take appropriate action against the attorney and advise the court of the violation. As it turned out, we did not find any violation of the rule by Justice Department attorneys in Washington or in the ninety-four U.S. attorney offices throughout the nation. It would have surprised me to find Justice Department lawyers making false pleadings or groundless appeals. My primary purpose in adopting the policy, which I announced in a Law Day speech at the University of Georgia Law School on April 28, 1979, was to set an example for private lawyers. It is too early to determine whether the policy announcement had the desired effect, although I must admit disappointment that no bar associations or other legal groups initiated drives to enforce Rule 11 or its state and local equivalents.

There is no counterpart to Rule 11 governing federal criminal procedure, but the American Bar Association's Code of Professional Responsibility for lawyers does provide that a public prosecutor or other government lawyer "shall not institute or cause to be instituted criminal charges when he knows or it is obvious that the charges are not supported by probable cause."[9]

In one of my first meetings as attorney general with the Justice Department's attorneys, I read to them Justice George Sutherland's admonition in the Supreme Court decision of *Berger* v. *United States:*

The United States attorney is the representative not of an ordinary party to a controversy, but of a sovereignty whose obligation to govern impartially is as compelling as its obligation to govern at all; and whose interest, therefore, in a criminal prosecution is not that it shall win a case, but that justice shall be done. As such, he is in a peculiar and very definite sense the servant of the law, the twofold aim of which is that guilt shall not escape or innocence suffer.[10]

A message carved on the rotunda of the Attorney General's office in Washington sounds the same theme: "The United States wins its point whenever justice is done its citizens in the courts."

We moved to assure that the emphasis on justice in criminal prosecutions was carried out in daily practice at the same time that we announced the Rule 11 policy. Our directive stated that a federal prosecutor would no longer recommend an indictment unless the evidence presented to a grand jury would be at least "likely" to produce a conviction. That meant that, except for highly unusual circumstances, a prosecutor would no longer seek indictment with only enough evidence to defeat a defense motion to dismiss the case at the close of the government's trial—the time such motions are routinely made. The standard is higher than the requirement in the Code of Professional Responsibility, which states charges be filed only where there is "probable cause" to believe that they were true. The new criterion applies to both the decision to prosecute and the selection of specific charges to bring. Besides increased efficiency, the goal was to increase public confidence in the good faith of federal prosecutions and to spare potential defendants the agony and expense of indictment and trial where the government's case is, at best, only marginal.

My desire to bolster the public's confidence in federal prosecutors was part of a larger concern about the way in which the Justice Department had been used—and abused—for political purposes in the recent past. That the attorney general be free from political influence is essential to public confidence in his office. The Watergate scandal and the corrosive effect it had on the public's faith in the honesty of government resulted partly from the fact that two consecutive attorneys general failed to exercise independent judgment and engaged in questionable practices. Plans for the Watergate break-in were discussed in then Attorney General John N. Mitchell's office before he moved from that job to head President Nixon's reelection committee. He subsequently was convicted of conspiracy to obstruct justice, obstruction of justice, perjury and making false statements to a grand jury. His successor as attorney general, Richard G. Kleindienst, pleaded guilty after leaving office to failing to testify accurately and fully to a senate committee about an order President Nixon had given him in an antitrust case. No previous attorney general had been convicted of crime.

Professor Daniel J. Meador of the University of Virginia Law School, who established the Office for Improvements in the Administration of Justice in the Justice Department when I was attorney general, has explored the importance of an independent attorney general:

> Some of our most fundamental tenets are not literally true. To say, for example, that we have a "government of laws and not of men" does not accord altogether with reality. Yet such propositions have great value, if there is any value in living under a legal order. And so it is with the idea that the attorney general serves us best when he functions independently as a quasi-judicial officer, applying and interpreting the law objectively and free of politics. If the executive branch of government, including the President himself, is to be governed by law, it is of crucial importance that there be a high-ranking officer such as the attorney general who can function as a relatively detached lawyer. Such an officer is essential not only to ensure that the executive branch operates within the law, but also to assure that the laws are applied to the citizens fairly and evenly both in fact and appearance.[11]

Under our present system, the attorney general wears so many hats that his independence is difficult to establish or sustain. He prosecutes violations of federal law, represents the United States in judicial proceedings, gives legal opinions on questions posed by other departments and agencies, provides comment as requested on pending legislation, proposes and steers Justice Department legislation through the Congress and advises the President on the appointment of federal judges and prosecutors. These responsibilities require varying degrees of contact and coordination with the executive branch on the one hand and independence from the executive branch on the other.

As Professor Meador concluded:

> This amalgam of different roles and the large growth in the attorney general's nonlawyering responsibilities have placed intense stresses on the historic and primary role of the attorney general as chief lawyer for the government. The resulting problems are sensed by many lawyers in the Department of Justice and elsewhere, but they are not widely understood. In the long run these problems are a potential threat to government under law. . . .[12]

Ever since the establishment of the office of attorney general in 1789, there has been ambiguity about its role and disagreement about the independence of the attorney general. The Judiciary Act of 1789 described the functions of the office without relation to the policy-making, politically rooted tasks of the rest of the executive branch:

> . . . to prosecute and conduct all suits in the Supreme Court in which the United States shall be concerned, and to give his advice and opinion upon questions of law when required by the President of the United States, or when requested by heads of any of the departments, touching any matters that may concern their departments.[13]

President Washington, in writing Edmund Randolph and urging him to become attorney general, indicated he was seeking a skilled, neutral expounder of the law rather than a political adviser:

> The selection of the fittest character to expound the laws, and dispense justice, has been the invariable object

of my anxious concern. I mean not to flatter when I say that considerations like these have ruled in the nomination of the attorney general of the United States, and that my private wishes would be highly gratified by your acceptance.[14]

Notwithstanding those promises of being removed from politics, our attorneys general soon came to know the tensions created when the independence of their deliberations collided with the policy preferences of their President. One such clash took place during the 1830 controversy over the national bank. President Andrew Jackson opposed the bank and consulted with Attorney General Roger B. Taney about finding new depositories for government funds:

> Consulting with his attorney general, he found that some doubts were entertained by that officer as to the existence of any law authorizing the Executive to do that act, whereupon Ole Hickory said to him, "Sir, you must find a law authorizing the act or I will appoint an attorney general who will."[15]

Attorney General A. T. Akerman, who was in office in 1870 when the Department of Justice was created, lost his job over independence. Akerman, the last attorney general from Georgia until I took the job, refused President Ulysses Grant's request that he execute the deed conveying western lands to the railroads. The signatures of both the President and the attorney general are needed to convey public lands. Grant fired Akerman. Later, Grant tried to make amends by twice offering to make him a federal judge, but Akerman turned down the offers.

The tension between the attorney general's duty to define the legal limits of executive action in a neutral manner and the President's desire to receive legal advice that helps him do what he wants has occurred in modern administrations as well.

In 1940, President Roosevelt was determined to provide the British, soon to be under siege by Nazi Germany, with fifty destroyers in return for long-term leases on British naval bases in the Western Hemisphere. However, the United States had proclaimed itself a neutral nation in 1939, a status that potentially barred such an exchange. The President asked then Attorney General Robert H. Jackson for an opinion.

Jackson's August 27, 1940, response permitted the exchange to be made as Roosevelt had hoped.[16] But his accommodation brought public criticism. A respectable, though by no means unanimous, body of legal opinion in the United States thought that Jackson had gone too far in accommodating the law to the exigencies of the time.

The 1962 Cuban Missile Crisis provides another contemporary illustration. President John F. Kennedy wanted to cut off the supply of Soviet missiles to Cuba, but there was concern within the government whether Soviet ships bearing arms to Cuba could be stopped and searched, because a blockade is normally considered an act of war. Attorney General Robert F. Kennedy was asked whether the ship searches could be called a "quarantine" and thus constitute a lawful defensive measure short of war. Despite the grave questions of constitutional and international law presented by the issue, pressure forced the attorney general's opinion to be hammered out in oral discussions between lawyers for the Justice and State Departments. Not surprisingly, it was favorable to the President's wishes.

In addition to reorganizing its own house and lighting beacons for the rest of the legal profession to follow, the federal government can seek to control the legal explosion by developing alternatives to going to court. Not long after rejoining King & Spalding, the law firm I had left to become attorney general, I was involved in such an alternative dispute resolution, one that illustrates the benefits of what I have advocated. A large corporation that was a client of King & Spalding had become enmeshed in a bitter dispute about severance pay with a senior officer who was resigning. Several hundred thousand dollars were involved, and a messy court fight could have ensued. But the outgoing officer had told the company's management he would accept anything I said was reasonable. I couldn't represent both sides, because that would be an impermissible conflict of interest. When management joined in urging me to try to settle the matter, I agreed only to find the facts of the matter, tell them my view of the facts and leave any resolution to them.

After talking first with the senior officer's lawyer, then the man himself and finally with our client, I established that none of them understood the facts. When I told them what I saw as the facts, the senior officer said, "I will agree to that." I said: "Don't agree with me. I'm not in the case. I'm just telling you what the facts are." The corporation's general counsel then arranged a meeting between the departing officer and the firm's president. They agreed on the facts and a settlement, avoiding a lawsuit. It didn't take a courtroom or a judge for this to be possible, only a fact-finder that everyone trusted.

The board chairman of a large West German steel company told me recently that one of the great disappointments he experienced when the company began to do business in America was our system of litigation. His greatest shock came from the proclivity of one businessman to sue another. In West Germany, he said, that would be bad form, but in America the climate has deteriorated to the point where the businessman might be accused of lacking vigor and aggressiveness if he settled out of court.

I can't help thinking of my days as a young lawyer when I heard Judge Joseph C. Hutchinson, Jr., of the U.S. Court of Appeals for the Fifth Circuit cut short an admiralty case that involved only $240. Weary of handling matters that had no business in court, Judge Hutchinson announced: "We will now suspend court and take up a collection in the courtroom to pay off this judgment."[17]

One possible solution is to make it mandatory for a prospective plaintiff to file a notice of intent to sue in which he describes his case. This notice would cause the prospective defendant to hire a lawyer who would be required to meet at least once with the plaintiff's attorney for the purpose of attempting to settle the case before it ever got into court.

Judges should actively encourage alternative means of resolutions. They could be more imaginative and innovative in using lawyers as fact-finders, mediators, arbitrators, special masters—whatever role the lawyer can play as an adjunct judge with his office as an adjunct courthouse. Judges could spur the transfer of nonadversarial matters from courts to nonjudicial agencies. The transfer is relatively simple for such matters as approving changes of name but more subtle for other nonadversarial matters such as uncontested divorces and child custody and adoptions. Yet the difficulties are not insuperable.

During my tenure as attorney general, the Justice Department took an important step in alternative dispute resolution by financing neighborhood justice centers in Los Angeles, Kansas City and Atlanta. At the centers, lay people were trained as mediators. The center in Atlanta functioned best because it was run by the state court system. Over half of the Atlanta center's cases were referred to it by the courts. Some fifty-five mediators still serve there, and their occupations run from a professor at Emory University to an IBM executive and a high school teacher.

The Los Angeles center was run by a bar association and the Kansas City one by the City Manager's Office. Particularly in Los Angeles, this put too much distance between the center and the courts where many of the cases began. Because the Los Angeles center attempted to identify with the community instead of with government or official channels, often it proved difficult to attract the landlord in a landlord-tenant dispute or the merchant in a merchant-customer argument. Nevertheless, the centers illustrate what the federal government can do to lead in easing the strain on the nation's legal system. A federal evaluation of the centers during their first fifteen months of operation found that nearly half of the 3,947 cases referred to them had been resolved. Six months later, a large majority of the disputants said the agreements were still in force and that they were satisfied with the process.

Another valuable experiment with mandatory, but non-binding, arbitration was undertaken by three federal judicial districts—the eastern district of Pennsylvania, the district of Connecticut and the northern district of California. Under the experiment, which began in 1978 and 1979, certain classes of civil cases were referred to a panel of three arbitrators. A party dissatisfied with the award could demand a full-scale court trial, but in two of the districts the party was penalized by having to pay the court costs or the arbitration fees unless the trial verdict gave him more than the arbitration award. The cases usually involved personal injury or contract actions in which no more than one hundred thousand dollars was sought.

An evaluation of the pilot efforts in March 1981 by the Federal Judicial Center in Washington found that about 40 percent of the arbitrated cases ended with the award being accepted while about 60 percent demanded a trial. But of those seeking a further hearing, 46 percent were settled before trial. In two of the districts—Connecticut and eastern Pennsylvania, the mandatory arbitration led to cases being disposed of more rapidly. The Judicial Center concluded that the experiments "show genuine promise."[18]

The idea of developing alternatives to taking disputes to court is a relatively new one. In a survey conducted in 1981, the American Bar Association found 141 dispute resolution programs operating, including programs in nearly every major city of the nation.[19] Ten years earlier, there had been fewer than six.[20] But to have a substantial impact on the legal explosion, the effort needs far more support from all levels of government and a sustained public education campaign so that those with disputes to resolve will know where to go. As Professor Earl Johnson of the University of Southern California observed in a 1978 report:

> . . . it is almost accidental if community members find their way to an appropriate forum other than the regular courts. Several other modes of dispute resolution already are available in many communities. Still, since they are operated by a hodge-podge of local government agencies, neighborhood organizations and trade associa-

tions, citizens must be very knowledgeable about community resources to locate the right forum for their particular dispute."[21]

Federal reinforcement of such plans seemed on the way on February 12, 1980, when President Carter signed into law the Disputes Resolution Act, which provided funds for new and existing centers to deal primarily with the resolution of consumer complaints such as small claims about shoddy goods or services. But the sudden wave of frugality in Congress eliminated most of the funds.

Professor Frank E. A. Sander of the Harvard Law School outlined at a 1976 national conference a "multidoor courthouse" that he saw coming into being around the year 2000.[22] Impressed by the concept when he proposed it, I find it even more promising now as a way of lightening the burden on the courts while delivering justice in a timely fashion. Inside the multidoor courthouse, disputes would be screened and assigned to appropriate forums. As Professor Sander explained:

> The room directory in the lobby of such a center might look as follows: Screening Clerk (room 1), Mediation (room 2), Arbitration (room 3), Fact Finding (room 4), Malpractice Screening Panel (room 5), Superior Court (room 6) and Ombudsman (room 7). . . .

> . . . a court might decide on its own to refer a certain type of problem to a more suitable tribunal. Or a legislature might, in framing certain substantive rights, build in an appropriate dispute resolution process.

> Institutions such as prisons, schools or mental hospitals also could get into the act by establishing indigenous dispute resolution processes. Here the grievance mechanism contained in the typical collective bargaining agreement stands as an enduring example of a successful model.

> Finally, once these patterns begin to take hold, the law schools, too, should diversify their almost exclusive

preoccupation with the judicial process and begin to expose students to the broad range of dispute resolution techniques."[23]

There is little chance that the American custom of turning to the law to solve problems can be altered significantly. Indeed, the idea that the law is there to serve us and that we all stand equal before it is basic to our system of government. But to make the idea work, we must change the way we administer the law. Proposals like Professor Sander's are the kind of imaginative approaches that can save us.

IX

DEALING WITH
THE MEDIA

When President-elect Carter called on me to be his attorney
general, I responded with considerable confidence. After all,
as a member of the United States Court of Appeals for the
Fifth Circuit, I had worked closely with the Department of
Justice for fifteen years and had been immersed in the principle legal questions of the era—civil rights, labor disputes,
consumerism, government regulation of business and the
like. My earlier years in private practice and in Georgia state
government had given me more than a nodding acquaintance
with the national scene. In short, like most others in Jimmy
Carter's circle of Georgians, I came to Washington with no
great trepidation, despite my lack of experience there.

And like most of my Georgia brothers, I was to learn all
too soon how much I did not know about operations in the
nation's capital. Nowhere, however, was my lack of knowledge
more acute than in my dealings with that Hydra-headed giant
known as the Washington press corps. Fortunately, perhaps,
my media baptism in Washington was in the born-again style
—total immersion. I got in trouble with the press even before
I arrived in Washington and stayed in trouble through my
Senate confirmation hearings. And from my swearing-in to

the day I left the Justice Department two and a half years later, there was hardly a day when I was not wrestling with a serious media problem of some sort. As a result, I had no choice but to concentrate a good deal of my time and attention on trying to understand the Washington press corps and figuring out how best to deal with it. On balance, I emerged reasonably satisfied with the results, but along the way I made some mistakes, not the least of which occurred in one major case when I forgot my own hard-earned lessons and got involved in a controversy that almost drove me to resigning as an embarrassment to the President.

As every schoolboy knows, the Founding Fathers attached so much importance to what we now call the news media that they made freedom of the press one of the handful of rights guaranteed in the Bill of Rights, along with freedom of religion, the right to assemble and petition for grievances and the right to be secure in our homes from unreasonable searches and seizures. Everyone in public life in America deals with the press—from selectmen in the smallest New England towns to governors of the largest, most populous states. Even judges do, including myself while I was on the bench in Atlanta, though in the comparative isolation of the federal judiciary I was rarely interviewed and never interrogated. Yet no amount of experience anywhere else is adequate preparation for doing business with the news media in Washington.

In large ways and small, the Washington press corps is unique. Politicians cannot escape it; they try to ignore it at their peril. Whether the newly arrived public official likes it or not, the press is, as Edmund Burke called it, "The Fourth Estate"—the fourth branch of government. Like the executive, the legislative and the judicial branches, the press does not possess absolute power; but it has enormous influence and can shape the issues government officials must deal with. It can color the public's perception of individual political leaders and their programs; and, most important of all, it affects the perceptions that officials in Washington have of one another. And the unique qualities—even idiosyncracies— of the Washington press corps make it likely that, no matter how well intentioned a neophyte public official may be, he will often find the press hard to understand and sometimes impossible to handle successfully. As a starting point, though, I found that one of the most useful skills to develop was to be able to put myself in the place of a reporter and see how a particular set of facts or statements would look to one who was observing, not participating.

One thing that sets the Washington press corps apart is its sheer size. There are more reporters in Washington—thousands more—than in any other American city. This means the competition there is keener and the pressures greater. On the whole, the product is better, too. Most Washington reporters had to win their assignments by demonstrating that they had sharply honed the skills of inquiry, analysis and expression. But because of overreaching caused by competition, because of too little expertise in highly technical matters and because of the time pressures, errors are inevitable. Unfortunately, the errors are hard to catch up with. Once in print, they tend to be picked up by other publications as gospel. Despite their supposedly skeptical natures, reporters and editors apparently are the last of the vanishing breed who really think you can believe everything you read. For example, a profile of me done for *The Washington Star* shortly after I arrived was riddled with inaccuracies and distortions, some of which were adopted—without any attempt to check their accuracy—by Washington correspondents for publications that appeared all over the nation. Similarly, when *The Village Voice* reported, falsely, that I had discussed with the U.S. attorney in Atlanta the legal difficulties of Bert Lance, President Carter's budget director and longtime confidant, *The Washington Post* and others published the falsehood, attributing it to the *Voice* without checking with me. At least the *Post* had the grace to publish a correction when we complained.

The fondness of the press for dealing in drama, conflict and inconsistencies—a characteristic of news no matter where in the Free World it is published—is especially pronounced in Washington. This stress on what is wrong or could go wrong—virtually never what is right—reflects a "herd" instinct. Reporters cover events such as news conferences and congressional hearings in groups; and the group, as the late Senator Everett Dirksen of Illinois used to observe as he scanned the press gallery from the Senate floor, too often operates like a pack of wolves or barracuda looking for mistakes on the part of potential prey. Also, Washington reporters are well aware that events in the nation's capital cast shadows across the country, as well as around the world. The result of this sense of being at the center of history's stage can be exaggeration and distortion, "hyping" the story, reporters call it.

The press corps' search for the negative was accentuated by the Watergate scandal. Previously, reporters had generally believed that corruption was something politicians left behind when they reached the highest levels. After Watergate, with characteristic vigor, the Washington press corps set out to eliminate the cancer, with reporters seeking to scale ever-new heights of investigative journalism. The ensuing lack of restraint meant that public officials became suspect, virtually guilty, until proven innocent, and this attitude did not leave town with Richard Nixon. How routine the post-Watergate perspective became is illustrated by the fact that *U.S. News and World Report* reported that "not until recently was it disclosed that the attorney general and Senator Eastland reached a secret agreement in December 1976" on using commissions to help pick nominees for federal appellate courts.[1] It is true that Senator James O. Eastland, chairman of the Senate Judiciary Committee, met with President-elect Carter and me in Atlanta a month before the inauguration and agreed to help get senators to accept the commission concept, a step that would reduce their patronage over the important judicial appointments. But there was nothing "secret" about the meeting or the subject matter. It was reported in *The Atlanta Constitution* the day after it happened.

However justified the media's attitude may have been during Watergate, it made things very difficult for officials who came later. And for the neophyte, the lack of previous dealing with the media was complicated by the difficulty of knowing what individual reporters were after from one moment to the next. I remember a day early in my confirmation hearings when the interrogation had grown tense. During a break, a reporter for one of the news magazines approached me as I sat at the witness table grinning and gritting my teeth.

"What did you have for breakfast, Judge, if you can remember?" she asked.

With some difficulty, I shifted my attention and recalled that I had consumed standard southern fare—grits. For a few seconds, as she jotted down my response in her notebook, I thought of telling her how to spell the delicacy and instructing her that the word always took the plural form, but I remained silent for fear of sounding condescending. Later, I learned that such details are the kind of information savored by reporters for a publication that appears only once a week. They use the extra bits of color to add drama and an "insider" aura to accounts of the basic news already published by their daily competitors.

Thus, one minute I was being questioned on a matter of profound legal policy, and the next a reporter wanted to know what I had had for breakfast. These shifts from the sublime to the ridiculous are so quick that it becomes difficult to keep your balance, and the unwary public official may make the mistake of regarding the exchanges with the press as a game rather than as a serious matter.

How serious a matter the Washington media really is I began to learn even before going to the capital. In Washington, the media not only deal in symbols, but have a lot to say about what those symbols will be. Not realizing this, I was taken unawares when, a few days after President-elect Carter announced that I was his nominee as attorney general, a reporter called my Atlanta home—I was still picking up my own phone in those days—to ask what I planned to do about my membership in private clubs. I belonged to several in Atlanta, including the Piedmont Driving Club and the Capital City Club, both of which had no black members. Without pausing for reflection, I told the reporter that I planned to retain my memberships. I viewed membership in private clubs as my private business, not realizing the media would use it as a symbolic clue to the ideology of the new administration. My attitudes were thought to be especially important both because I was viewed as a close friend of the President-elect and because my Cabinet post was most responsible for protecting civil rights.

My nomination had already disturbed some traditional Democratic liberal constituencies who had candidates of their own and who were wary of Jimmy Carter and the Georgians around him. From the beginning, these liberals had doubted the new President's commitment to equal rights, even though blacks had given him strong support in the election. Now, in my too hasty defense of the clubs, they thought they saw the old southern bigotry they had feared all along. Using their ready access to the eastern press, they turned the glowing coal of my private club comment into a damaging fire. It did not matter that most federal judges in Atlanta belonged to the same clubs, including my friend Elbert Tuttle, whom the civil rights movement regarded as a hero, or that several of us had sought to integrate other clubs such as the Atlanta Lawyers Club.

My wife, Mary, being more attuned to symbols than her husband, helped put out the fire. She recalled that a controversy over club membership had erupted during the Kennedy administration. The question then was how the President's brother and attorney general, Robert F. Kennedy, could maintain his membership in the Metropolitan Club, an English-style men's club in Washington that banned blacks and women. Mary reminded me that Robert Kennedy had resigned his membership, saying it was important symbolically for an official who was responsible for enforcing civil rights laws. Realizing he had set an admirable precedent, I issued a statement that I, too, would resign from the clubs upon becoming attorney general. The statement dulled the club controversy but did not prevent my being scrutinized more closely during the pre-inaugural period than any other Carter appointee, except the President-elect's short-lived selection of Theodore C. Sorensen, the former aide to President John

F. Kennedy, as CIA director. My senate hearing was televised live daily by Public Broadcasting, and my confirmation was delayed a week beyond Inauguration Day, when the other Cabinet members were sworn in. I survived the baptism and learned a thing or two about the media and symbolism in the process.

In some ways, the most worrisome characteristic of the Washington press corps to me is its northeastern bias. Former Vice-President Spiro T. Agnew's complaint that the influence of the Northeast dominates what is reported and how it is presented in print and on the air throughout the nation should not be dismissed just because a disgraced officeholder voiced it. I detected the slant immediately, referring to it as the bias of the Northeast Strip, the urban cluster running from Boston in the North through New York City to Washington at its southern end.

It is displayed in the values reporters and editors apply in defining what is important enough to qualify as news. Reflecting the Northeast, Washington journalists are somewhat internationalistic, attaching more importance to events in Europe than in Kansas City; they place a high premium on formal education, preferably at an Ivy League school; they come down on the liberal or left side of civil rights and civil liberties issues; they regard federal programs as a solution for many of the nation's ills; and they see economic questions through the prism of Keynesian training rather than through that of some other theoretical analysis, monetarism, for example, or supply-side economics. They also suffer from a provincial tendency to attach very little importance to what happens west of the Hudson or south of Washington, D.C.

The impact of the prejudice is felt throughout the nation, reflecting the power of such major city dailies as *The New York Times* and *The Washington Post.* The headquarters of the news operations of the television networks are also in the Strip, as are the weekly news magazines and the press or wire associations. These media leaders feed upon each other in determining what is news and how it should be viewed. Their choices are adopted by news outlets throughout the country and, to a lesser extent, the world. *The New York Times* is particularly listened to. I've been told by a reporter for one of the news magazines that fresh, insightful observations of government activities have been rejected when he or a colleague proposed them as stories, because the *Times* had seen the event differently—or not at all.

If you run afoul of a Strip operation, the consequences are likely to be far greater than if your critic is from another sector. The pervasive role in news selection played by one region may partially explain the public distrust of the media that pollsters have been recording in recent years—a lack of faith I find disturbing. The power and population of the nation is heading west, but the news leaders and their values are still firmly implanted in a narrow, unrepresentative corridor of the country.

Despite experiences with newspapers and television that drove me to exasperation and threatened some of the most important work I was trying to accomplish as attorney general, I left Washington convinced that the press is—however imperfectly—a surrogate for the public at large.

In addition to monitoring government for their readers and viewers, the news media have a voice in setting government's agenda. A President can propose programs and Congress can take them up, but if the news media don't pay attention, both the Congress and the President will find it difficult to make headway against special interests who are in opposition.

It has been written that we live under a government of men and women and morning newspapers, an observation that I found to be on the mark during my service as attorney general. On many days, an examination of the morning newspapers caused my agenda to be reset. A prime example of this took place during the administration's first year in office when *The New York Times Magazine* ran on its cover the photograph of a man wearing a loud suit that complemented the cocksure expression on his face. "Mr. Untouchable," the magazine's cover proclaimed. "This is Nicky Barnes. The police say he may be Harlem's biggest drug dealer. But can they prove it?"[2]

President Carter saw the picture and read the article, and at the next Cabinet meeting asked me why the government couldn't do something about Nicky Barnes. I promised to look into the matter and called Bob Fiske, then the U.S. attorney for the Southern District of New York. Fiske, because of the call, decided to prosecute the case himself. Six months later, Leroy "Nicky" Barnes, Jr., "Mr. Untouchable," was convicted, along with ten codefendants, of conducting a criminal enterprise—what Fiske described as "the largest, most profitable, venal drug ring in the city."[3] He was sentenced to a term of life in prison by U.S. District Court Judge Henry F. Werker on January 19, 1978. I cannot contend that the President's interest in the matter, which spurred my call and Fiske's decision to take charge himself, was solely responsible for the salutary result of taking Nicky Barnes off the streets of New York. But I do know that the prosecution received top priority once the President concluded from reading the newspaper article that Barnes was a national menace and, thanks to *The New York Times,* a widely recognized one.

In a way, the saga of Mr. Untouchable illustrates the power of the press of the Northeast Strip. The story had a visibility in the White House that it would not have if it had been carried only by the *Kansas City Star* or the *Des Moines Register and Tribune,* in part because such an article from Kansas City or Des Moines would probably not have been included in the news summaries of articles of interest that are compiled daily and circulated in the White House and Cabinet departments. The action against Mr. Untouchable was more than the government's responding to a particularly strong newspaper, of course. It also sprang from President Carter's intuitive response to a problem that millions of Americans worry about all over the country—the vulnerability of their children to drugs; but because the article had appeared in *The New York Times,* the case had a symbolic impact, even on the President, that it would not otherwise have enjoyed.

Along with resetting my agenda, the press indirectly helped me stay on top of my job by providing significant information, not just in what I read but also from what I gleaned from reporters' questions and comments in news conferences and interviews. The regularity of these confrontations proved useful in another way. When we traveled outside Washington for speeches and conferences, my practice was to meet with reporters in each area we visited—all part of the effort to rebuild confidence in the integrity and neutrality of the Department of Justice. To prepare for these encounters, Dean St. Dennis, a veteran member of the department's public information office, would compile a briefing book that spelled out in exhaustive detail what the Justice Department, including the FBI, the DEA, the Bureau of Prisons, and the LEAA, was doing of interest in each spot we stopped. St. Dennis's briefing papers became a highly useful synopsis of substantive Justice Department activities.

Unfortunately, the press sometimes goes too far in being the public's monitor of the other three branches. It can get carried away by the sheer momentum of a breaking story and be influenced by values, priorities and even fads that prevail inside the corps. During my years in Washington, "Koreagate" was an example of that. Koreagate was the label attached by the press to the government's inquiry into attempts by the South Korean Central Intelligence Agency to buy influence on Capitol Hill. The label implied that the scandal approached or surpassed the scale of Watergate. Story after story speculated on the number and names of members of Congress involved in the Department of Justice's investigation. The numbers ran from seventy to ninety and even to more than a hundred.

The conjecture prompted me to state publicly several times that very few present and former members of Congress were seriously involved in the investigation. In the end, one ex-member, Richard T. Hanna, Democrat of California, was sent to prison on a guilty plea. Another, Otto E. Passman, Democrat of Louisiana, was indicted but acquitted. And three sitting members, Edward R. Roybal, Charles H. Wilson and John J. McFall, all Democrats from California, were reprimanded by the House of Representatives. Hardly worth comparing to Watergate.

Because of the importance of communicating to the public what you are seeking to accomplish as a public official, I never stopped trying to improve my skills in dealing with reporters. At the same time, I must acknowledge that part of presenting a credible case is doing what comes naturally. Making yourself accessible and being open and candid are good starting points. I tried always to speak "on-the-record," a relatively rare way of communicating in Washington in which the reporter is able to attribute to you by name everything you say. Perhaps even rarer is the practice of admitting your mistakes rather than ignoring them or blaming them on subordinates or on the faceless bureaucracy. Above all, I found the use of one's sense of humor, particularly a self-deprecating one, went a long way.

My standard for candor was set even before the Senate confirmed me. At a hearing, Senator Mathias extracted a pledge from me to post publicly each day a log of my contacts with persons outside the Department of Justice. These included calls or meetings with members of Congress, judges, private attorneys, Cabinet officers and the White House staff —even the President. The log, which did not include people I saw at social receptions outside the office or calls to me at home at night or during the weekend, appeared daily in the Justice Department press room, down the hall from the attorney general's office. Early editions of the log included such significant data as my crossing Pennsylvania Avenue to use the FBI gymnasium, which promptly appeared in *The Washington Post,* and a visit to the barber in the Sheraton Carlton Hotel, which also was published. Occasionally, we would exercise some editing restraint. For example, when I was telephoning prospects to head the FBI, prospects whose names had not yet been made public, we would list on the log "conversation with a possibility for FBI director—name to be supplied later." I am convinced that the log helped persuade reporters who covered the department that we meant to carry out Jimmy Carter's pledge of an open administration. One of Attorney General William French Smith's first official acts during the Reagan administration was to do away with the logs. He contended that because they did not cover contacts over the weekend and away from the office they were not valuable in keeping track of the attorney general. Aides to the new attorney general said his decision reflected the fact that he "is a very private man." I must say that I gave Attorney General Smith my views on the value of the log system, stating that, while it helped me, the Republic would not fall if he discontinued it, especially since no other government official was following the practice.

As attorney general, I held frequent press conferences, gave scores of individual interviews and, particularly during my last year, invited reporters, columnists and television commentators to the attorney general's dining room for lengthy, informal conversations over quail, grits and rooster pepper sausage, a little-known South Georgia delicacy that Charlie Kirbo and I introduced to Washington. Reporters traveled with me on government planes and in commercial airliners, and I spent much of the time in flight responding to their questions.

Before I was confirmed, the Justice Department's Office of Public Information gave me a detailed explanation of the strange jargon that the media and the government use in communicating with one another. Ground rules under which the communication is conducted begin with "on-the-record" and range downward in terms of the official's willingness to be quoted and to be held publicly accountable for his statement through "on-background," to "deep-background" and, of course, "off-the-record." When a Justice Department official speaks "on-background," his comments can be attributed to "a senior Justice Department official," or if the official feels that's too close to home—and the reporter agrees ahead of time—to "an administration source." When a reporter accepts information on "deep-background," he usually is agreeing to write it on his own, attributing it to no source, as if the information came to him from out of the blue. "Off-the-record" means that the reporter will not publish the information being given him and that he is accepting it only for the purpose of helping him to better understand the situation being discussed. Some reporters use off-the-record information as a lead to pry the same details from another official, under less restrictive rules of attribution. Others treat off-the-record the same way as they treat deep-background, reporting the details but giving no hint of their origin.

I found these tiered levels of decreasing responsibility offensive, believing that if something is important enough to be said, it is important enough for someone to say it publicly and take the responsibility for saying it. I must acknowledge, though, that my staff, particularly Terry Adamson, my special assistant and the department's chief spokesman, used all the guidelines of attribution in talking with the press. Adamson contended there were many times he needed to convey facts but that he couldn't do so if they were to be quoted as the official comments of an aide to the attorney general or those of the chief spokesman for the department. I can understand his argument, but I cannot be comfortable with it. When a government official backs away from standing behind what he tells the press, he injects deceit into his relationship with the public that he is supposed to serve.

Admitting mistakes seems so fundamental, especially when you want to convince people of your honesty, that it should not have to be mentioned. But it is apparently something extraordinary in the nation's capital. One of my initial ideas for reorganization was to merge the Drug Enforcement Administration into the FBI, a proposal that caused a stir, especially at DEA headquarters. When, as I wrote in Chapter VII, we sent a team of FBI experts to study the DEA, their report made clear that the merger would be a mistake. Reporters soon were asking what had happened. I told them it was one of those ideas that sounded good when you first heard it but that further study showed would be impractical. Not all notions for reorganization are good ones, I added, and it's better to consider a whole host of proposals than only advance those you are certain will work out. I gave this explanation several times, and each time reporters reacted as if the emperor were confessing that he had no clothes.

Another example of how unaccustomed the Washington

press corps is to confession of error took place at the White House when I announced the President had selected Judge William H. Webster to be FBI director. Implicit in the announcement was the fact that we were not appointing any of the candidates proposed by the prestigious committee we had created to prepare a list of the best-qualified persons. Naturally, when I was making the announcement, a reporter asked about the committee:

> *Q:* Does that mean that the previous system the President instituted is out the window? (Laughter)
>
> *Attorney General Bell:* I will have to say that, number one, the President didn't institute it. I will have to take the blame for that. That was one of my brainstorms. (Laughter)
> *Q:* He bought it, though.
>
> *Attorney General Bell:* He sometimes has too much confidence in his attorney general. (Laughter) I have seen some sign of that lately. (Laughter) . . . It looked like a good thing to do at the time.[4]

My friend Reg Murphy, now publisher of the *Baltimore Sun*, has a sign behind his desk advising those who would take on the press that it is never wise to do battle with anyone who buys ink by the barrel. But there are times, particularly for the public official, when an erroneous account is so damaging that it must be challenged, and vigorously. For me, *The New York Times* published such a story on December 2, 1977, when its Pulitzer Prize-winning correspondent, Seymour M. Hersh, wrote in a front-page piece that I had delayed a "planned appointment" of a U.S. attorney in Pittsburgh "under pressure from investigators" in the Justice Department.[5] The implication was that I had been about to appoint a man of questionable honesty. Hersh wrote that sources he identified only as "officials of the Federal Bureau of Investigation and the Justice Department" had charged that we "had improperly delayed a full-scale investigation" into payments from the candidate for U.S. Attorney, George E. Schumacher, to Representative Joseph M. Gaydos of Pennsylvania.[6] There were many things in that story that were wrong, including several statements in the first paragraph. First, I was under no pressure. Second, the appointment was not planned but only under consideration. Third, our investigation of whether there had been payments and, if so, whether there was anything improper about them, had been proceeding for several weeks. Hersh had interviewed me and Associate Attorney General Michael J. Egan the previous day and reported correctly that both of us denied the accusations.

I called a press conference within hours after reading the story and denounced the article as "scurrilous, irresponsible and completely out of keeping with anything I thought *The New York Times* stood for." Hersh had reported that "one well-informed government official" told him that everyone in the investigation "is scared."[7] That was too much for me. If there is anything the Justice Department and its investigative arm, the FBI, can do without, it is frightened investigators. I told the press conference I was sending the head of the Justice Department's Office of Professional Responsibility, the department's internal watchdog, Michael E. Shaheen, Jr., "to find out just what the trouble is there." Shaheen, whose reputation for independence later gained national attention through critical reports he issued concerning my successor, Ben Civiletti, and the President's brother, Billy Carter, had already demonstrated that he would report the facts as he found them, no matter how uncomfortable for anyone.

Shaheen's investigation unearthed FBI agents who readily acknowledged talking to Hersh but who insisted they had not told him they felt pressured. In the end, I decided not to recommend the nomination of Schumacher to the President —but not for any reasons Hersh had mentioned. Later, after I left office, Hersh told Terry Adamson that my reaction to the story had surprised him and that upon further investigation he had satisfied himself that I was telling the truth.

That departure from accurate reporting occurred because one of the nation's leading newspapers let its hunger for "investigative" journalism, a field in which it trailed during the Watergate era, overpower its good judgment. U.S. attorneys' posts are sought-after jobs, with rival factions supporting rival candidates. In the Schumacher case, I think *The New York Times* was used by one politically motivated side in the drive to obtain that appointment, which leads to the obvious conclusion that the reasons for providing a reporter with information should be a subject of that reporter's scrutiny before he runs the story.

Lack of restraint would be less of a problem if the press practiced more self-criticism. Our First Amendment's free-press guarantee would not be harmed if the media began to hold itself accountable to the media. The increasing use of ombudsmen by newspapers to monitor their own performance is a step in the right direction.

Misdirected zeal does not afflict only reporters in the Washington press corps. Columnists can also be bitten by the bug. One such was William Safire, author of an occasionally clever, frequently acerbic and almost always critical column for *The New York Times.* Safire had been an aide in the Nixon White House, and many in the Carter administration counseled me against meeting with him because, they said, his column was just a never-ending apologia for the Nixon years. If Safire could demonstrate that other administrations played fast and loose with government, then the sins of the Nixon period would seem less sinful. Thus, he labeled the department I presided over as the "Carter Department of Political Justice." In his thrusts at the President, the Democratic party and the department, he sought to make every allegation or investigation another Watergate. Thus, Safire hung the label "Koreagate" on the inquiry into alleged payoffs to Congressmen by a representative of the Korean CIA. Investigations involving President Carter's brother, Billy, were shorthanded in Safire's column as "Billygate." Although Safire invariably ascribed the basest of political motives to those the Nixon White House would have regarded as enemies, there was frequently a germ of truth in his observations.

Despite the advice to the contrary, I talked several times

with Safire. Although I found him charming and engaging, I had sufficient sense of self-preservation to keep my defenses up. Because I tried to treat him as I treated other journalists, I think he often gave me the benefit of doubt in his column. Frequently, when I figured in his pieces, he would append to my name, "though he is an honest man." Maintaining direct lines of communication with Safire helped me and the department over the long run.

If I learned from my successes, I learned more from my errors. And it is not surprising that my darkest days as attorney general came from a case that could qualify as Exhibit A on how not to handle a media event. The case quickly became known as the Marston affair, named for the Republican-appointed U.S. attorney in Philadelphia, David W. Marston. The setback was so great that I seriously considered resigning from the Cabinet as an embarrassment the President did not deserve.

We made grave mistakes from start to finish in handling the matter. For one thing, I let the case simmer far too long without appreciating the context in which it was taking place. Because I had no sense of how it would play in the press, I failed to perceive it accurately on two levels. Locally—that is, in Philadelphia—I did not understand how much Marston had come to be regarded as an anticorruption crusader; and at the Washington level I did not foresee how the Marston affair would fit so well into Watergate-bred suspicions about public officials. To make the matter worse, I also neglected most of the techniques for dealing with the press that I cited earlier.

To understand the Marston affair, you have to go back to the 1976 Democratic convention where then-candidate Jimmy Carter told the platform committee that "all federal judges and prosecutors should be appointed strictly on the basis of merit without any consideration of political aspect or influence."[8] After the election and before the inauguration, he and I met with Senator James O. Eastland of Mississippi, the longtime chairman of the Senate Judiciary Committee. Judges and U.S. attorneys are examined by that committee, and those proceedings, as I indicated earlier in the chapter, are a vehicle for the exercise of Senate patronage. Eastland agreed to support the naming of commissions to pick candidates for the federal circuit courts of appeal—a first step in delivering on the President's pledge to introduce a merit system. No such agreement was reached on district court judges or U.S. attorneys. Thus, the President followed the practice of his predecessors and selected U.S. attorneys by relying on the recommendations of Democratic senators. If a state was unwise enough to have no Democratic senators, President Carter would turn to the congressional delegation or to the political committee of the state concerned. By the time of the Marston affair, we had named about seventy U.S. attorneys— all of them Democrats—and had retained about twenty— most of them Republicans—that the preceding Republican administration had put in office.

David W. Marston, then thirty-five years of age, was an unlikely character to play the role of nonpartisan white knight to my partisan black knight. The series of incidents that followed set back by months my attempt to gain control of the Justice Department and to make it recognized as a neutral zone in government. After being beaten twice in races for the Pennsylvania legislature, Marston in 1973 joined the staff of Senator Richard Schweiker, Republican of Pennsylvania, as a legislative aide. Three years later, in the waning days of the Ford administration, Schweiker was instrumental in his being appointed U.S. attorney in Philadelphia. When Jimmy Carter won the election, one would have thought Marston's days as U.S. attorney were numbered. It was customary for U.S. attorneys to submit their resignations, although we did invite them and their hundreds of assistants to advise us if they wanted to be considered for retention under a merit system. Marston, in my view, was not likely to be retained. Not only had he come to the job straight from a Republican senator's office, which made his appointment appear political, but he had no trial or prosecutorial experience.

We did not move immediately to replace Marston, however. Mike Egan, the associate attorney general who normally handled such matters, and Pete Flaherty, the deputy attorney general and a veteran Pennsylvania political figure, both advised against removing him. Marston had taken over an office blessed with some of the top federal prosecutors in the country as assistant U.S. attorneys. The FBI field office on which he depended for investigations was probably the most vigorous we had; it was headed by a maverick, Neil Welch, who aspired to be head of the FBI and who became a key Marston ally. And the target of their efforts was one of the most notorious systems of political corruption in the United States. Historically, state and local prosecutors had been removed when they grew too serious about rooting out corruption. The highly skilled lawyers under Marston, however, successfully prosecuted such powerful Democratic Philadelphia state legislators as former House Speaker Herbert Fineman and State Senator Henry J. Cianfrani. Egan and Flaherty warned that removing Marston would touch off a media furor. Another factor that delayed action was that the Democratic congressional delegation from Pennsylvania—the state had no Democratic senators—was split over who should succeed Marston, though the congressmen undeniably wanted Marston out. Representative Joshua Eilberg of Philadelphia, an important Democrat on the Judiciary Committee, told me repeatedly in the spring of 1977 how unhappy he was over seeing Marston still in office.

In June of 1977, trying to soothe the unhappy congressional delegation, I offered the job to Jerome Shestack, a Philadelphia lawyer of considerable repute. He turned me down, suggesting we leave Marston alone because the U.S. Attorney's Office had just begun an especially sensitive brutality case against the Philadelphia Police Department. Replacing Marston might be misinterpreted as a move to undermine the case. I decided to continue searching for a replacement and to retain Marston at least for the rest of the year.

But Eilberg had grown unhappy with me over my failure to act and over my opposition to his proposals for "reforming" grand juries. On November 4, 1977, he telephoned President Carter and said that Marston had to go. Eilberg gave no reason, and the President didn't ask. Instead, he called me in the attorney general's limousine as I was headed for shopping at Brooks Brothers in Washington. Knowing the radio phone lines were not secure, I rode on to the store and spoke to the President from the manager's office. The President said there was pressure from Democrats in Pennsylvania to replace Marston and asked why it had taken so long. I told him that I had stopped talking with Eilberg. He replied, "I know. That's why I had to take his call." Aware of Eilberg's abiding interest in replacing Marston, Frank Moore, assistant to the President for congressional relations, was flabbergasted that Eilberg had got through to the President. I think Jimmy Carter talked with Eilberg because he badly wanted the congressman's support for pending energy legislation and because Eilberg was chairman of the House Judiciary Subcommittee on Immigration, Refugees and International Law, another area the President was trying to reform.

Neither the President nor I knew when Eilberg urged the President to oust Marston that the congressman's law firm was involved in an investigation by Marston's office into irregularities in the construction of Hahnemann Hospital in Philadelphia. But in the afterglow of Watergate, the Caesar's wife, cleaner-than-a-hound's-tooth doctrine prevailed, and appearances became more important than reality. Hahnemann Hospital was being built with a $14.5 million federal grant and $39.5 million from state and local agencies that had been obtained with the assistance of Eilberg's law firm. The investigation, in a very preliminary stage at the time, was not targeted at Eilberg; nor was he even considered one of the subjects of the probe. In August, two and one-half months earlier, an aide to Marston had mentioned to an official in the Justice Department's Criminal Division that a unit of the U.S. Attorney's Office in Philadelphia was investigating a transaction that might involve Eilberg. Later testimony established that I had no knowledge of that investigation until the following January, a key month in the Marston affair.

My response to the President's call was to advise Egan that the President wanted Marston's removal expedited. A few days later, while Marston was in Washington attending a conference for U.S. attorneys, Egan told him he would be removed because of "pressure from on high."

Nearly two months afterward, on January 8, 1978, the *Philadelphia Inquirer* reported that I was trying to replace Marston—at the urging of Congressman Eilberg who, the newspaper noted, was connected with an investigation being conducted by Marston's office. Four days later, President Carter told a news conference that he had "not interfered at all" in the Marston matter and that he had not discussed "the case" with me. Only when pressed did the President concede that he had spoken with Eilberg, that Eilberg had asked that Marston be removed quickly and that the President had then telephoned me. Trying to limit the damage, I immediately held a press conference and pointed out Marston's shortcomings, saying it was my intention from the start of the administration to replace him. Moreover, I said I knew of no investigation involving Eilberg and that if there was one Marston had been "negligent" in not telling me about it. Later, I came to modify that view, realizing that it had been my own Department of Justice staff that had neglected to tell me of the investigation related to Eilberg. To prevent a recurrence of that kind of disaster, I set up a system under which I would be notified whenever a "public figure or entity" became the subject of a Justice Department investigation.

It took me several days to confirm that Eilberg was being investigated. President Carter made matters worse by telling a group of Democratic congressmen, one of whom relayed it to the press, that the Justice Department had not been able to establish that Eilberg was under investigation. Marston then told reporters we were "dead wrong" in stating we could find no investigation of the congressman. Despite the beating we were taking, I remained convinced that Marston had to leave. I sent three department lawyers to Philadelphia to assess whether the decision to replace Marston had jeopardized investigations into political corruption in Pennsylvania. They reported that over the long run replacing him would not affect the investigation, though one said it could cause problems in the short run.

Marston agreed to come to Washington to meet with me, an invitation that was another mistake on my part. Setting up a confrontation between the attorney general and a young, rebellious U.S. attorney escalated the conflict. Instead of getting directly involved myself, I should have dealt with Marston through an agent, removing the newsworthy person of the attorney general. This would have led reporters to downplay the event as a news story and allowed the public to focus on issues rather than on personalities.

The media's interest in the confrontation was further whetted when Marston and an aide were delayed for several hours through no fault of their own, and reporters, cameramen and TV technicians paced the corridor of the department outside my office waiting and swapping speculation and rumor. In our meeting, I asked Marston to remain in his job until a replacement could be appointed. I told him his successor would have to be at least Marston's equal in ability, character and integrity, and that I would have to be convinced that replacing him would not impede any investigation or prosecution. Marston turned down the bid to stay in his job, saying he would remain only on condition that he serve a full four-year term. This amounted to a subordinate dictating terms to his superior, and I could not go along with it. Marston stepped out into the corridor and told reporters who engulfed him that he had been "fired."

That's where I made another big mistake. Forgetting the emphasis on openness and accessibility, I did not step out into the hallway—or have a subordinate do so—to challenge Marston's account. I, in effect, abandoned the field. When we finally figured out that it looked as if we had fired Marston peremptorily and issued a statement listing the facts, it was too late—at least for the TV journalists. They reported on the evening news a few hours later that Marston had been fired. There was time for some print reporters to learn the truth and produce accurate accounts, which took note of Marston's misrepresentation. But an estimated 80 percent of Americans depend on TV—not newspapers—for their prime source of information.

A few days later, I learned on a flight across the country to Portland, Oregon, how costly the Marston affair had been. The pilot of the United Airlines flight came back to the passenger cabin and stopped at my chair. He said he had written President Carter a letter to protest the discharge of Marston. When I asked why, he said: "I really felt deeply grieved that the President interfered with a pending prosecution of a congressman and helped him."

"Do you really believe that?" I responded.

"That's the way it looked," he said.

I felt terrible in reflecting that when the President contacted me about Eilberg's call to him, I didn't know enough facts to say immediately: "Mr. President, you shouldn't have had that conversation with Congressman Eilberg. He's under investigation." As I told my staff at the end of the Marston episode: "If I were the President, I believe that I'd find me another attorney general, one who could find out what's going on around his department."

There are two postscripts to the Marston affair that should be noted. Marston declared his candidacy for governor of Pennsylvania two months after he left his U.S. attorney's post. He lost in the Republican primary. In November 1979, he made his fourth try for elective office and lost in the general election his bid to be mayor of Philadelphia. As for Eilberg, the House Ethics Committee charged him in September of 1978 with accepting more than one hundred thousand dollars from his law firm in connection with its work for Hahnemann Hospital. He lost his reelection contest in November after federal prosecutors—under the leadership of the new U.S. attorney in Philadelphia, Peter Vaira, an experienced prosecutor and a veteran of ten years in the Justice Department who had no public association with partisan politics—obtained a grand jury indictment of him for conflict of interest in receiving compensation for advocating private cases before a federal agency. He pleaded guilty and was placed on probation for five years and was fined ten thousand dollars. Eilberg, under terms of the statute to which he pleaded guilty, was barred for life from holding any federal office.

If Marston serves as Exhibit A of how not to handle a

media firestorm, my dealings with Jack Anderson could stand as Exhibit A of how a public official should respond to an error-prone gossip columnist whose writings are widely carried nationally. But the column is just the base of what *The Wall Street Journal* described as "a veritable multimedia conglomerate." Anderson appears several times a week on network television and radio, lectures for fees around three thousand dollars and spawns various entrepreneurial projects under the umbrella of journalism.

As with Safire, I invited Anderson to an early lunch at the department for a general discussion. Ironically, I told Anderson at this first lunch that he was then President Carter's favorite columnist. I did not know that Anderson had by this point already approached Ben Civiletti, assistant attorney general in charge of the Criminal Division, with the message that Anderson would be "favorable" to him in his column and broadcasts in return for "good information." Civiletti turned him down flat.

The battle I eventually had with Anderson illustrates what I think are several important points. Not least of these is that there are times, as I wrote earlier, that a public official must confront the media head-on for the good of both.

To go after a widely circulated journalistic falsehood with hammer and tongs is no denigration of the First Amendment, the role of the press in our society or the public interest. To do so bolsters each. The Supreme Court, in its landmark decision of *New York Times* v. *Sullivan* in 1963, held that the Constitution required that before a public official can recover for libel he must show that the libelous statement was made with knowledge of its falsity or with reckless disregard of whether it was false or not. This rule was based in part on the greater access that public officials enjoy to channels of effective communication, giving them a more realistic opportunity to counteract false statements than private individuals normally enjoy. Though the opportunity for rebuttal seldom suffices to undo the defamatory falsehood, there are times when all available access should be used in an attempt for the truth to catch up with the lie.

My major clash with Anderson was over Robert L. Vesco,

a financier who fled the United States in 1972 to avoid being tried on charges that he and associates had looted $224 million from Investors Overseas Services, a foreign-based mutual fund, and had made a $200,000 illegal contribution to President Nixon's 1972 reelection campaign. The stakes were a lot higher for me in the struggle with Anderson than in the Marston affair, because Anderson initially alleged that high administration officials were involved with a criminal in what amounted to old-fashioned corruption.

We first heard of Anderson's allegation late on Friday, September 8, 1978, while President Carter huddled with Anwar Sadat and Menachem Begin at Camp David, hammering out what became the Camp David Accords. Several reporters began calling the Justice Department to ask about a column by Anderson that their papers had received for publication the following Monday. In it Anderson charged that Hamilton Jordan and Charles Kirbo were linked to a ten-million-dollar "political fix" which resulted in the Justice Department's dropping its efforts to extradite Robert Vesco. Anderson's allegation involved extraordinarily complex facts, and he dealt with them in numerous columns, some versions of which he still publishes to vindicate his reporting. I find it heartening that few news organizations, if any, picked up Anderson's original charge but instead reported on the columnist's confrontation with the administration, on Anderson's various versions of the events, his admission of "reconstructed" evidence and on Anderson's own relationship with the fugitive financier, Robert Vesco, and United States senators interested in the matter.

As *The Atlanta Constitution* had reported in late July 1978, long before Anderson, Vesco had indeed approached some Georgians in an attempt to get the charges against him dropped. The key intermediary was an ex-convict, R. L. Herring, who was in prison on a swindling conviction and was subsequently convicted in Virginia of first-degree murder. Another participant in the scheme was a young Albany, Georgia, lawyer named Spencer Lee, a boyhood friend of Hamilton Jordan, President Carter's chief aide. Later grand

jury investigations determined that Lee met in the early weeks
of the administration with a White House aide named Richard
Harden, who had been head of the Georgia Welfare Department under Governor Carter. Thereafter, Harden spent
about five minutes with President Carter, who wrote me a
handwritten note in early February, stating "Please see Spencer Lee when he requests an appointment—J.C." I do not
remember reading the note, but whether I did or not, it ended
up in a file for pending appointments in the desk of my counselor and scheduler, Mike Kelly. There it sat for the next year
and a half. Lee never requested nor had an appointment. A
federal grand jury returned no indictments, and no evidence
was ever produced that Jordan, Kirbo or anyone else in the
administration had made any efforts to act on behalf of Vesco.

But Anderson implied continuously, and still does, that
the scheme succeeded in obtaining favorable Justice Department action for the accused fugitive. In characteristic fashion,
Anderson presents selective facts and innuendo, repeating his
core implication in carefully worded but misleading fashion.

Following the calls that first Friday, my aide Terry Adamson quickly reviewed his notes and Justice Department files
concerning Vesco in order to respond to the inquiries of
reporters from *The Los Angeles Times, The Atlanta Constitution,
The Washington Post* and *Newsday.*

With Adamson present, Anderson had interviewed me in
my office the previous Monday. At that meeting, Anderson
inquired about three approaches said to have been made to
me concerning the Vesco case. My logs, appointment records
and staff notes demonstrated at that meeting that none of the
three contacts had been made, and Anderson's columns
never referred to them. Adamson's notes of my meeting with
Anderson reflect that Anderson asked in passing and only
generally about extraditing Vesco and why the department
had decided not to pursue it. He did not inquire about our
reasons or whether any other move was being made to secure
Vesco's return for trial.

Since Adamson was holding a briefing on Saturday for
reporters who had inquired about the Anderson charge, An-

derson called to complain that the briefing was being held before his column had appeared and that he had been left out. At that time, Anderson was briefed on details of the extradition question.

Anderson then revised his still-unpublished column, eliminating the allegation that Jordan and Kirbo were linked to a "political fix" to drop the extradition proceeding and added a disclaimer: "There is in fact no hard evidence that either man [Jordan or Kirbo] lifted a finger in Vesco's behalf with Attorney General Griffin Bell or the President." The accusatory lead of the original column was softened to state that "the Justice Department quietly switched tactics in the spring of 1977" in its campaign to bring Vesco to Justice, and that this "major change in tactics was made in the aftermath of a high-pressure lobbying campaign directed at two of President Carter's closest political confidants"—Jordan and Kirbo.[9] The revised column implied—but did not state explicitly—that the change in tactics represented a lessening of effort to apprehend Vesco.

Despite the changes Anderson made, delays and difficulties in transmittal of the revised column by Anderson and Anderson's distribution syndicate, United Features, resulted in differing versions of the column running in various newspapers around the country. What Anderson had obtained—but did not reflect in his revised column—was the actual documentation of the Justice Department's action and its rationale concerning Vesco. This documentation, which also was released to other reporters Saturday and Sunday, showed that when Rosalyn Carter was in Costa Rica in 1977, reporters asked her about U.S. efforts to bring Vesco back and try him. Vesco's presence, long a sore point in Costa Rica, was an important issue in the upcoming presidential elections there. The press inquiry to Mrs. Carter prompted National Security Adviser Zbigniew Brzezinski to write me for a progress report on the Vesco matter.

The request was forwarded routinely to the department's Criminal Division, which sought advice from the U.S. attorney of the Southern District of New York where the criminal charges were pending against Vesco. That U.S. attorney, Robert Fiske, was a holdover appointment from the Ford administration who distinguished both administrations. He advised that extradition had already been attempted unsuccessfully at great cost to the U.S. government. The difficulty was in showing that the laws Vesco was charged with violating were covered by the existing extradition treaty between Costa Rica and the United States. In a memo, Fiske proposed that efforts be made to induce the Costa Rican government to expel Vesco "and coordinate such expulsion so that he may be apprehended by the United States as a fugitive." At the top of the memo, I wrote: "I concur, Griffin B. Bell, June 15, 1977." Adamson forwarded the package with his own summary memo to Dr. Brzezinski on June 16. It was returned to me a day later with the President's handwritten note at the top, "Take AG advice, okay with me, J," to which Dr. Brzezinski had added: "I have informed the State Department that the President has decided that extradition procedures may be too complicated and time-consuming, and hence a better route is simply to request Costa Rica to expel Vesco."

In subsequent conversations with Anderson that Sunday, Adamson pressed Anderson to give the Justice Department's Criminal Division any evidence he might have of pro-Vesco activity by administration officials. A meeting was set for 6:00 P.M. Sunday in my office, with Anderson, Assistant Attorney General Civiletti, Fiske, Adamson, my special assistant, Phil Jordan, and me attending. Despite the fact Anderson would write many times that he had turned over his evidence at this meeting, Anderson only outlined orally some facts he said he had uncovered. He sent the department a portion of his "evidence" the next week.

In a second column, Anderson suggested that he had an "incriminating letter" written by Spencer Lee to Hamilton Jordan that implicated Jordan in the scheme. Though Anderson wrote that Lee "vehemently denies writing the letter and Jordan denied receiving it,"[10] the column supported the Anderson thesis that something improper had caused the Justice Department to drop its extradition plans. Later, Anderson had to write that this letter and others purporting to be to Jordan or Kirbo were fake, although Anderson called them euphemistically "reconstructions."[11] Adamson continued to press Anderson to explain in his column why the Justice Department had decided against extradition and particularly that the decision meant no lessening of effort to secure Vesco's return for trial. Anderson indicated that he was going to repeat the charge on his commentary on ABC's "Good Morning, America." By this time, Adamson's secretary was listening to and transcribing his telephone conversations with Anderson, who was advised of the monitoring.

Adamson, who had gained experience as a newspaper libel lawyer in private practice, then called ABC Executive Vice-President and General Counsel Everett Erlich in New York to inform him ABC was on notice of the falsity of Anderson's charge and the defamatory content. He told Erlich that if ABC broadcast Anderson's charge, the department wanted to respond and would consider other legal action. ABC withheld Anderson's taped commentary on Vesco from the next morning's show and ran in its place a commentary on another subject already in their tape storage. Before the morning broadcast, ABC sent Adamson a commentary Anderson had rewritten that dropped the charge that the Justice Department was no longer vigorously trying to bring Vesco back for trial. ABC gave the department an opportunity to respond, which, given Anderson's changes, we chose not to do.

I had asked the Civil Division of the department earlier that week to advise me whether the United States may bring a tort action for defamation arising from a libel of the Department of Justice. Though hardly surprising to me, the answer was no. I thanked the division in a memo, and added: "The First Amendment clashes with the right to sound government if there is no remedy against false charges of corruption . . . the people have a right to know or the right to know the truth? Which?"

Vesco's attempt to buy favorable treatment grated on me the more I thought about it and the more I recalled published reports of Vesco's efforts to influence previous administrations. Because President Carter was totally absorbed in the Camp David peace talks, I had been delaying action on a matter involving foreign intelligence that eventually would require his attention. Using that as an excuse, I flew by helicopter to Camp David, taking Director Webster of the FBI with me. We arrived at the President's lodge and found him alone and reading. After quickly dispensing with the "official" reason for our visit, I told the President that it was a travesty that Vesco apparently believed he could "buy" favorable legal action from the Office of the President of the United States and that I was outraged. I said that we should make every effort to press the Bahamian government, where Vesco had by then fled, to pursue the expulsion plan outlined by Fiske in the 1977 memo. The President was as incensed as I; he reached for the phone and asked Secretary of State Vance to come to the lodge. When Vance, who was on the tennis court, arrived in his tennis whites, President Carter reported our indignation and asked that we coordinate and intensify our efforts to force Vesco's return. We established a joint Justice-State task force for the Vesco project, and I am confident, without knowing details, that Vesco has begun to feel the fruits of our efforts.

Just two months after his Vesco columns, Anderson smeared me again, but this time his "reporting" was even more careless and irresponsible. And the attack extended to my son, Griffin B. Bell, Jr., then an attorney in Savannah, Georgia. In a November 14, 1978, column, Anderson charged that I had influenced a decision by the Justice Department to favor my son. Specifically, Anderson suggested I had prevailed on Justice Department attorneys to withdraw their objection to a proposed annexation of land by the city of Savannah because Griffin, Jr., was counsel to the Savannah school board. Anderson said the dropping of the federal government's objection to the annexation plan—which the Justice Department initially feared might be designed to dilute black voting strength in Savannah—came about as a result of "slick, down-home politics."[12]

The Savannah Morning News ran a story on its front page the day the column appeared pointing out that Anderson was wrong in nearly all of his facts. But of course that story did not appear in the hundreds of newspapers across the country which published Anderson's column. As the *News* correctly noted, the school board, which my son was serving as counsel, had "no political connections with the city council" or to the city administration, the mayor of Savannah did not meet with me and the black community had voted heavily in favor of the annexation—all contrary to the column's assertions.[13] What Anderson seemed determined to ignore was that the Department of Justice had a perfectly valid reason for dropping its objections: The annexation represented no threat to black voters and, indeed, a majority of them had voted in favor of it.

When it received the prepublication copy of Anderson's column, *The Savannah Morning News* was so distressed that it assigned a reporter to check back with the columnist. The reporter pointed out the errors to Anderson before the column's publication date. Anderson told the reporter that an associate had gathered the "facts" entirely by telephone. Anderson said he "profusely apologizes" for the "technical errors" in the column, the *News* reported, "but defended the column as being 'essentially accurate.' "[14]

The *News* story further quoted Anderson as surmising: "It's not likely that [Drew] Days [assistant attorney general for civil rights] would have reversed himself as drastically as he did on Savannah's annexation plan if he hadn't been under pressure from Attorney General Griffin Bell."[15]

My son, the school board, the mayor of Savannah and Justice Department spokesman Terry Adamson, on my behalf, demanded retractions by Anderson.

On November 27, a paragraph subtitled "Correction" ran in Anderson's column, which focused on another subject. The paragraph corrected some of the "technical errors" Anderson had referred to, but repeated the implication that the decision to withdraw the plan, which "our sources continue to insist . . . discriminated against blacks," was made because of my intervention.[16]

The correction had corrected nothing about the original column's unfair innuendo. Griffin, Jr., sent a lengthy and indignant letter of rebuttal to leading newspapers around the country, but only the Savannah and Atlanta papers printed it. United Features, which syndicates Anderson, refused our demand that it send its subscribers our unedited response. I then directed Adamson to get a list of the subscribers so that I could write them, but United Features again refused to cooperate. Through Adamson, I told Anderson that the Justice Department would write every daily newspaper in the United States, and Adamson's staff actually began addressing the necessary envelopes. Anderson must have realized that I meant business, for he proposed as a compromise that the column would run an unedited response.

On December 2, 1978, Anderson circulated a new column in which he repeated the basic false charge, and wrote: "In the original column, we cited a Justice Department statement disputing our findings. We later cleared up a couple of technical errors. The attorney general still isn't satisfied that his side of the story has been told fairly. He feels strongly that our column impugned his integrity. We offered, therefore, to publish an additional unedited statement from him. Here it is:

> I want to thank Mr. Anderson for giving me a few unedited words to respond to the attack on my son and me. He said, for instance, that my son was appointed counsel to the Savannah school board by the "city fathers" while the fight over redistricting was going on. In fact, my son was appointed by the countywide independent school board, which has no political connection with the city or the city council. I had nothing to do with that appointment, although I was proud of my son when I learned that he had been selected. The legal issue of the redistricting was discussed with me by my associates, Mr. Egan and Mr. Days, at their request, which is appropriate in such matters. But the decision was later made by them. Mr. Anderson also said the annexation was a successful effort by the "white establishment" to dilute black voting

power in Savannah. In fact, *The Savannah Morning News*
pointed out, "the black community voted overwhelmingly . . . to approve the annexation." The column as-
serted that the mayor of Savannah made several trips to
Washington to lobby for the annexation and implied that
lobbying of me "paid off." In fact, I never met with the
mayor of Savannah or anyone else from that city on this
issue. I am told that the mayor made one trip to Washington and met with the head of the Civil Rights Division. The suggestion that there was any connection
between the department's decision on annexation and
my son's appointment is blatantly false. His only connection was by accident of geography (he lives in Savannah)
and accident of birth (he is my son). I recognize the First
Amendment need for full, free and even unfair comment
by the press on public officials and public affairs. Ordinarily, I would not respond to a column such as Mr.
Anderson's, but dragging in my son was beyond the
pale.[17]

In my summary of these two cases, more has been said
than Jack Anderson is worth. So far as he himself is concerned, I share the view of my old warhorse lawyer friend,
Ham Lokey, who wrote to Griffin, Jr., after his indignant letter
concerning the Savannah column appeared in *The Atlanta Constitution:* "I thought your letter to Jack Anderson was a master-
piece. You said to him what needed to be said. However,
considering the man, I doubt that he can be reformed. You
just can't carve rotten wood."

Yet there are times when one must tackle a journalist such
as Anderson head-on, even if there is little chance of changing
the individual. When a journalist with the circulation and thus
the power of an Anderson errs in a significant way, the victim
in government must confront him or suffer a loss of effective-
ness.

The lack of professionalism and ethical behavior that I
found in Anderson's operation, however, was the exception
in my dealings with the Washington press corps. Most often,

the problem for the neophyte government servant is not how to deal with smears but how to remember that the media—frustrating as some of their actions may be—have become an integral part of the Washington apparatus. The media, imperfect as they are, can shape public policy by reporting and analyzing its development and, sometimes, simply by ignoring the development. The public official who denies or challenges that reality is banging his head against a printing press. I view myself as a champion of the First Amendment rights of reporters and editors and I salute them for serving our country as much—and sometimes more—than if they were in the government.

X

REFORMING GOVERNMENT

It is hard to imagine anyone spending two and a half years as a member of the Cabinet, working intimately with the President and the Congress and career federal officials, without gaining profound new respect for our system of government. The closer I came to the complexities of the federal system, the more impressed I was at how well our government manages to function.

It is equally true, however, that anyone deeply involved in government service will realize that serious problems exist. Adaptable as the system created by the Founding Fathers has proved to be, there are things about it that do not work well in the world of today. And it seems to me that the kinds of changes occurring—the revolution in communications, the increasing social and economic interdependency of regions and nations, the proliferation of ever-more terrible weapons —make these weaknesses more and more costly. As a nation, we have tended to shy away from proposals for major changes in our institutions on the assumption that the inherent strengths of the system would enable us to muddle through. But that belief may no longer be valid. Although our Founding Fathers were historical giants, we are not helpless inheritors of a wondrous mechanism unable to understand both the virtues and the shortcomings of what we have. Devising constructive changes is not beyond us.

In that spirit, I venture to offer suggestions. I am a lawyer, not a scholar, and I do not pretend to have comprehensive vision. Much less do I know precisely what should be done about every problem. Yet there are some changes that my experience has led me to feel strongly about.

Most fundamental, perhaps, is the term of service of the President. We should carry the Twenty-Second Amendment to the Constitution, which limits a President to serving two four-year terms, to its logical conclusion. The President should serve a single six-year term.

There are those, such as Thomas E. Cronin, a scholar on the presidency, who contend that the Twenty-second Amendment is a mistake because it would not permit a man like Franklin D. Roosevelt to continue serving in a unique period like the early 1940's.[1] I reject that view. It is unthinkable that anyone could be a good President beyond eight years. The job is so incredibly difficult that a President burns out. I voted against Roosevelt for that reason.

Allowing a President to serve two terms usually means that the officeholder exercises excessive caution during the first four years because he is too concerned about avoiding anything that might hinder his reelection. When critics charge that President John F. Kennedy was overly timid on civil rights and on judicial appointments during his thousand days in office, Kennedy defenders often say, "But it would have been different had there been a second term and he didn't have to worry about reelection." The defense misses the point: We must have a President whose judgment is based on what's best for the country. Even if a President can put aside self-interest during his first four years, there is virtually no chance of his having a staff that can, because the personal careers of individual aides are too bound up with his reelection.

I found the White House staff obsessed by President Carter's reelection almost from the start. Its single-minded-ness was all the more startling because I left office more than a year before the election and did not even experience the phenomenon at its peak. When Senator Kennedy and I were at odds over corporate merger policy in 1979, Hamilton Jordan worried that my stance might offend the potential Democratic rival. I attribute much of the pussyfooting about delivering a crime message to the fact that domestic policy experts at the White House were uncertain about the possible political fallout.

Opponents of the single-term presidency contend that having to be reelected can force a President into action he might not otherwise take, citing as an example President Nixon's decision to withdraw U.S. troops from Vietnam, a nearly four-year-old campaign promise, when the 1972 election became imminent. Yet the chaotic manner in which our troops were withdrawn hardly bolsters their argument. Instead of forcing action, approaching elections more often suspend it. The general rule for officeholders in an election year is to do as little as possible to rock the boat.

Defenders of the status quo also argue that the two-term system allows the citizenry to try a President out for size. Obviously, however, the presidency is not something we can afford to experiment with. Having a single term would not diminish accountability any more than standing for reelection after four years diminishes accountability during a second four-year term.

Moreover, the premium that opponents of the single-term proposal attach to a second term seems misplaced. We haven't had a President since Dwight D. Eisenhower who served two full terms. Only one subsequent President, Richard M. Nixon, actually won a second term. Nixon was reelected with a record victory, but many of the abuses that forced his departure from office had been committed during his first term—hardly evidence that the prospect of an election compels responsible conduct.

We probably could continue to get by if a President could be reelected and have four additional years to devote solely to the duties of the office. But a President is now judged several times a day by the instant media, much of the judgment during prime time, and every decision is so second-guessed that the Chief Executive eventually becomes worn down. Our one-term President would function more effectively if his term were for six years.

Trying to find time to be a President was a debilitating experience for Jimmy Carter. Without the need to worry about winning in November 1980, he would have been far more able to devote himself to the job. The political hazards are compounded by the realities of the budget process. When a President takes office, he is operating under a budget drawn up by his predecessor. The budget for the fiscal year that begins nine months after inauguration also is his predecessor's. Not until the third year does a new President get his own budget—and the government—in place, since the budget controls the government. He can move to change the budget for the fiscal year that begins in October of his first year in office, as President Reagan did, but the effort required is so substantial that practically all other matters take a backseat—as happened with the Reagan administration.

I grow weary of the standard reaction to the six-year, single-term proposal, which is that it is not a new idea. That's right. It was discussed as far back as the Constitutional Convention. But I do not believe that anyone attending that convention could foresee the demands placed on a President today or the highly centralized government that would develop, despite the emphasis that the Founding Fathers placed on federalism. Times have changed, and a successful system of government must adjust. In Congress, the six-year term was first proposed in 1826, and it has been reintroduced at least 160 times since then.[2] Presidents Johnson, Nixon, Ford and Carter all came to believe that the United States would be better off if Presidents could serve a single six-year term. Despite this support by leaders who have experienced the pressure and demands of the Oval Office, a substantial number of newspapers have editorialized against the change, perhaps because a single term might make the President feel less accountable to the press.

Sometime in 1982, we will be launching a nationwide campaign to amend the Constitution to provide for a single-term, six-year Presidency. Those serving with me on the steering committee of the campaign include William Simon, secretary of the treasury during the Nixon and Ford administrations, Milton Eisenhower and Cyrus Vance. Some on the committee want to broaden the drive to limit the number of terms a member of Congress can serve, but I'm opposed on grounds that this would be trying to do too much at once, even if a case could be made for such a limit. Initially, the campaign will seek the required support of two thirds of the state legislatures to call a constitutional convention rather than follow the traditional route of persuading two thirds of both houses of Congress to propose the amendment. I am convinced that we would have trouble getting the amendment through the Congress. Many special-interest groups would be staunchly opposed because a single-term President would be less vulnerable to their pressures than would a President concerned about winning reelection.

Many in Washington are upset by the notion of amending the Constitution through a convention. During the Carter administration, there was much talk of such a convention to require a balanced budget. Washington panicked. Then Vice-President Mondale, along with many others in the White House, thought that the prospect of the states forcing the federal government to let the people vote on amending the Constitution was one of the worst possible eventualities. A movement was started to wipe out the provision in the Constitution that allows amendment by convention as an alternative to amendment through both houses of Congress. The fear was that the Constitution might be rewritten in a wholesale fashion. Fortunately, the movement did not go far. The provision for a constitutional convention was probably the wisest single move of the Founding Fathers. It was and is a safeguard against Washington's getting out of hand. The state legislatures, with the approval of the people, can bring the central government under control. The appeal of trying to accomplish the single, six-year term change through a convention called solely for that purpose is that the issue could be debated without danger of other amendments being presented. The resolution for the convention could state explicitly that no other question could be voted on, destroying exaggerated, Washington-bred fears of revisions running amok.

If a single six-year term for the presidency is an idea whose time has come, then requiring national service for all eighteen-year-olds is an idea whose time should have come years ago and that can still benefit our system immensely. Hearings by the Senate Watergate Committee provided an example of the need for national service. Gordon Strachan, a former aide to H. R. Haldeman, President Nixon's chief of staff, was asked by a senator whether he had advice for other young people who might be considering working for the government in Washington. Strachan let his own involvement in the scandal influence his answer. "Stay away," he said. To me, his response is appalling. Yet much of the present college-age generation seem to be heeding Strachan's advice and shunning government service like the plague. They are said to be afflicted with "me-ism"—to be overly concerned with themselves, interested chiefly in charting financially rewarding careers and lacking the idealistic drive that caused the Peace Corps to be flooded with applicants during the Kennedy administration. I think this is so because we as a nation have stopped instilling a sense of patriotism and duty in our children. National service could go a long way toward changing that.

Just as many persons feel they owe a tithe to their religion, I think we all, particularly the young, owe a tithe to our nation. Our country cannot flourish unless talented individuals make whatever personal sacrifice is necessary to contribute at least some of their time and ability to making the system work. We have never had a hereditary class of governing officials, no tradition of noblesse oblige. The genius of our system has been that in each generation men and women from all walks of life have dedicated some portion of their productive lives to their government. For some, the service constitutes personal sacrifice. The task of governing is difficult and the pressures can be great. But the satisfactions are lasting, and foremost among them is knowing that you have paid your tithe as a citizen.

Selective Service was a form of national service that reached only able-bodied men during World War II and the Korean War, both accepted by Americans as wars in which the country should have been involved. Seldom heard during those years was the complaint so common now of young persons feeling "lost" after high school, sampling various colleges and work experiences and often wandering for months or years before finding themselves. A year or two of national service required of every eighteen or nineteen-year-old man and woman would help cut short such aimless wandering.

The service could involve work in forest projects, education, health and recreation—whatever was needed. Because the military would be one of the options, the need for a volunteer army would end and we could stop boosting salaries to lure men and women into the military. That saving would help offset the cost of a national service program. Unlike a committee that studied such a program in 1979 and recommended that it be on a voluntary basis, I would make it mandatory.[3] To be fair, it would have to be universal. We cannot afford another Vietnam-type experience in which practically all who wish to avoid serving their country could do so.

More important, you're not going to break up the ghetto with a voluntary program, and breaking up the ghetto would be a principal goal of the national service I envisage. It would accomplish what the Comprehensive Employment and Training Act (CETA), a milestone among boondoggles, never could achieve: removing the younger residents from the ghetto and showing them a different life. CETA did not take people out of their environment. They worked in menial jobs and remained where they were, some of them representing the fourth generation in their family to be living in low-rent housing supplied by public authorities. A good many of those who entered national service from the ghetto would receive more than they gave. The illiterate among them could be made literate, in part by others who had been more fortunate. The unhealthy could be made strong, and those who lacked skills could be trained to perform paying jobs.

As short-range devices for easing the immediate pain of unemployment, approaches like CETA may suffice. But we've reached the point in America where we have to think seriously about where we will be fifty years from now. Unless we take dramatic steps, we will have barrios and ghettos in urban areas that will be little different from Indian reservations, except that they will hold hundreds of thousands more Americans than the reservations ever have. They will be tinder-dry, ready to go up in flames because there will be so little promise for the inhabitants. Eventually, someone will throw a match, and that will begin the Second American Revolution.

National service as a means of avoiding an urban Armageddon would be like the military conscription of World War II, when the benefits, stretching far beyond the war years, were immense. We extended greater education to much of a generation that came back from service vowing to live a better life than it had left.

One of my notions for improving the way the federal government works drew laughter when I mentioned it to employees of the Justice Department. The idea is that we should disperse the central government, moving some of our larger agencies like Housing and Urban Development and Health and Human Services to states like Kansas, Oregon and Texas. Career federal workers assumed I must be joking, and that response helps make one of the points for the dispersal. The buildup of the bureaucracy in Washington has created a parochialism unequalled anywhere else in America, and this Washington-knows-best attitude has contributed to the growing resistance to centralized government among the people. It has also made it almost impossible for Washington to receive fresh ideas from what many in government regard as "the provinces."

Proposing that we move the Agriculture Department to

Des Moines, for example, does not mean I harbor ill will toward Des Moines. Economic benefits would accrue to the new sites. Why should Montgomery County, Maryland, and Arlington County, Virginia, monopolize the high per capita income they derive from serving as bedrooms for hundreds of thousands of government workers? What I'm suggesting is an updated version of the share-the-wealth plan of the 1930's. The annual survey of spendable income in the nation's major urban markets by *Sales & Marketing Management* magazine provides a measure of the financial rewards of federal employment.[4] Metropolitan Washington led the country in terms of real affluence. The average household income after taxes in the area was $29,648 in 1980, which exceeded the average of the other nine top markets by 17 percent and the national average by 34 percent. On a per capita basis, the area's spendable income was $10,902—37 percent above the average for the United States.

Of course, there are limits to what government departments you could move. The Pentagon, for example, has too much invested in its base across the Potomac River to be shifted. And the presence of the Department of Labor has led many unions to build their international headquarters in Washington. Relocating that Cabinet agency would prompt unfair labor charges against the government. At the same time, all the regulatory reforms imaginable would not equal the salutary effect of a systematic dispersal of the federal agencies. Ideally, almost nothing else would remain in Washington except the Executive Office of the President, the Congress and the Supreme Court. The breakthroughs that have been achieved in high-speed telecommunications eliminate the argument that the bureaucracy would slow down, and the dispersal would reduce the number of meetings that waste so much of government's time.

A much more important benefit would be lessening the influence of the lobbyists, who operate less visibly but no less effectively in the halls and offices of the Cabinet departments and regulatory agencies than they do on Capitol Hill. Relocation would mean that some "Lotus Eaters"—those who came to Washington in some governmental capacity and stayed on to make their fortunes as influence peddlers—would have to settle elsewhere. I call them "Lotus Eaters" because they remind me of the story in Homer's *Odyssey* of the men who were washed ashore in the Land of the Lotus Eaters and, after eating the lotus, stopped caring about going home.

James E. Stewart, chairman and chief executive officer of Lone Star Industries, Inc., another advocate of dispersal, said that government could profit from the lesson of private industry, which often builds a new factory with new technology when faced with excessive payrolls and loss of productivity.[5]

Washington was chosen as the nation's capital because it was close to the geographical center of the original thirteen states, a reason that still makes sense. If we followed that concept today, we would move the capital to Lebanon, Kansas, now the geographical center of the United States, excluding Alaska. Stewart and I differ on the matter only in that I favor spreading the government around, while he advocates single-point dispersal. I fear that in time Lebanon would grow into another Washington, with the attendant provincialism and stale thinking.

At the same time, I would set a tight cap on the number of aides and other staff members that a President, a member of Congress or a judge can employ. Staffs, in a very real way, run the government, and fortunate is the officeholder who is able to select and retain the most able assistants available. But bigger staffs invariably mean more government control, and if we are serious about reducing this control we must reduce the size of the staffs. I have included all three branches of the government because no proposal for limiting a public official's capacity to employ assistants could have any chance of adoption unless it restricted all branches equally. I'm reminded of the time Chief Justice Earl Warren was asked by a group of reporters whether he would favor setting a mandatory retirement age for judges and justices of the Supreme Court. The occasion was Mr. Warren's Seventy-fifth birthday. With a twinkle in his eyes, the Chief Justice said he would be for that as soon as the other two branches did the same.

Much of my energy as attorney general was devoted to seeking changes in the judicial selection process, particularly trying to reduce the amount of political patronage involved, so that the President could concentrate more on merit. The selection process is outlined by Article II, Section 2 of the Constitution, which provides that the President shall nominate and, with the "advice and consent" of the Senate, appoint judges. Senate confirmation, then, is one of the checks and balances of our constitutional system: One branch nominates; another advises and consents through confirmation hearings and a vote. But the meaning of the words "advice and consent" have been debated throughout American history. Almost from the beginning, the process developed in a way that seemed to contradict the intention of Article II, Section 2. Senators of the President's party from the area where a judgeship vacancy existed in effect nominated an individual by giving his or her name to the White House. The President consented and the Senate confirmed.

In place of this political approach, President Carter, relying on his experience as governor of Georgia, instituted a commission system—initially for the federal circuit courts of appeal. Prominent lawyers and others in each of the judicial circuits recommended three to five possible candidates for each vacancy. Our hope was that eventually the commission system would be extended to the much more numerous federal district judgeships, and senators from eighteen states did set up district judgeship commissions on their own. Unfortunately, President Reagan's first action on judicial appointments was to rescind the executive order by which President Carter had established the commissions.

Officials of the Reagan administration charged that the commissions had neither reduced nor eliminated the role of politics in picking judges. The critics, while acknowledging that we had delivered on our goal of ensuring the appointment of women and minorities to the federal bench, cited the fact that the commissions were overwhelmingly composed of Democrats and, more importantly, that the judges they recommended also were Democrats.

I am not wedded to the commission system, but I will

endorse it until someone develops a better means of examining the qualifications for a judgeship. I think the criticism of the commission system was too broad and missed the point, which was to find a way to interpose a merit-oriented institution between the President and the senators of his party. From my reading of every FBI file on federal judges chosen while I was attorney general, I can say that many were politically independent, particularly in presidential races, and were not down-the-line Democrats. Carolyn D. Randall, of the U.S. Fifth Circuit Court of Appeals, had me arrange her first meeting with by then former President Carter in Plains some two years after she went on the bench. She simply wanted to thank him for selecting her and to tell him that it was a rewarding experience. Mrs. Randall was a regular supporter of the Republican party, and her appointment, along with many others I could name, undercuts the charge that political affiliation was the prime requisite.

If the commission system did not entirely remove political considerations, it did substantially raise the qualifications of those becoming appellate judges. It was a common occurrence for the Republican district judges whom President Nixon or Ford had appointed to apply to one of President Carter's commissions and seek elevation to an appellate court. Under the commission system, the Democrats selected had to be at least equal in qualifications to the Republican contender. The commission system also raised qualifications by increasing the number of persons applying for appointment, particularly those with no strong political ties to a Democratic senator. The abandonment of the commission system marks a step backward from the goal of selecting judges on merit.

Equally in need of reform is the process of appointing United States attorneys. Those posts are considered rich plums in the patronage basket of senators of the incumbent President's party, and the long tradition of senatorial patronage—senators play the same role with U.S. attorneys that they play in picking federal judges—casts an unfortunate aura over the appointees.

Unlike judges, U.S. attorneys are part of the executive

branch, so·the role of the legislative branch in selecting them is also an unseemly interference with the President's powers. The ninety-four U.S. attorneys are the highest federal law enforcement officers in their districts. Because they are key officials in the prosecution and enforcement of law, the circumstances surrounding their appointments are more sensitive than in the selection of other federal executives. The people understand how important it is that the laws of the land be faithfully executed, without fear of favor and in a fair and even-handed way toward all.

In this regard, it is not wrong—nor, of course, surprising —that U.S. attorneys usually are of the same political party as the President. The authority they have for making policy and their responsibility to the attorney general, who, in turn, is responsible to the President, make their party affiliation almost inevitable. But the present appointment system casts doubt on their qualifications by suggesting they have obtained their offices only because of political influence.

The surest way to correct that impression, which, whether accurate or not, undermines law enforcement and the people's respect for their government, is to let the attorney general appoint U.S. attorneys without Senate confirmation. In theory, the confirmation should be a form of quality control. But historically senators have turned the process into patronage, often picking lawyers who have assisted them in their Senate election campaigns.

Senate confirmation of U.S. attorneys, as distinguished from judges, is not mandated by the Constitution. Article II, Section 2 states that the Congress may provide for the "appointment" of "inferior officers," which means Congress could change the present system simply by passing a law.

Giving sole power to the attorney general lies within the constitutional and statutory framework by which the President, the attorney general and the U.S. attorneys all function. The President, as head of the executive branch, is charged with enforcing federal law. The attorney general is the chief executive officer through whom the President carries out that duty. In turn, the attorney general discharges a large part of his responsibility through the U.S. attorneys, who must be people in whom he has complete confidence. Only by making U.S. attorneys entirely accountable to their superiors in the executive branch can we expect to achieve consistent and effective administration and enforcement of the federal laws.

My final proposals for reform draw not only from my experience as attorney general and as a federal judge but from a lifetime of participation in, and observation of, our political system. The all-accommodating Democratic party tent that Franklin Roosevelt tried to pitch, under which Americans of all persuasions could find shelter, is no longer practical. There simply is no longer a way to put the southern conservatives in with the northeastern liberals, or those exponents of social welfare in the large cities with well-paid, blue-collar workers or with the midwestern or Rocky Mountain farmer and rancher. The realignment, which I regard as inevitable, will split the Democratic party so that for a time we may operate with a three-party system, or at least with a large bloc of independents who would constitute a swing vote. Over the long run, I see us returning to a two-party system divided along clearer conservative-liberal lines. There is an alternative: Moderates could take control of the Democratic party. But I think this is unlikely because of the dominant voices in the party today. Union leadership could bring about that change, but given the current union leaders, that seems unlikely, too.

Whatever party system emerges, leaders must resume leading. Very few public officials do that today. Most office-holders are guided by polls and act only in tune with what is perceived to be majority opinion. The result is that the country has neither leadership nor representative government. Our form of government is based on the premise that we elect leaders to use their judgment within broad parameters and basic principles. To do so, leaders must expose themselves to risk—even the risk of not being reelected. A good many of the problems on the local, state and federal levels are caused by a failure of leadership, though that is part of the responsibility of taking office.

The American political system—unique in the world—is constructed to enable a huge and diverse people to live in freedom, avoiding the twin scourges of human history—despotism on the one hand and anarchy and chaos on the other. To achieve that difficult goal, our system places a duty both on those who serve in the government and on the people.

The duty of the people is to participate in the democratic process—speaking out, lobbying, voting for candidates of their choice—but then accepting and supporting the decisions of the majority and the actions of government officials responsible for carrying out those decisions. As citizens, each of us owes that support to our public officials even in cases where the vote did not go our way and the policies being pursued by government may not be serving our personal interests. Of course, where a citizen disagrees strongly on principle, he can work to have a decision revoked. But until it is, the citizen must accept the decision. If citizens do not meet their obligation, our system of government cannot survive.

It may seem odd for a southerner to cite the Civil War as a catastrophic illustration of what happens when masses of people refuse to accept the decision of a majority of their countrymen. But I salute—as I do every time I pass his monument in Washington—Abraham Lincoln, who went to the heart of the matter in his first inaugural address:

> Plainly, the central idea of secession is the essence of anarchy. A majority, held in restraint by constitutional checks and limitations, and always changing easily with deliberate changes of popular opinions and sentiments, is the only true sovereign of a free people. Whoever rejects it, does, of necessity, fly to anarchy or to despotism. Unanimity is impossible; the rule of a minority, as a permanent arrangement, is wholly inadmissible; so that, rejecting the majority principle, anarchy or despotism in some form is all that is left. . . .[5]

At the same time, those who wield the power of central authority must always remember that they are there to serve the people and to follow the will of the majority, restrained and tempered by the constitutional provisions which are meant to keep the majority itself from becoming a despot.

Public servants must keep clearly in mind that they are the government. It is they to whom the people look, and it is they who are accountable to the people. The only limits to reforming our system lie in us. I'm reminded of an experience Justice Harry A. Blackmun had several years ago. Visiting in Aspen, Colorado, he got into conversation with a five-year-old boy named Matthew. That night, when Matthew's mother put him to bed, Matthew said to her: "I met the nicest man tonight."

"Who was it?" she asked.

"I don't know," Matthew said, "but I think he was the government."

The government is us—every public official.

NOTES

Prologue

1. Alexis de Tocqueville, *Democracy in America*, Vol. II, ed. Henry Reeve and retrans. Francis Bowen (New York: Vintage Books, 1945), pp. 335–37.

Chapter One

1. Comprehensive Employment and Training Act of 1973, Title II, Part D, 29 U.S.C. §841 *et seq.*
2. Ibid.
3. *Regents of the University of California* v. *Bakke*, 438 U.S. 265 (1978).
4. Daniel J. Meador, *The President, the Attorney General and the Department of Justice* (Charlottesville: The University of Virginia, 1980), p. 130.
5. Jimmy Carter, Remarks to the Los Angeles County Bar Association, May 4, 1978, *Presidential Documents*, Vol. 14, No. 18 (Washington, D.C.: Government Printing Office, 1978), pp. 834–41.

Chapter Two

1. William McCleery, "The Emerging Crisis over the 'Imperial Bureaucracy,'" *Princeton Alumni Weekly* (Princeton, N.J.: January 15, 1979), pp. 13–17.
2. Ibid, p. 14.
3. Hugh Heclo, *A Government of Strangers* (Washington, D.C.: Brookings Institution, 1977), p. 226.

Chapter Three

1. *Watergate Special Prosecution Force Report* (Washington, D.C.: Government Printing Office, 1975), p. 136.

2. *Congressional Record,* Senate 10940, July 31, 1979 (remarks of Sen. Charles Percy).

3. *Government Regulation: Achieving Social and Economic Balance,* Joint Economic Committee, Special Study on Economic Change (Washington, D.C., Government Printing Office, 1980), p. 14.

4. *Regulatory Reform,* Hearings before the Committee on the Judiciary, U.S. Senate, 96th Congress, 1st Session, Part II (Washington, D.C.: Government Printing Office, 1979), p. 4.

5. Arthur Andersen & Co., *Cost of Government Regulation Study for the Business Roundtable* (New York: 1979).

6. *Reform of Federal Regulation,* Joint Report of the Committee on Governmental Affairs and the Committee on the Judiciary, U.S. Senate, 96th Congress, 2d Session (Washington, D.C.: Government Printing Office, 1980), p. 5.

7. Stuart E. Eizenstat, Speech to the National Press Club, Washington, D.C., December 4, 1980.

8. K. Chilton, *A Decade of Rapid Growth in Federal Regulation* (St. Louis: Center for the Study of American Business, 1979).

9. *State of Texas* v. *Environmental Protection Agency,* 499 F. 2d 289 (5th Cir. 1974), *stay denied,* 421 U.S. 945 (1975).

10. *Regulation: The View from Janesville, Wisconsin, and a Regulator's Perspective,* U.S. Regulatory Council, February 29, 1980, as published in Regulatory Reform Hearings before Senate Judiciary Subcommittee on Administrative Practices (Washington, D.C.: Government Printing Office, 1980), Part 3, pp. 272–333.

11. *Benefits of Environmental, Health and Safety Regulations,* Senate Committee on Governmental Affairs, 96th Congress, 2d Session (Washington, D.C.: Committee Print, 1980).

Chapter Four

1. *Jagdish Rai Chadha* v. *Immigration and Naturalization Service,* 634 F. 2d 408 (9th Cir. 1980).

2. In matter of Jagdish Rai Chadha, U.S. Department of Justice, 1974, reported in *Chadha* v. *INS,* 634 F. 2d 411 (9th Cir. 1980).

3. *Chadha* v. *INS,* 634 F. 2d 421.

4. Ibid, p. 429.

5. Ibid, p. 430.

6. Ibid, p. 433.

7. "Congress Ruled Out of Bounds on Deportation," *Los Angeles Times,* December 25, 1980, p. 1.

8. Statement on Department of Justice appeal of *Chadha* v. *INS,* Jimmy Carter, *Presidential Documents* (Washington, D.C.: Government Printing Office, January 20, 1981), p. 2883.

9. Jimmy Carter, *Presidential Documents* (Washington, D.C.: Government Printing Office, June 26, 1978), p. 1148.

Chapter Five

1. Sir Thomas Erskine May, *Constitutional History of England,* Vol II (London: Longmans, Green & Co., 1912), pp. 149–150.

2. *Intelligence Activities and the Rights of Americans*, Final Report of the Select Committee to Study Governmental Operations with Respect to Intelligence Activities, U.S. Senate, 94th Congress, 2d Session, Book II (Washington, D.C.: 1976), p. 103.

3. Ibid.

4. Gerald R. Ford, *Presidential Documents* (Washington, D.C.: Government Printing Office), Exec. Order 11905, February 18, 1976, p. 234.

5. Jimmy Carter, *Presidential Documents*, (Washington, D.C.: Government Printing Office), Exec. Order 12036, January 24, 1978, p. 194.

6. *United States* v. *Truong Dinh Hung, United States* v. *Ronald L. Humphrey*, 629 F. 2d 920 (4th Cir. 1980).

7. Phil Wechsler, "Spy Trial Judge Forbids Secrecy," *Washington Star*, October 10, 1978, p. 1.

8. Fred Barbash, "Two Soviets Get 50-Year Terms in Spying Trial," *Washington Post*, October 31, 1978, p. A14.

9. Dan Fisher, "Kremlin Accuses Ex-U.S. Envoy of Role in Murder," *Los Angeles Times*, June 13, 1978, p. 1, quoting *Izvestia* of June 12, 1978.

10. Barbash, *op. cit.*

11. Nathaniel Sheppard, "Spy Trial Focusing on Security and CIA," *New York Times*, November 12, 1978, p. 35.

12. Robert C. Toth, "Cia 'Mighty Wurlitzer' Is Now Silent," *Los Angeles Times*, December 30, 1980, p. 1.

13. George Lardner, Jr., "CIA Security on Classified Papers Lax, Trial Is Told," *Washington Post*, November 10, 1978, p. B19.

14. "The Use of Classified Information in Litigation," Hearings before the Subcommittee on Intelligence, 95th Congress, 2d Session, 9, 10 (1978).

Chapter Six

1. Stansfield Turner, "The CIA's 'Unequivocal' Right to Prior Review," *Washington Post*, December 7, 1977, Opposite Editorial Page.

2. *United States* v. *Snepp*, 456 F. Supp. 176, 179 (E.D. Va. 1978).

3. Ibid, p. 180.

4. Ibid, p. 180–181.

5. Ibid, p. 180.

6. *Snepp* v. *United States*, 595 F. 2d 926 (4th Cir. 1979).

7. *Snepp* v. *United States*, 444 U.S. 507 (1980).

8. Ibid, p. 516–526.

9. Debate with Reid Irvine, Chairman of Accuracy in Media, June 14, 1979 (Washington, D.C.: Committee to Defend the First Amendment, 1979), p. 37.

10. *New York Times Co.* v. *United States*, 403 U.S. 713 (1971).

11. Ibid.

12. *United States* v. *Progressive, Inc.*, 467 F. Supp. 996 (E.D. Wisc. 1979).

13. Ibid, pp. 994–995.

14. Robert Gillette, "Letter Seems to Offer Exposure of H-Bomb Data," *Los Angeles Times*, September 19, 1979, p. 23.

15. Anthony Marro, "Helms Is Fined $2,000 and Given Two-Year Suspended Prison Term," *New York Times*, November 5, 1977, p. 1.

16. Ronald J. Ostrow, "Helms Given Suspended Sentence, Fined $2,000," *Los Angeles Times*, November 5, 1977, p. 1.

17. Ibid.

18. Charles L. Heatherly, ed., *Mandate for Leadership* (Washington, D.C.: The Heritage Foundation, 1981), p. 933.

19. Ibid, p. 934.

20. Ibid.

21. Ibid.

22. George Lardner, Jr., "CIA's Deputy Assures Senators He Does Not Favor Spying in U.S.," *Washington Post*, March 14, 1981, p. A13.

Chapter Seven

1. *To Establish Justice, To Insure Domestic Tranquillity,* Final Report of the National Commission on the Causes and Prevention of Violence (Washington, D.C.: Government Printing Office, 1969), pp. 44–45.

2. *Prisoners at Midyear,* Bureau of Justice Statistics Bulletin (Washington, D.C.: Department of Justice, 1981).

3. "Prison System Gates Open for Some 'Bad Actors,' " *Atlanta Constitution and Atlanta Journal,* March 29, 1981, p. 1.

4. Ibid.

5. *To Establish Justice, op. cit.,* p. 43.

6. "Crime in the United States 1978," FBI Uniform Crime Reports (Washington, D.C.: U.S. Department of Justice, 1979), p. 40.

7. Harry Scarr, testimony before Attorney General's Task Force on Violent Crime in Washington, D.C., April 16, 1981, p. 33 of transcript.

8. "Crime in the United States 1979," FBI Uniform Crime Reports (Washington, D.C.: U.S. Department of Justice, 1980), p. 37. Scarr, *op. cit.*

9. John C. Ball, Lawrence Rosen, John A. Flueck and David R. Nurco, "The Criminality of Heroin Addicts When Addicted and When off Opiates," Paper presented to International Congress on Alcoholism and Drug Dependence, Medellin, Colombia, December 3–6, 1980, p. 21.

10. Ibid, p. 24.

11. Ibid.

12. Ibid, pp. 7–22.

13. Ibid, p. 25.

14. Harry Scarr, assistant to the associate attorney general, paper presented to the Attorney General's Task Force on Violent Crime, April 16, 1981, in Washington, D.C., pp. 12–22 of transcript.

15. "Prisoners in State and Federal Institutions on December 31, 1980," U.S. Department of Justice, Bureau of Justice Statistics (Washington, D.C.: Government Printing Office, 1982), p. 33.

16. Colin Lofton, Paper presented to Attorney General's Task Force on Violent Crime, June 18, 1981, in Detroit, Michigan, pp. 50–80 of transcript.

17. Ibid.

18. Attorney General Griffin B. Bell, Memorandum on Crime Program, "Ten General Principles for Delivery of Criminal Justice," October 13, 1977.

Chapter Eight

1. W. J. Bate, ed. *Edmund Burke, Selected Works,* (New York: The Modern Library, 1960), p. 127.
2. Alexis de Tocqueville, *op. cit.,* Vol. I, p. 290.
3. Jerrold K. Footlick, "Too Much Law?" *Newsweek,* January 10, 1977, p. 47.
4. Jethro K. Lieberman, *The Litigious Society* (New York: Basic Books, Inc., 1981), p. 187.
5. *Congressional Globe,* 41st Congress, 2d Session, 3036 (1870).
6. John Davis, Department of Justice Control of Agency Litigation 17, Report to the U.S. Administrative Conference (Washington, D.C.: Government Printing Office, 1975).
7. Erwin N. Griswold, Statement of Solicitor General concerning Securities Exchange Act H.R. 5050 before Subcommittee on Commerce and Finance of the House Committee on Interstate and Foreign Commerce, 93rd Congress, 1st Session, 11 (Washington, D.C.: Government Printing Office, June 7, 1973).
8. Erwin N. Griswold, "The Office of the Solicitor General—Representing the Interests of the United States before the Supreme Court," (Columbia, Mo.: Missouri Law Review, Vol. 34, 1969).
9. American Bar Association, *Model Code of Professional Responsibility and Code of Judicial Conduct* (Chicago: American Bar Association, 1980), p. 37.
10. *Berger* v. *United States,* 295 U.S. 88 (1934).
11. Meador, *op. cit.,* p. 43.
12. Ibid, p. 24.
13. Judiciary Act of September 24, 1789, ch. 20, 1 Stat. 73.
14. Luther A. Huston, Arthur S. Miller, Samuel Krislov, Robert G. Dixon, Jr., *Roles of the Attorney General of the United States* (Washington, D.C.: American Enterprise Institute, 1968), p. 44.
15. Ibid, p. 51.
16. Ibid, pp. 57–58.
17. Judge Joseph C. Hutchinson, Jr., Statement made in presence of author (Bell).
18. E. Allan Lind and John E. Shapard, "Evaluation of Court-Annexed Arbitration in Three Federal District Courts" (Washington, D.C.: Federal Judicial Center, 1981), p. 94.
19. *Dispute Resolution Program Directory* (Washington, D.C.: American Bar Association, 1981), p. Introduction.
20. Daniel McGillis, "Recent Developments in Minor Dispute Processing," memorandum for former Attorney General Griffin Bell, August 1979.
21. Earl Johnson, *Courts and the Community,* National Center for State Courts Task Force Report (Williamsburg, Va.: 1978).
22. Frank E. A. Sander, "Varieties of Dispute Processing," Paper presented at National Conference on the Causes of Popular Dissatisfaction with the Administration of Justice (the Pound Conference), 70 Federal Rules Decisions 79 (1976).
23. Frank E. A. Sander, "The Multi-Door Courthouse," *Barrister* (Chicago: American Bar Association, Summer, 1976), p. 20.

Chapter Nine

1. *U.S. News and World Report,* February 6, 1978, p. 25.
2. Fred Ferretti, "Mr. Untouchable," *New York Times Magazine,* June 5, 1977.
3. "Drug Kingpin Nicky Barnes Gets Life," *New York Daily News,* January 20, 1978, pp. 2, 8.
4. Briefing by Attorney General Griffin Bell, Office of White House Press Secretary, January 19, 1978, p. 10.
5. Seymour M. Hersh, "Bell Puts Off Naming U.S. Attorney Pending an Inquiry Into Payments," *New York Times,* December 2, 1977, p. 1.
6. Ibid.
7. Ibid, p. B4.
8. *The Presidential Campaign 1976* (Washington, D.C.: U.S. Government Printing Office, 1978), Vol. I, Part I, p. 226.
9. Jack Anderson, "Vesco Bid Aimed at Jordan, Kirbo," *Washington Post,* September 11, 1978, p. C27.
10. Jack Anderson, "Letter Ties Jordan to Vesco Payoff Bid," *Boston Globe,* September 12, 1978, p. 19.
11. Jack Anderson, "Vesco Case Papers 'Reconstructions,'" *Washington Post,* September 26, 1978, p. B8.
12. Jack Anderson, "Squabble on Savannah Redistricting," *Washington Post,* November 14, 1978, p. B15.
13. Eddie Fleming, "Anderson's Savannah Exposé Called 'Lies,'" *Savannah Morning News,* November 14, 1978, p. 1A.
14. "Jack Anderson Defends His Column," *Savannah Morning News,* November 14, 1978, p. 3A.
15. Ibid.
16. Jack Anderson, "Senate Aide's Firing Makes Waves," *Washington Post,* November 27, 1978, p. C23.
17. Jack Anderson, "Libyans at FAA Academy Disciplined," *Washington Post,* December 2, 1978, p. C11.

Chapter Ten

1. Thomas E. Cronin, "Should Presidents Serve One Six-Year Term?" *Common Cause,* October 1980, pp. 22–23.
2. Hearings before the Subcommittee on Constitutional Amendments of the Senate Committee on the Judiciary, Senate Joint Res. 77, 92nd Congress, 1st Session, October 28–29, 1971.
3. *Youth and the Needs of the Nation,* Report of the Committee for the Study of National Service, The Potomac Institute (Washington, D.C.: 1979), p. 1.
4. William H. Jones, "Evidence Shows D.C. Economy Most Affluent," *Washington Post,* Washington Business section, July 27, 1981.
5. James E. Stewart, "Let's Move Washington to Lebanon," *New York Times,* October 29, 1980, p. A31.
6. *Inaugural Addresses of the Presidents of the United States* (Washington, D.C.: Government Printing Office, 1974), pp. 119–126.

INDEX